The Quality of Federal Policymaking

The Quality of
Federal Policymaking
Programmed Failure
in Public Housing

Eugene J. Meehan

University of Missouri Press
Columbia & London, 1979

Library of Congress Cataloging in Publication Data

Meehan, Eugene J
    The quality of federal policymaking.

    Bibliography: p. 223
    Includes index.
    1. Public housing—Missouri—St. Louis.
I. Title.
HD7304.S2M433   301.5′4   78-27663
ISBN 0-8262-0272-1

Photographs 1, 2, 4, 13, 14, 15, 16, 20, and 21 courtesy
St. Louis Post-Dispatch; photograph 3 courtesy *St. Louis
Globe-Democrat*; photographs 5, 6, 7, 8, 9, 10, 11, 12, 18, 19,
and 22 courtesy the St. Louis Housing Authority.

To Alice

Acknowledgments

Like its predecessor, this volume is the product of an experiment in collaboration between a state university and a public agency that has proved highly advantageous for both parties. For several years, the St. Louis Housing Authority has provided me with unlimited access to historical and current data relating to housing program operations. The staff has tolerated my endless and sometimes difficult questions with remarkable good humor. I cannot hope to thank them all properly, but my indebtedness to former Director Thomas P. Costello, who made it possible, and to Charles Schultz, Harry Dew, Barry Williams, and their respective departments is beyond payment. Special thanks are also due to Marjorie Wilson, who led me through the intricacies of the accounting system, to Mary Ann Becker, who knew what was in the files and where to find it, and to Marjorie Taylor, who helped me to learn about contracts and legal actions. Barbara Freeland very graciously allowed me to "borrow" the results of her work with the Target Projects Program (TPP). Addie Ward and Malinda Bailey, both unfortunately now deceased, allowed me to share their wide experience in public housing, and I remember them with much warmth and gratitude. John Stevenson, who developed the computerized records and accounts system for the Housing Authority, both supplied me with tapes and allowed free use of his detailed analyses. For his work on the projected impact of the Brooke amendment alone, he deserves to rise one rank in Dante's Inferno. Larry Westermeyer from the Computer Center at my own university earned much gratitude if no monetary recompense by the excellence of the data processing. And Mary Ann Burke of the Housing Authority staff continued to serve as guardian angel to the enterprise, reading and correcting, explaining, suggesting sources, and most of all, encouraging. What I have learned of the operation of public housing during these past seven years is largely a result of her prompting.

Although this volume could not have been written without their assistance, none of these kind people is in any way responsible for either the accuracy of the data or the acceptability of the conclusions, judgments, and recommendations. Indeed, they may disagree very strongly with them. Responsibility for what follows is solely mine.

One minor technical point: unless otherwise noted, all data refer to a fiscal year that begins on 1 October and ends on 30 September.

E.J.M. — St. Louis, 6 February 1979

Contents

I.

Introduction

The study on which this volume depends began in 1971 as an innocent, and perhaps innocent's, attempt to determine more precisely the reasons for the internationally famous disaster in St. Louis public housing.[1] Detailed examination of the evolution of the "conventional" public housing program (housing developed, owned, and operated by a public agency) from the 1940s through the end of the 1960s demonstrated beyond doubt that neither the particular circumstances in the city of St. Louis nor the "culture of poverty" that characterized the tenant environment was a primary cause of the disaster—though they may have exacerbated it. In effect, asserting such "causes" was only a subtle form of "blaming the victim." The principal culprits implicated were a set of policies programmed for failure, impossible to implement successfully in the long run, and a set of institutions unable to correct or improve them. The disaster was built into the program and guaranteed by the institutional arrangements. A combination of norms adjusted to another era and policymaking institutions unable to develop competent policies and unsuited to adjusting and improving them in the light of program performance over time literally forced the outcome.

The conclusion that under existing institutional arrangements the society could not avoid programmed disaster and could not expect program improvements in response to failure has truly horrendous implications for the future. The public housing program offers an ideal locus for a test. The human and social significance of public housing should ensure the best efforts of those involved. Public housing is one of the primary means used by a very large industrial society to provide its less fortunate members with one of their most elemental needs. The costs of error or inadequacy are very high in both material and human terms. Nationally, public housing has a well-documented history; detailed records of the effects of policy changes on program operations in one large city were readily

1. See Eugene J. Meehan, *Public Housing Policy: Myth Versus Reality*.

1

available. The test could therefore be carried out under near-optimum conditions. Because St. Louis is sufficiently representative of the very large cities in which the bulk of the public housing program was located, the findings should hold for a very significant range of individual programs. Finally, public housing went through a series of major crises in the late 1960s and early 1970s, and the reaction of federal policymaking institutions to these crises provides a good measure of their capacity to perform.

The focus throughout is critical rather than descriptive. That is, the primary concern is with the effects of policy rather than the reasons specific decisions were made. The latter focus, which is central in most studies of policymaking, leads to emphasis on the changes that are possible within the framework of existing institutions. My own preliminary conclusions suggest that the institutions themselves must be questioned.

The inquiry concentrates on six basic points in the development of public housing policy: first, the original program design, dating to the late 1930s; second, the introduction of federal operating subsidies; third, the decision to use private developers to produce housing facilities for public authorities, the so-called turnkey program; fourth, the use of private agents and tenants to manage housing operations; fifth, the sale of apartments to individual tenants; and sixth, the lease of privately owned facilities for use as public housing. Together, these points include all the central features of the public housing program from its origins in New Deal legislation through the late 1970s.

The evidence generated by the study is extensive, detailed, and consistent; the effect is uniformly damning in its indictment of existing institutional arrangements. The record shows change without improvement, experience without learning, distressing insensitivity to the plight of the unfortunate, and action in blatant disregard for consequences. With respect to public housing, the social institutions involved are clearly awry. Moreover, a very tentative and preliminary inquiry suggests that the same institutionalized incapacity is to be found in other major areas of governmental activity. More specifically, there are three fundamental dimensions of policymaking in which performance is ominously weak. First, the quality of the information employed in the policymaking process is uniformly poor, the reasoning is inadequate, and the conventional wisdom on which action is based is frequently mistaken but rarely examined. Second, the underlying normative structure—the set of priorities actually being satisfied in action—is almost grotesquely distorted. The reward system is little less than perverse. Finally, there is little if any evidence of learning from experience and applying the learning to future action; indeed, there is little sign of any systematic effort to learn. Moreover, the administrative apparatus is opaque, at the federal level particularly; hence it is almost impossible to see how it operates and how it might be improved—as constituted, the bureaucratic structure is radically incorrigible even if the will to correct were present. The importance of such findings, in an era where governmental actions are the dominant influence in the lives of countless millions of persons, hardly requires elaboration here.

Perhaps the most significant and far-reaching dimension of the findings, however, is the support they provide for localism, for a systematic and extensive decentralization of authority and resources to the particular locality where effective action is required. What is involved here is not a simple matter of reducing levels of taxation along the lines of the California "tax revolt" of the late 1970s. If anything, experience seems to suggest that centralized taxation is more equitable and efficient than local taxation, other things equal. But the design and administration of policies aimed at local institutions and local populations, typified in the provision of goods and services for low-income populations, are in principle unsuited for centralized control. If policy is to be reasoned and improvable over time, a powerful element of local control is unavoidable. Given past history, such transfers of authority to the local level are likely to incur serious short-run costs, particularly if they are carried out without adequate preparation. But learning and improvement are at least possible in principle at the local level; centralized control rules out, for all practical purposes, reasoned action. Those who operate massive centralized agencies do not and cannot calculate the implications of their actions at the level of particular persons and places excepting a few special cases—even the effects of a period of military service will vary in some degree with the person. The source of the difficulty is not the development of professional administrators and the widespread belief that policymaking can be divorced from the substance to which policies refer and the persons affected by them. That problem is now endemic in both public and private operations and growing more serious daily, but it exaggerates and does not cause the dilemma. But if policies are to be judged and improved in terms of their particular consequences, particular, not aggregate, information must be available to the policymaker. In practice, this means either local control or complex reporting and massive, centralized data handling systems. Both are impractical.

Evaluating "Policies"

Systematic evaluation or criticism of policies and policymaking depends on a fairly complex set of assumptions about the meaning of "policy," the purposes that policies can satisfy, and the conditions in which they can function successfully. Usually, such fundamentals are simply assumed; and in such well-developed fields as agriculture or medicine where the basic assumptions are well articulated and fully incorporated into professional training, that causes no serious problems. But in social science, the meaning of "policy" is differently construed and criteria to be applied to research strategies or governmental performance are often hotly disputed. Even in such new and specialized fields as "policy analysis" or "policy evaluation," individual conceptions of the nature of the enterprise differ greatly. A brief summary of the concept of "policymaking" adopted here is essential to expose the criticism to further criticism and open the way for cumulative improvement.

The meaning of "policy" varies enormously in use, even among professional scholars. Traditionally, policies were simply identified with governmental actions or proclamations, and that tended to concentrate attention on the reasons given for acting, the formal machinery for making decisions, and the strategic principles employed in the conduct of public affairs—with an occasional glance at the informal networks involved. The conception of "policy" used here comes from a more concise and technical approach to analysis, perhaps best articulated in foreign affairs.[2] There, policies are treated as *guides to action*, rules of choice that apply priorities to specific

2. See, for example, Eugene J. Meehan, "The Concept 'Foreign Policy,'" in Wolfram F. Hanrieder, ed., *Comparative Foreign Policy: Theoretical Essays* (New York: McKay, 1971), or Eugene J. Meehan, "Science, Values, and Politics," *American Behavioral Scientist* 17:1 (September/October 1973):53–100.

decisions. Two basic points justify the usage: first, it links policy to the satisfaction of human purposes, which gives it human significance; second, such policies are corrigible over time on the basis of human experience within the limits of human capacity. The criteria for adequate policy are minimal and quality can vary greatly. The guidance provided by a policy may be slight. Improvements in quality are difficult even under the best of circumstances. Nevertheless, any genuine guide to action must be precise enough to *force* a specific outcome; therefore, it will have discernible consequences when employed and is in principle open to improvement over time on the basis of experience. Without such a rule of choice improved human performance is solely a matter of luck. The rule, not the action, should be the focus of efforts to improve.

The implications of this innocuous-sounding conception of "policy" are surprisingly extensive. For if a policy is a guide to action, it is tested and improved only in the particular application, exactly as prescribed methods for treating illness are improved only by results obtained from the particular case. Policy evaluation requires an intensive and detailed case study, an examination of the results of specific applications. Aggregate data can indicate program failure but cannot suggest why the program failed nor suggest ways in which failure could be avoided. One of the more serious methodological anomalies in contemporary social science is the coexistence of a widespread denigration of "case studies" with a demand for more analysis and evaluation of public policy—tantamount to asking for improvements in medicine while ridiculing treatment of individual patients. The question why a program succeeded or failed is *not* equivalent to the question how successful programs differ from unsuccessful programs. There is no need to answer one question in order to answer the other and answering one does not automatically answer the other. Indeed, knowing the causes of failure is not necessarily useful for learning how to succeed. But whatever the focus of concern, answers must be sought in the particular case. In fact, the case need not be typical of all other cases; it need only be a member of the generic class. That is, even if St. Louis were the only city in the United States where public housing failed to meet expectations, and that was certainly not the case, the failure in St. Louis would be a criticism of the overall policies incorporated into the program, whatever the results obtained elsewhere.

Policies are evaluated in terms of the results they produce in any situation where they are supposed to apply, just as prescribed medical treatments are judged by the cases in which they are employed. For each case, policies are judged by all the results of use and not just a selection.

Construed as guides to action, policies are independent of either their authors or their users; evaluation focuses on the policy. The actor who makes use of a policy may or may not be held responsible or blamable if the result is not satisfactory. In general, responsibility is limited to what could reasonably be anticipated by the actor at the time of action. A policy, however, is "responsible" for all the consequences that follow from its use, foreseen or not. Identification of the actor involved is important in policy evaluation only because the set of choices available will in some measure depend on who is involved. That produces some genuine problems for the critic when actions are a result of the authority attached to office or status. It is relatively easy to stipulate the legal scope of congressional authority, for example; but choices must be genuine and not merely legal possibilities, and that is exceptionally difficult to determine. The decision rules in the Congress serve to aggregate individual actions in ways that determine how the collective authority of the body is used. But the reasons an individual congressman votes for or against a bill may be unrelated to its content and the consequences of voting one way or another may be quite different for each person. The machinery aggregates votes in the same way that a basket "aggregates" apples, pears, and peaches. The voters are homogeneous only with respect to legal meaning. Analysis is complicated still further when the actual decisionmaking procedures are not known, as was the case with the Department of Housing and Urban Development (HUD). For it is almost impossible to hold an agency responsible for the results of its actions unless it can be forced to state its expectations in advance of action, thus allowing the critic access to the theories employed, and to outline the options from which a choice is being made, thus opening its priorities to public examination. Such prior commitment is rarely required by Congress or volunteered by an agency. While it is easy to attack an agency whose actions consistently produce results considered reprehensible, there is no way to justify the criticism without knowledge of the available alternatives and no way to suggest improvements until the decisioning procedures, and the assumptions attached to them, are made public.

Every guide to action or policy necessarily involves an empirical and a normative element and criticism may focus on either or both of them. If policies are guides to choice, and since choice refers necessarily to the future (it would be pointless to speak of "choosing" the past), policies necessarily refer to future outcomes that can be produced by human action. Projection of such anticipated results requires adequate theories (or "scientific" explanations). Because social science is notoriously deficient in theory, the projections will usually be weak and highly problematic. Social policymaking will therefore depend far more on improvement through trial and error or successive approximation than does agriculture, engineering, or medicine. It follows that agencies responsible for social policy require particularly well-developed machinery for gathering the results of action and linking the results to the policymaking apparatus in ways that will allow for speedy adjustment and modification. Further, social policy must rely more on "natural state experiments" or historical records and analogies than does policy in the harder sciences. The handicap need not be fatal, but it does imply a systematic effort on the part of social agencies to find evidence in recorded experience that relates to present concerns, to record experience that seems likely to have future importance, and to design current activity with an eye to learning how to deal with important classes of cases.

As guides to action, policies provide the various intervention strategies used to achieve desired outcomes in the environment. The precision and reliability of those intervention strategies are a direct function of the quality of the theories on which the policy depends. Increased knowledge and more sophisticated technology are often as important for the efficiency in action they make possible as for the goals they allow us to achieve. The weakness of social science is reflected in the crude and often wasteful techniques that are used by social policymakers—defining eligibility for food stamps and other welfare benefits loosely enough to ensure coverage of all those in need, for example, and thereby opening the way to widespread abuse by establishing eligibility for groups the program was not intended to benefit. Wasteful or inefficient intervention strategies are not limited to social matters, of course. It is common practice in medicine to vaccinate very large populations against such diseases as smallpox, even though only a very small number of persons actually need the protection. The procedure may be justified when the cost of each action is small, the difficulty of isolating and identifying those who genuinely need treatment is great, and the side effects of the action are minimal. But such techniques are wasteful and open the way to serious abuse. The practice of greasing the squeaky wheel solves the distribution problem in the short run by rewarding those who yell soonest and loudest, but it encourages research into loud and timely yelling rather than into equitable allocation procedures and the state of need. Similarly, distributing resources by conducting a lottery, which is another hidden cost of ignorance or unwillingness to deal seriously with problems, seems grossly unfair or improper if the knowledge needed for equitable distribution can be produced. All such dimensions of policy are a challenge for the evaluator.

Policies are evaluated in terms of their consequences, by comparing outcomes produced to available alternatives. Ultimately, consequences are specified in terms of effects on human populations. For man, man is necessarily the measure of all things. Such aspects of society as social stability or personal safety, economic growth or ease of access to education can be very important, obviously, but they are valued only because they can be linked to changes in the human condition and not intrinsically. Unless it can be shown that tenants in public housing benefit unmistakably in known ways from scatter-siting, for example, there is no reason to support that policy. It might be tried experimentally if it were expected, for some theoretical reason, that desirable effects would ensue, but that is a different issue. Evaluated in terms of their consequences, adequate policies must (1) identify a specific target population; (2) identify the amount and kind of change to be made in the lives of that population; and (3) provide a descriptive account of the present condition of the target population that can be used as a baseline for determining the actual effects of action. Policymaking and policy improvement involve a special kind of inventory management; without an initial inventory, the effects of action would be indeterminate and the policy cannot be tested or evaluated. Inducing change is not enough: policy improvements depend on information relating to amount of change, rate, time spans involved, and a variety of potential side effects. Collapsing these dimensions of action suppresses costs and benefits and thus eliminates the possibility of reasoned improvement.

Perhaps the best model available for social policymakers is found in the careful and painstaking planning, testing, and refinement used in medicine or agriculture. They combine a steady flow of information into the decisioning unit and organization of the administrative machinery in ways that will translate feedback information into policy modifications. Simply generating feedback is not enough; the information flowing from the field must be integrated with information relating to the current status of all the relevant subpopulations through an appropriate decisioning mechanism. A continuing choice of choices is required in any society not prepared to freeze its allocation system into a hard and fast mold. Unfortunately, the facilities and traditions needed for such ongoing evaluations are not incorporated into most governmental structures and are increasingly difficult to design as the structure grows in absolute size and complexity. Such considerations are prerequisites to elaborating an acceptable and justifiable allocation system for social benefits and costs.

Indicators of Public Housing Performance

Analytically, what is usually referred to as "public housing policy" is in fact a bundle of policies relating to a wide range of activities and generating a variety of consequences for a great many different persons. Among those affected directly and indirectly by what is done in public housing, for example, there are lawyers and bankers, architects and administrators, construction workers and taxpayers, security guards and tenants. Some classes of persons are affected directly and immediately by specific policy changes. Other effects appear in the broader features of society, in the social climate or even the physical terrain. And the effects of inaction and omission must be included in the consequences, for a family that is excluded from public housing by eligibility requirements adopted in Congress or by a local housing authority is affected just as much as a family that is eligible for entry but chooses to remain in the private sector. All such effects, to the extent they can be determined, are part of the cost–benefit calculations by which policies are evaluated.

The full impact of major public actions is beyond determination, in practice if not in principle. But if a target population has been identified, policy evaluation can begin by focusing on that group, trying to determine whether or not the changes expected to flow from the policy are actually produced, and seeking desirable and undesirable side effects. A policy that does not produce the expected outcome in the target population, whatever its side effects, is a clear failure. The side effects, serious or trivial, also cannot be fully anticipated, particularly with respect to large-scale operations. That is why policies must ultimately be tested in use—evaluation refers to effects actually obtained and not merely to projections. Moreover, different intervention strategies may have different side effects while producing a common outcome, and that provides an opportunity to increase efficiency or decrease costs. Technological advance furthers more efficient resource utilization as well as man's capacity to control ever larger areas of the environment. Of course, the primary focus of the policy must be maintained at the center of evaluation: it would be a travesty to count the millionaires created by medical practice and ignore the effects of treatment on the patients. But, so long as decent housing is provided for persons of low income, it is perfectly reasonable to prefer a method of construction that increases the available job supply to a method that does not if there is no significant decrease in the amount or quality of housing actually made available and if costs remain stable or even increase slightly.

Unfortunately, public housing policies were rarely conceived or asserted precisely enough to allow careful evaluation or improvement. The target population was simply "persons of low income," and the Congress neither attempted to aid all of the members of that class nor specified the kinds of results to be achieved. Federal and local authorities alike confined themselves to general statements about the amount of housing to be produced, costs, administrative regulations, and eligibility for participation. There was no effort to determine the size of the need for housing or to inventory the population needing housing and thus provide a baseline for measuring program performance. The decennial census data are much too badly flawed with respect to precisely the population that was the target for the program to be of much use. In consequence, evaluation of public housing from housing records alone is analogous to trying to determine the quality of the taxi service in a large city on the basis of taxi records alone. Even if the records were complete, accurate, and reliable the evaluation would be incomplete and in some respects inadequate—certain crucial questions could not be answered from those records. With respect to public housing, there is no way to decide from housing records alone whether the effects produced could have been generated more efficiently by other means. An adequate evaluation would have to take into account the amount and quality of housing provided and its relation to need, the alternative uses to which the resources might have been dedicated, and so on. The evaluation program is complex, and in practice almost impossible to carry out, but that is because the society does not habitually keep records of such matters.

The fact that taxicab records cannot establish the quality of the taxi service does not mean they are not worth careful study. Valuable information can be obtained relating to types of services provided, costs, characteristics of the recipients, potential lines of improvements, and even program performance along certain limited continua. If the need for the service is demonstrably greater than the supply—a question that can be answered from such records—then increasing the supply is reasonable, other things equal. If existing facilities are not fully utilized though a shortage has been established, that is a good indication of performance failure somewhere in the operation. Conversely, full use of available services indicates need satisfaction within the limits of available resources at an acceptable if not an optimal level. The measures are gross, but if facilities and needs can be differentiated, that may suggest ways of improving performance.

In public housing, the best practical indicator of performance, other things equal, is occupancy, the ratio of facilities occupied to time available for occupancy. Since the statutes and regulations supply fairly narrow standards of eligibility, all tenants are automatically part of the target population—low income persons or families. There is no implication of equal need, obviously. Demonstrating that the need for housing assistance in St. Louis was much greater than the supply of public housing is an easy task. As late as 1970, there were some

44,000 renters in the St. Louis metropolitan area earning less than $2,000 per year and another 37,000 renters earning between $2,000 and $4,000 per year.[3] Some 80,000 families therefore lived at or below the official poverty level for a family of four—$4,200 in 1973 and $5,000 in 1974. A large part of this population lived in the inner city; about two-thirds of them paid more than 35 percent of their income for rent. Concurrently, there were fewer than 9,000 units of public housing altogether. Clearly, far more families "needed" housing assistance than public housing could supply, even on very conservative estimate—assuming, for example, that those paying more than one-third of income for rent needed help. Further, urban renewal was reducing the supply of very cheap but poor quality housing in the area, thus reducing the options available to those willing to trade quality for lower price.

In those circumstances, significant vacancy levels in public housing clearly indicated program inadequacy. Reasons for the inadequacy could vary. The local authority may not have been able to supply housing on acceptable terms; external factors such as habit, tradition, or reputation may have interfered with the transformation of need into demand. And, if effective demand was very low in some projects but very high in others, as was the case in St. Louis, that reinforces the conclusion. Unfortunately, local housing authorities have little impact on the demand for public housing. Effective demand is not a response to legislative fiat but results from a complex set of calculations involving factors over which public authority has little control. The renter does not simply weigh something called the "cost of housing"; he rents a complex amalgam of real and imagined factors by applying principles that are not always consistent. Information about the rules of action actually employed in house selection are difficult to obtain and dangerous to infer. The fact that a family rents an apartment that *is* cheap does not mean that it was rented *because* it was cheap, though that may have been the reason. All that can be inferred from observation is that certain priorities and rules of choice are not being applied. That is, the family that rents a ground-floor apartment rather than an identical top-floor apartment does not prefer elevation to proximity, other things equal. Beyond that, the data are inconclusive.

The associated indicator of housing performance is, obvi-

3. Sue Dubman, *Poverty in St. Louis*.

ously, cost. While the primary costs of housing are monetary, not all money costs are recorded, and nonmonetary costs and benefits may be very important. Such direct costs as rent paid by the tenant and subsidies supplied by the federal government and by other public agencies are readily determined—though the nature and incidence of subsidies may be disputed. Indirect costs borne by the local community through forgone taxation, additional services required (police, garbage collection) and so on are more difficult to calculate, as are the collective benefits to the community. Monies expended by private and public agencies outside the federal government—local housing authority nexus, such as welfare organizations, church groups, child-care centers, and so on—are difficult to identify and compile. And the psychic costs and benefits to those involved with public housing, the headaches, the moments of pride and shame, the stigma, are quite beyond calculation but not unimportant. This study relies mainly on housing authority records and for that reason is incomplete, but the data are sufficient for the purposes in hand and other money costs are included where they can be identified.

Evidence relating to the physical condition of the public housing supplied to the low-income population is available only sporadically and in aggregate. There are occasional vignettes of apartment conditions in the records. The *Comprehensive Consolidated Management Review Report* prepared by HUD late in 1970 and published the following year contains an invaluable overview of physical conditions in the conventional developments; I have had to rely on it very heavily. The cost of reconstructing an adequate sample of specific apartment and building data would have been prohibitive given the state of the records and the size of the St. Louis Housing Authority's holdings. Had an adequate and systematic maintenance program been enforced, the records would have indicated the physical state of the housing when tenants entered or left; the extent and frequency of maintenance would have suggested the amount of damage incurred from tenant use. Unfortunately, the maintenance program in St. Louis was relatively ineffectual and unsystematic. Therefore, a "unit of housing" may refer to a wide range of apartment conditions.

Finally, there are significant amounts of information available about the tenant population; such things as age, income, size of family, number of minor children, and so forth are accurately recorded. Such data indicate the extent of the need for different kinds of housing and help identify the portion of the target population actually reached by the program. How the tenant population resembled the low-income population remaining in the private sector, and where they differed, simply is not known. That has unfortunate consequences. Knowing the characteristics of the tenants can be useful for refining policy, say, to exclude certain groups presently eligible for services. Such data cannot assist in policy revision that would bring other groups into the program. The point is not always appreciated fully. For example, when it was discovered that existing legislation allowed persons clearly excluded from the target population to obtain food stamps (unemployed young drifters, for example, or wealthy college students) the angry denunciations aimed at the malingerers ought properly to have been aimed at the legislation. Unless those who were angered by the results of applying the policy were suggesting that (1) it was not meant to be applied literally, or (2) administrators should be allowed to pick and choose the persons to whom such legislation provides benefits, anger was simply out of order. The only way in which policies can be improved is through literal application and careful scrutiny of the consequences.

Organization of the Materials

The evolution of public housing policy, including local and national regulations issued from the administrative units, is traced in Chapter II. The results of applying those policies in the city of St. Louis between 1939 and 1969 are summarized in Chapter III. The impact of policy changes is traced out in Chapters IV through VI. Chapter VII contains the major findings.

II.

The Evolution of Public
Housing Policy

Like so many other social programs in the United States, public housing was a product of the New Deal era. The basic assumptions and procedures that guided its development and operation were hammered out in the 1930s, in the National Recovery Act of 1933, the Housing Act of 1934, and the George-Healey Act of 1936, among others. The approach to public housing that emerged in the Housing Act of 1937 and was reproduced in its essentials in the Housing Act of 1949 dominated the public housing program for the next four decades. Two basic modes of operation were used to supply housing services to low-income families. The original prototype, known as the "conventional" public housing program, was characterized by the use of a public agency to develop, own, and operate the housing facilities; by the end of 1974, more than 860,000 units of housing, amounting to 66 percent of the total public housing supply, had been developed by this method. Another 230,000 units, about 18 percent of the total, were produced by a variant known as "turnkey" housing; the units were developed by private interests, then sold to a public agency, usually a local housing authority. The Housing Act of 1965 authorized an alternative approach to supplying public housing for the poor, lease of privately owned facilities. By the end of 1974, leasing accounted for more than 13 percent of the total supply, some 169,000 units of 1,316,000. The changes in operating philosophy introduced by the Housing and Urban Development Act of 1974 foreshadowed a major increase in the role played by leased housing in the overall public housing program. Indeed, if the 1974 act were to be implemented systematically and rigorously and without major change it could put an end to the traditional form of public housing in relatively short order. Some of the reasons for the new approach, and its implications, are explored in this chapter.

Conventional Public Housing

The public housing program incorporated into the Housing Act of 1937 was very much a child of the times. The first Roosevelt administration faced a staggering array of problems when it took office in 1933: the economy was stagnant, unemployment was extremely high, wage levels were badly depressed, the monetary and fiscal system was in shambles, and public confidence in government and private enterprise alike had been shaken by the stock-market collapse and its aftermath. The housing industry was but one of many sectors of the economy in urgent need of assistance. In the cities, large concentrations of aged and dilapidated buildings, lacking in amenities and badly needing repairs, posed a hazard to the health of the inhabitants and, so it was believed at least, a danger to the social health of the community. Everywhere there was an acute shortage of decent housing for persons of low income, and overcrowding of the kind indicated by the 1940 census of housing had been common for years. In the circumstances, it is hardly surprising that the public housing program was viewed as a multipurpose activity, a way of simultaneously reducing the level of unemployment in the country, assisting the beleaguered housing industry, eliminating slums and their concomitants, and increasing the supply of cheap and decent housing available to the poor.

Development of a program that could serve a number of masters was very powerfully reinforced by various other circumstances of the times. There were wealthy and powerful interests to be placated—in real estate, banking, construction, and the labor unions—and their aims were not always compatible. The prevailing ideology was characterized by built-in opposition to public ownership or even to extensive governmental intervention into the social and economic life of the nation. The tradition of self-help remained strong, and there was a marked tendency to assume that poverty was deserved and avoidable by hard work. Finally, the superiority of a profit-maximizing economic system, euphemized in school and press as a "free enterprise system," was taken for granted by rich and poor alike. The corollary assumption that private enterprise is invariably more efficient and productive than any form of governmental activity was accepted as an article of faith by most elements of society. While such propositions may be tautologically true in Adam Smith's economics, the empirical evidence is sparse and inconclusive. In any case, even if the superior efficiency of private enterprise could be demonstrated with respect to the past, there is no reason in principle why it should continue into the indefinite future regardless of the direction taken by society as a whole. Nevertheless, these beliefs have been much reinforced, quite illegitimately, by uninformed and irresponsible generalizing about "the failure of public housing," though the evidence suggests quite a different set of conclusions.

Unfortunately for the public housing program, multipurpose activities make for ambiguous policies and uncertain target populations; they in turn make it difficult if not impossible to criticize, evaluate, or improve the program. In both the 1937 and 1949 housing acts, the major articulated concerns were unemployment and slum clearance; the provision of housing for persons of low income was a peripheral rather than a central goal.[1] And with respect to housing, primary emphasis was placed on development and construction and not on the provision of housing services. In consequence, progress tended to be measured in terms of dollars spent, units of housing produced, construction wages generated, or number of units of dilapidated housing demolished rather than the amount and quality of housing-in-use supplied to the poor. Yet measuring the success of a public housing program in terms of employment provided, slums cleared, or even units built is as much a travesty as measuring the success of a medical operation in terms of amount of time taken, number of persons involved, or the surgeon's fee. Indeed, if the emphasis in the legislation is taken literally, the Pruitt and Igoe developments in St. Louis, commonly ranked among the more prominent disasters in the history of public housing, ought properly to be counted among its greatest successes, for they were built at great cost, they lasted a very short time, and they were quite expensive to liquidate. In brief, they contributed more to the local economy in the short run than any other housing development in the city's history.

1. The best general historical survey of the early days of public housing is Robert M. Fisher's *Twenty Years of Public Housing: Economic Aspects of the Federal Program.* Other useful background works include Robert Ellickson, "Government Housing Assistance to the Poor"; Robert Taggart III, *Low Income Housing: A Critique of Federal Aid*; Leonard Freedman, *Public Housing: The Politics of Poverty*; plus the periodic surveys in the *Congressional Quarterly.*

Ownership and Administration

Given the economic circumstances in which public housing evolved, the locus of ownership and operational control over facilities was a matter of prime importance. Public housing provided a major opportunity for breaking the established mode of economic activity and demonstrating an alternative. The profit-maximizing production and distribution system then operating responded only to effective demand (desire *plus* capacity to pay); it had clearly failed to provide for the housing needs of large segments of the population. That is, it had produced housing that was too expensive for many, as well as the many for whom housing was too expensive. How to deal with the situation? An effort to maintain private ownership and yet to control the price of housing to the consumer would have foundered unless production costs were controlled or rents were subsidized. Cost control was anathema to owners and unions alike. Direct cash subsidies, much favored by real estate interests, were considered far too expensive overall, since they would overstimulate demand for an inadequate supply of decent housing and thus provide unwarranted returns to the owners of old housing of poor or marginal quality. Public ownership offered a more efficient means of divorcing the cost of housing to the tenant from the cost of development. Capital could be obtained at preferred rates, taxes avoided, and the return to capital (profit) retained in the public coffers. In the long run, ownership is cheaper than renting or leasing. Nevertheless, in 1974, pressure from interest groups made public subsidy of privately owned housing the central thrust of the public housing program, suggesting that in economic matters sheer persistence is more likely to be rewarded by government than is good argument.

Given the strength of the opposition to public ownership in American society, congressional agreement to public ownership of housing was a tribute to the strength of the critique launched against the performance of the economic system. Until 1965, public housing in the United States meant publicly owned housing. The program was one of the few large-scale experiments in public ownership in an area traditionally regarded as part of the private sector. In the early days of the New Deal, ownership was vested in the federal government and operations were controlled by a centralized bureaucracy. An adverse court ruling in 1935 that prevented the use of eminent domain to obtain land for public housing sites coupled with popular distrust of "big government" forced a change in the rules. The Housing Act of 1937 gave title to local housing authorities (LHAs) which were agencies of local government, created within a framework of state enabling legislation. If public housing has been a dismal failure, as is often charged, there would be little reason to experiment further along the same lines or in parallel areas. In fact, the failure is grossly exaggerated and misconstrued. What failed was a particular form of public housing, foreseeably programmed for failure no matter how earnest, willing, or competent the administration. The attack on "public housing" is perhaps the most arrant example of condemnation without trial in the annals of the society.

In principle, public ownership of housing facilities enables the government to supply housing to persons according to need rather than capacity to pay, making up the difference between rents charged and actual costs from the public treasury. But public ownership alone is not enough. Other conditions must also be satisfied for the program to succeed. Had the federal government created enough decent housing to supply all of society's needs and underwritten the difference between operating costs and the rent that tenants could afford to pay, program administrators could have simply located the needy and housed them as expeditiously as possible. But to the degree that the available housing was of poor quality or was significantly less than the need, or that operating costs were inadequately subsidized and could not be met from tenant rents without imposing serious hardships, the program could not operate properly.

Tragically, the necessary conditions for a successful public housing program were nowhere met consistently or adequately, primarily because of the way in which the program was designed. The quality of building construction was often poor and sometimes grossly inadequate. Poor construction and inadequate resources for maintenance, reinforced by a social climate in which vandalism was sometimes positively encouraged, rather than impeded, produced significantly accelerated deterioration of facilities in the 1960s. The method of financing adopted by the Congress forced local housing authorities to transfer the burden of rapidly increasing maintenance and operating costs, reinforced at times by very serious inflation, to the tenants. By the end of the 1960s, the combination of policies and circumstances had brought most of the larger housing authorities in the nation to their financial knees. Nevertheless, the amount of public housing actually developed—disregarding quality for the moment—was far less than the actual need. The absence of accurate data relating to need prevents a precise estimate of the degree of inadequacy. Fewer than 160,000 dwelling units were authorized and built under the 1937 Housing Act; the Housing Act of 1949 generated 1,115,000 units to the end of 1974. But in 1949, it was estimated that 810,000 units of housing, the amount authorized by the 1949 act, was only one-tenth of the total need. The shortcomings of the public housing program condemned millions of persons to paying an inordinate share of their income for shelter of the poorest quality for years and years, despite the humaneness of the goals articulated by Congress in 1949. Governmental unwillingness to accept responsibility for satisfying the urgent and primary need for decent shelter produced scarcity that was socially induced and therefore avoidable, though at cost. In time, government policy tended to exclude from public housing the very persons the program was designed to serve—the working poor.

Development Policies

The program created by the 1937 Housing Act was built on a local–federal arrangement from which the state was virtually excluded once enabling legislation was passed. Over time, Congress tended to concentrate on four basic areas of housing policy, leaving most other matters for administrative decision: First, the amount of housing authorized for addition to the public housing stock; second, the cost of developing the facilities; third, the fiscal arrangements that controlled program operations; fourth, the conditions of tenancy. Federal administrators exercised a great deal of control over the program through budgetary oversight, allocating resources for new development, auditing, and monitoring everyday operations. Local governments could influence the program in their areas through the formal cooperative agreement required by statute and, less formally, through appointment of the governing body that directed the program. In practice, local governments had

veto power over certain critical aspects of development, notably the size, location, design, and staffing of the facilities. The
local housing authority, under the overall direction of the governing body, had a voice in site selection, choice of architect,
design, and so on; it also controlled such aspects of daily operations as tenant selection, maintenance and repairs, legal actions against tenants, staffing, and general administration.
Until the 1970s, the LHAs were given wide latitude in operations by the federal administration; central control over details
of day-to-day operations increased substantially after 1969.

The direct cost of public housing to the local community was
spelled out in the required federal–local agreement. The LHA
was granted a tax exemption in return for a payment in lieu of
taxes amounting to 10 percent of gross rent less utility costs.
Whether the payment covered the actual cost to the community, particularly during those periods when rents were high
and occupancy was virtually complete, is much debated and
probably not determinable. On the other hand, the collective
benefit obtained from public housing development certainly
outweighed any additional direct cost to the community. Curiously, the positive benefits derived from public housing were
usually ignored. The 1937 act required local governments to
eliminate one unit of substandard housing for each unit of
public housing built, but the impact of the "equivalent elimination" rule was slight and it was abandoned in 1949. Finally,
local governments were to provide such normal municipal services as police and fire protection, garbage removal, paving,
and street lighting. In practice, the obligations proved difficult
to enforce. In St. Louis, the local authority was forced to employ
private security guards by the beginning of the 1960s and
complaints about the quality of garbage collection, street lighting, and so on were common. The net effect of such performance
failures by local governments was a major increase in the
managerial burden placed on the LHA and ultimately a large
increase in the cost of operating the facilities.

There were two curious lacunae in the development policies
generated within the federal government: first, little effort was
made to control the quality of the housing produced; second, the
cost of the site was not limited by any of the statutes. The 1937
Housing Act placed a ceiling on the overall cost of each dwelling unit and on the cost per room; established limits could be
adjusted upward 25 percent in "high construction cost" areas,

usually the larger cities where powerful construction unions operated. In 1949, limits on overall cost per unit were eliminated leaving cost per room as the sole criterion available for controlling development cost. Since room cost limits were included in the legislation, they applied to the country as a whole. In 1970, Congress adopted a "prototype" cost base for dwelling units of various sizes and types of construction and HUD was charged with establishing suitable limits and revising them annually. Again, the limits could be exceeded by 10 percent without waiver and by another 10 percent with federal approval. Land costs remained uncontrolled and no qualitative construction controls were specified in the statutes.

The effect of weak control over development costs and construction quality is readily foreseen. Site costs were often unconscionable, particularly in the 1950s when the rate of development was high and projects were deliberately located in cleared slum areas—and forced to absorb clearing costs. In the long run, the economic inefficiencies generated by land speculation were probably less important than the common practice of paying premium prices for apartments so shoddily built that a choir of angels could not have abided in them regularly without producing serious disrepair. Poor quality cannot be ascribed to federal miserliness. In St. Louis, the Housing Authority paid for its projects at costs equal to or greater than the cost of luxury housing in the suburbs. It did not receive value for money from the housing industry.

The principle underlying the failure is not hard to find. A profit-maximizing economic system also minimizes performance. Unless performance criteria for the end product are specified fully, in which case there is likely to be a major increase in cost, the producer is bound by the rules of the game and perhaps by the "facts" of economic life to maximize profits within the limits of the contract price. The most accessible route to additional profit is a reduction in the quality of the product. The clearest evidence of the pervasiveness of the principle is found in the recent experience of federal agencies engaged in space exploration or defense whose purposes demand very high levels of performance. To obtain quality performance, specifications must be developed in great detail and with precision, otherwise cost overruns of great magnitude can be anticipated from the effort to achieve required performance through trial and error. The result is in either case a massive increase in end-product cost. The same trend appears in the general market for consumer goods. In principle, the producer whose goods perform poorly or whose services are less than what they should be is supposed to lose his customers to a better producer. In practice, information flow among consumers is incomplete and the gap between promise and performance is so common that it seems to have little impact on consumer behavior, perhaps because advertising practices reinforce unconcern. Whatever the reason, the producer who can choose between a significant improvement in product performance at some known cost and artificial demand stimulation for an unimproved product at much greater cost is apparently well advised to choose the latter. The old adage about building a better mousetrap and having the world beat a path to the door no longer holds, if ever it did. Patent medicine is not always driven from the marketplace by disclosing that it is only patent medicine or even by development of a genuine cure for the illness the patent medicine purports to treat.

Conditions of Tenancy

The more important of the congressional policies relating to tenancy in public housing dealt with eligibility for admission and continued occupancy, rent levels, definitions of tenant income, and priorities assigned to different classes of applicants. The consistent central concerns have been the amount of income that a prospective tenant could earn yet enter or remain in public housing and the kinds of income that could be excluded from such calculations. Under strong pressure from real estate interests, the prime goal of federal policy was to exclude from public housing anyone with enough income to obtain housing on the private market. Understandably, those interests sought to keep the income level of public housing tenants at a minimum. Since income limits were partly determined by local rent levels, which in turn were based on information supplied by local real estate interests, they were often quite influential. Over the long run, pressure for low ceilings on tenant income, taken in conjunction with other fiscal policies, contributed materially to the aggregation in public housing of a highly dependent population whose incomes were very low in relation to the rest of the community and changed much more slowly than general wage and price rates. For example, between the early 1950s and the mid-1970s the consumer price index for St. Louis more than doubled, while the median family income for public housing tenants rose from about $2,400 per year to just over $3,700 per year, far less than was needed to keep pace with inflation even if the initial income level had been adequate—clearly not the case.

The procedure used to determine income limits for those admitted to public housing was fairly complex. The LHA went to the local housing market (newspapers, agents and brokers, and so forth) to determine the current price of decent rental accommodations of various sizes. The income needed to "afford" such housing was calculated by a five-to-one ratio (six-to-one for families with three or more minor children). That is, if the going price for a three-bedroom apartment was $100 per month, it was assumed that a family with an income of $500 per month could afford it ($600 per month when there were three or more minor children). The maximum allowable income for admission to public housing was 80 percent of that amount, or $400 per month. Federal policy required a "20 percent gap" between the income sufficient to afford needed housing and the maximum allowable income for admission to the developments. If other factors remained constant, the tenant whose income increased to 25 percent over admission limits was required to leave public housing. He would then be earning enough to "afford" housing on the private market. In principle, the policy was expected to keep everyone with enough income to purchase housing on the private market out of public housing. However, estimates of available housing tended to significantly overestimate the amount of "decent" housing available and significantly underestimate the going price and thereby to exclude from public housing many of its "best" potential tenants. The relative value of the facilities afforded by public housing, even in areas where they were badly deteriorated, is attested by the length of housing authority waiting lists.

Given the formula used to calculate eligibility for admission to public housing, the question what kinds of income should be excluded from the calculation was a major concern for both tenant and LHA. The 1937 act, which simply counted all income from all sources, soon produced hardships that clearly contravened the spirit, if not the letter, of the program. The 1949 act allowed an exemption of $100 per year for each of the first three children in the family and the first $500 of earnings by a minor. The $100 exemption was later extended to all minors in the family and, over time, exemptions were allowed for child care, tuition costs, medical expenses, certain kinds of work expenses, and so on. In some cases, special arrangements were allowed because of peculiar local circumstances; the arrangements that settled the St. Louis rent strike in 1969, for example, enumerated income exemptions considerably broader than those allowed by normal regulations. The Housing and Urban Development Act of 1974 consolidated and reduced exclusions, allowing (1) $300 for each minor, (2) nonrecurring income, (3) the first $300 of earnings by the spouse, and (4) 5 percent of gross income (10 percent for elderly families). The "20 percent gap" was then dropped.

Once prospective tenants satisfied the income limits required for admission, various priorities established by Congress or administrative action came into play. Precedence was given to war veterans and persons displaced from their homes by such public actions as slum clearance in both the 1937 and 1949 housing acts. In 1954, a hostile Congress limited admission strictly to persons displaced by public action, but that policy proved untenable and was rescinded the following year. The impact of such priorities probably varied from city to city but seems not to have been very great. Between 1966 and 1973, for example, fewer than 12 percent of all families entering public housing had been displaced by public action, and only 1.2 percent were uprooted by either urban renewal or housing development. In 1956, the elderly were given priority in admission, and an increase in construction costs of $500 per room was allowed for housing designed specifically for use by the elderly. That priority was extended to the disabled shortly afterward.

The negative priorities involved in racial segregation were ignored by the Congress and by the federal and local administrations. When the public housing program began, developments in many cities were racially segregated and blacks were excluded from white projects, or vice versa, as a matter of course. Formal segregation ended in 1954 when the U.S. Supreme Court refused to overturn a California ruling that admission to public housing could not be refused on racial grounds. Within fifteen years, local social and economic conditions in many areas combined to resegregate public housing, this time with respect to the rest of the community, by aggregating large numbers of minority group members in the developments.

The rent paid by public housing tenants was linked to family income and not to the amount of space occupied. A large family with little income might pay less for a five-bedroom apartment than was charged a smaller family with a larger income for an apartment with a single bedroom. Technically, the portion of tenant income paid for rent was not limited, though in practice the administrators tried to maintain rents at minimum levels. As housing authority operating costs soared after 1960, minimum and average rents climbed steadily, far more rapidly than tenant income. By 1969, such cost pressures had created very serious problems for most housing authorities. Some of the very poorest tenants were forced to pay as much as three-fourths of their income for rent, and payments equal to one-half of gross income were common. That condition, among others, led to the 1969 rent strike in St. Louis and to significant disturbances elsewhere. The outcry produced one of the so-called Brooke amendments in 1969, limiting the amount that could be charged a tenant in public housing to 25 percent of adjusted income—less for persons of very low income. Unfortunately, that limitation sometimes led to reductions in state welfare payments; such reductions were forbidden by another Brooke amendment in 1971. The 25 percent limit was apparently taken from the rent supplement provisions of the 1965 Housing Act. Why it was considered proper is uncertain; by European standards, 25 percent of income is a very high rent level. Perhaps the American propensity to relatively expensive single-family housing accounted for the size of the standard. In 1974, the structure was simplified, though the base was retained: rent could vary from 25 percent of income for persons earning 80 percent or more of the median income in the area to 5 percent of income for persons with very large families (six or more minors) or very low incomes (less than 50 percent of the area's median income). The act required LHAs to fill at least 30 percent of their units with families from the very-low-income group. However, the act also required each LHA to collect at least 20 percent of the total income of its tenants as rent. The confusion engendered by the regulations lasted well into 1977. Median income levels are virtually impossible to determine with any accuracy for a metropolitan area, and the meaning of the median in this context is most uncertain. If the median is calculated from the tax rolls, those who do not file, mainly persons of very low income, are omitted, and that tends to raise the median level. If medians are calculated from census data, the results are even more likely to be artificially high. Neither the method to be used for the calculation nor the reason for using such standards in the first place was made clear in the legislation or in the discussion that preceded it.

Fiscal Policies

The public housing program created by the Congress moved toward financial disaster as inexorably and predictably as any Greek tragedy. Inadequate policies with respect to quality and costs virtually ensured physical structures of minimal quality. The limits imposed on tenant income guaranteed a very modest rent yield to the LHA. The self-destruct system was completed by adopting fiscal policies that were foreseeably unworkable and sticking to them for more than thirty years in the face of all evidence. To put the matter as starkly as possible, the federal government undertook to pay all capital costs on public housing as they came due, it guaranteed the mortgage payment leaving all other expenses the responsibility of the local housing authority. The LHA's sole source of income was rent. No operating subsidy whatever was provided by Congress until 1961. Had the matter stopped there, the program could not have survived very long. Economic collapse was rendered even more certain by imposing four additional fiscal burdens on the LHA, to be met from its rental income alone.

First, utility costs were included in the rent charged the tenant. From the tenant's point of view, utilities were a free good, rent was unaffected by the amount of utilities used. Predictably, utility costs became a major burden on local housing authorities, even before utility prices began to climb in the energy-scarce climate of the 1970s.

Second, 10 percent of gross income from rent less utility costs had to be turned over to local government each year as payment in lieu of taxes. Until 1937, public housing was owned by the federal government and therefore was automatically exempt from state and local taxes. To offset the cost of municipal services to the developments, 10 percent of gross rent was turned over voluntarily to local governments. When ownership of public housing was vested in local authorities, they became subject to local taxes. However, the Congress required local support for the housing program amounting to 20 percent of the federal contribution, a requirement that local governments could meet in full simply by waiving local taxes. In return, the LHA was permitted to pay 10 percent of gross rent minus utility costs in lieu of taxes. In 1954, the waiver of taxes was made a program requirement and the payment in lieu of taxes was mandated rather than allowed.

Third, the cash reserves that could be accumulated by any LHA were limited by administrative action to 50 percent of one year's rent. That very effectively precluded the LHA from building up the funds needed for capital replacement or even for major maintenance such as roof repairs. As the apartments aged, major maintenance was deferred and handled piecemeal. Unfortunately, an iron law of escalation in damages operates in even the most expensive and luxurious apartments: the amount of damage to a building or area increases directly and exponentially with the time delay between damage and repair. Maintenance deferral is an open invitation to vandalism, regardless of the age, sex, ethnic background, income level, occupation, or rent level of the tenants.

Fourth, in any year in which an LHA "showed a profit," in which rental income exceeded gross expenses plus allowable transfers to reserves, the surplus was used to pay capital costs—to reduce annual contract contributions. From 1945 until 1953, the federal government paid less than 50 percent of the capital costs of public housing, and in the peaks years of 1948 and 1949 the LHAs paid nearly 85 percent of their own capital costs. Congress added insult to injury in 1954 by requiring the LHAs to repay 55 percent of capital costs from rental income. The requirement had little practical significance given the steady deterioration in the financial position of LHAs, but it does provide a good indication of the blindness to long-range impact common among those responsible for policy decisions relating to public housing.

The fiscal arrangements made by Congress were the most important single factor in the eventual breakdown of the conventional public housing program. Combined with inadequate control over housing quality and relatively poor administrative performance (HUD inefficiency is notorious, even among Washington bureaucrats, and it was very unlikely that LHAs

could recruit adequately trained and experienced administrators given their fiscal position and political vulnerability),
they doomed the program, *foreseeably and inescapably*! The
point is vital. It was both humane and reasonable to base the
tenant's rent on ability to pay rather than space occupied by the
family, and it was altogether appropriate to restrict occupancy
to persons of low income. It was also reasonable to expect local
housing authorities to operate their developments with the
income obtained from rent once capital costs were secured. But
imposing *both* requirements without additional subsidy was an
act of folly, particularly in the light of the known periodicity of
the economic system. The housing program could succeed only
if costs, rents, and tenant incomes remained in relatively stable relationship for fairly long time periods. Since economic
activity tends toward very rapid shifts in costs and prices and
the incomes of the poor do not keep pace with rising costs, the
logic of the fiscal arrangements guaranteed a cost–income
squeeze for the LHA in any period of rapidly advancing wages
and prices.

Even without inflation, the fiscal apparatus was lethal. The
LHA's income was a function of the price of housing on the local
market and the income of the tenants. The LHA's expenses
depended on the size, quality, durability, design, and so on of
the developments; the kinds of tenants who occupied the premises; and basic trends in the overall economy. There was no
reason to suppose that the income needed to operate the developments would be generated out of the interplay of this set
of pressures. In the private sector, the rental income needed for
successful operation of multifamily apartments is calculated
by a rule of thumb that states that roughly one-sixth of development costs must be generated each year in rent. In the
1940s and 1950s, about 40 percent of the total rent (6.4 percent
of development costs) was needed to cover operating expenses;
by the 1960s, it was safer to assume that about 50 percent of
rental income was required for that purpose. In effect, the
private sector estimated that between 6.4 percent and 8.0 percent of development costs must be yielded each year from rents
just to cover operating expenses. An equal amount was needed
to pay capital costs, taxes, and return to the investor. Utility
costs were normally borne by the tenant and do not figure in
the calculation. The gross level of revenues required in the
private sector is approximately the same as the HUD estimate

that $754 in annual income is needed for each $10,000 of investment in a public housing development.

Public housing authorities rarely obtained as much as 6 percent of their investment costs in annual rentals; in St. Louis, the return averaged just over 4 percent for more than two decades. Moreover, an adjustment is needed to cover the utility costs and lieu of taxes paid by the LHAs; it brings income requirements to about 10 percent of development cost per annum. Such sums were far beyond the capacity of housing authority tenants to pay; and even if that much rent had been collected, regulations governing reserves would not have allowed the LHA to set enough aside to meet future replacement costs. Finally, private sector estimates assume good design, sound construction, and proper care by tenant and management alike—conditions not easily met in public housing, particularly after 1960. In the circumstances, the most surprising thing about the collapse at the end of the 1960s is that anyone was surprised. Mere survival was in some cases a major accomplishment.

Changing the Basic Pattern: Subsidies and Privatization

The operating pattern for public housing established in 1937 continued with only minor changes until the 1960s. Both opponents and supporters of public housing tended to what might best be called "mindless incrementalism" in their approach to policymaking. Reasoned decisions increase or decrease resources allocated to specific purposes on the basis of careful study of the effects of operation. Mindless incrementalism is marked by increases or decreases in allocations that are unrelated to performance or even perverse in the light of performance. Such procedures are a good indication of failure somewhere in the policymaking process, usually in either the supply of information or the manner in which the information is used. In the case of public housing, the failure occurred in both areas: too often, the data needed to correct and improve policy were not available; in most cases the conventional wisdom that served as a base for decision was mistaken or misdirected. Since the initial conditions to which these policies applied were not determined and the target population was only vaguely identified, there was no way to decide the amount and kind of change produced by specific actions, to locate the major side effects of policy, or to make a reasoned assessment of impact. The program was radically incorrigible until it collapsed; the way it collapsed virtually guaranteed that any lessons the experience might have taught would not be learned.

In fairness to supporters of public housing, incrementalism was in some degree forced by the opposition; both nationally and locally, hostility to public housing remained widespread, vocal, powerful, and implacable. It was difficult just to obtain a simple increase in the number of units authorized in a given fiscal year. Supporters of the program may well have felt that asking for policy innovations was too risky. There is considerable evidence to support that point of view.[2] The opposition in Congress and in the country was strong enough to delay enactment of a new housing law from 1945 until 1949, even though the proposed bill had Republican support (from Sen. Robert Taft and others). The public housing provisions of the 1949 Housing Act escaped deletion in the House of Representatives by only five votes. In 1949, Congress authorized development of 165,000 units each year for five years, but only 250,000 units were actually funded in the whole decade of the 1950s. As the Eisenhower administration grew increasingly hostile to governmental intervention in the economic sphere, mere survival of the public housing program became increasingly uncertain.

On the other hand, the special circumstances in which public housing operations began in the 1940s made the first generation of developments (authorized in 1937) conspicuously successful in the early years, masking the fact that the program was living on borrowed time. World War II brought about a rapid shift in population to urban war production centers and placed enormous pressure on the existing housing supply. Relatively full employment and higher earnings, coupled with a special dispensation that allowed the use of public housing by war workers, created a bonanza for local housing authorities not entailed by federal policies. War workers kept the apartments full. Tenant incomes far in excess of the levels intended by regulations meant premium rents and ample incomes for LHAs operating new developments requiring little major maintenance or capital replacement. Even after the war ended, occupancy remained high, some of the overincome workers

2. See particularly, Freedman, *Public Housing*, and Daniel R. Mandelker, *Housing Subsidies in the United States and England*.

remained, and most of the tenant body were employed, hence rental income remained relatively high until the end of the 1940s. Difficulties began when overincome tenants were forced from the developments, occupancy began to fall, and maintenance costs and capital replacement needs began to rise rapidly.

Again, the multipurpose character of the public housing program tended to impede evaluation of its performance. Additions to the program were usually sold to the Congress during periods of moderate-to-severe economic recession as a way of stimulating the construction industry while serving good purposes. Even as late as 1974, public housing was linked legislatively to community development and then indirectly to such diverse functions as rational use of land, integration of income groups, and preservation of historic properties. While such mixed associations may help gain votes in Congress, they increase the difficulties associated with performance evaluation. In practice, program supporters tend to emphasize the positive aspects of performance and ignore failures; the opposition follows the same strategy but emphasizes different factors. The *balance* of benefits and costs, which is crucial to reasoned policy improvement, tends to be ignored by both sides.

The Changing Social Environment

While public housing policy remained more or less frozen in its original mold, operating on principles borrowed from the traditional private sector, social change was proceeding rapidly in the housing developments as in the wider community. World War II much accelerated certain trends established earlier, such as the shift of population from the central city to the suburbs. Persons in the higher income brackets headed for the suburbs early in the century; federal housing and tax policies after 1945 encouraged blue- and white-collar workers to follow. New industries and old industries alike moved to the cheaper land on the city's outskirts as they expanded; a burgeoning trucking industry and an expanded highway construction program hastened the process by increasing accessibility. The erosion of the city's tax base was hastened by urban renewal, transportation construction, and subsidies to housing and other construction. Despite the countless billions of dollars poured into the central cities in an effort to preserve what was mistakenly identified as "the city" as a whole, anticipated investment did not materialize. The inner city became increasingly an isolated clump of older business facilities surrounded by a widening belt of deteriorated housing occupied mainly by the very poor, the black, and the permanently unemployed. Neighborhoods previously characterized by long-term residence and stable social behavior crumbled and fragmented as the elderly died off and the younger workers moved to the suburbs seeking homes they could afford, desirable schools and neighborhoods, and physical separation from the expanding inner-city ghetto. The end of the World War II employment boom hardened the differences between inner city and suburb. The recession of 1956–1957 had a profound impact on most large cities, and for some the recession of 1961–1962 was merely a continuation. Lack of employment, particularly among the young, the black, and the disadvantaged, increased out-migration of the working-age population; those left behind were mainly the permanent poor, the very young and the very old, the disabled, the relatively helpless and dependent, the recipients of public assistance.

As in other things, the public housing developments mirrored the course of events in the wider community. Public housing ceased to be a way station for the working poor en route to a family-owned dwelling and became a haven for concentrated masses of dependent persons with little possibility of improving their lot through their own efforts. The indicators of their helplessness were classic: real wages that lagged persistently and significantly behind local and national levels; unemployment rates several times the national average; extreme transience in employment; marginal jobs; frequent and often sustained reliance on public assistance; and heavy concentrations of the very young and the very old, usually members of a minority group. In some cases, two or three generations of a single family were tenants in the same public housing development. Tragically, factual helplessness was actually increasing at the very time when the dependent population was being urged most strongly to entertain rising expectations about the quality of its own life and the life its children could anticipate. In the past, the liberal rhetoric of national politics had been counterbalanced effectively by the conservative practice of local authorities. After 1945, the federal government became a direct and meaningful participant in local affairs, often bypassing state and local jurisdiction. Unfortunately, the rhetoric of national politics was seldom funded at a level that allowed the entire poor population to benefit. Most commonly, rhetoric was implemented through lotteries in which a few cities were successful and most were not or through legal changes that could not be enforced without costs the government was rarely prepared to accept—the busing controversy of the early 1970s is a good illustration of the process.

Of course, rhetoric has an impact on attitudes, opinions, and behavior that may exceed the effects of funded programming. To the extent that legalistic liberals supported the pursuit of principle without regard for the consequences, they played an important role in the general dissolution of internalized social controls that characterized the 1960s. The subsequent course of events was dramatic evidence of the inability of such institutions as law, police, courts, schools, churches, and families to maintain stability and order when the underlying priorities of society are challenged blindly and persistently. Crimes against person and property increased relentlessly despite enormous expenditures for security and the introduction of highly sophisticated technologies for maintaining social control. Abandoned houses were vandalized systematically rather than allowed to decay unmolested. Public property of all sorts, and not public housing alone, was subjected to alarming abuse in every area of society. Both personal and collective behavior were freed from a significant range of prior restrictions. Claims to rights and prerogatives increased exponentially while obligations long taken for granted were questioned or simply abandoned. The social climate, in brief, became stormy, threatening, subject to extreme perturbations.

Local housing authorities were caught in a broad flow of events they could not hope to master, bereft of resources, married perforce to inadequate and relatively inflexible federal policies, harassed by a clientele that desperately needed their services yet increasingly could not afford them. The cities were helpless, caught in the same whirlwind; the states, for the most part, looked the other way. Declining productivity in the housing industry worsened the LHAs' situation by increasing capital and maintenance costs without improving quality or increasing productivity. The real costs of housing began to rise rapidly just as public housing development began expanding. Various contributory factors can be identified: profit-maximizing entrepreneurs used technological improvements to maximize profits, union power forced the inefficient use of expensive labor. It cost more and more simply to maintain the quality of a basic unit of housing; the effort to reduce costs apparently led to an overall decrease in construction standards.

A parallel transformation of the population of public housing undermined the survival capacity of the LHAs in every part of the country. There was a steady decline in the number of employed workers, a steady increase in the number of families wholly or partially dependent on public assistance. Predictably, the amount of income available to each family tended to decline relative to incomes and prices in the wider community. The number of female heads of household increased with a concurrent expansion of the number of relatively undisciplined young persons living in the developments. In border cities such as St. Louis, racial segregation based on income became the rule. Public housing became the prime repository for the very poor: the black, the elderly, the female head of household and her brood of children, the unemployed, and the unemployable. Rents declined, expenses soared, the meager reserves were soon expended; the financial position of the LHAs weakened rapidly and seriously. Declining revenues forced deferred maintenance, which led to deteriorating physical conditions, which stimulated vandalism, which further depressed the quality of the housing supply. The end result was too often a ghastly landscape of mutilated buildings, broken glass, empty apartments, abandoned automobiles, litter, and garbage; a wasteland hostage to the criminal, vagrant, truant, and street gang; a hazard to the passerby; and a nightmare to the resident.

Subsidies

Money alone would not have solved the problems of the LHAs; but, without significant additions to their incomes, efforts to improve design, tenant selection, management, maintenance, or other aspects of performance were futile. Public housing deteriorated in a shocking manner predominantly because of the money shortage; so long as funds were available, most developments operated reasonably well. The two St. Louis developments completed in 1942, for example, were exemplars of the kind of public housing intended by the legislators so long as even modest resources were available to maintain them. Although the federal government allowed periodic increases in construction costs, modest rent increases, and in rare cases allocated special funds for refurbishing some of the more conspicuous disasters, no regular operating subsidy of any kind was available until 1961 and there was no effective operating subsidy before 1972. Yet, so long as the LHAs were wholly dependent on rent, the fact of low tenant income meant that they could not obtain enough revenue to operate the developments. Under the pressure of rising costs and deteriorating physical plant, the LHAs were literally forced to behave like the slum landlords they had become, increasing rents and reducing services until the tenants finally balked and refused to pay. The only possible source of relief was a subsidy; the only realistic source of subsidies was the federal government. The poor were being squeezed dry.

Ironically, and it is tempting but perhaps unfair to say typically, the first subsidy, when it finally arrived, did little to ease the basic problem. Instead, Congress subsidized the provision of housing for a whole new class of tenants by offering a bonus for housing elderly families. The Housing Act of 1956 allowed a special premium of $500 per room for the construction of housing for the elderly; the Housing Act of 1961 provided the LHAs with an additional $120 per year for each elderly family housed in the developments. In combination, the two subsidies made the elderly poor into the favored darlings of the public housing program; their numbers increased spectacularly in the 1960s and 1970s. Since the only special features required for "elderly" housing seemed to have been a few feet of handrail in halls and bathrooms and a warning device to be pulled (if time permitted) should cardiac arrest set in, the increased construction allowance was a significant windfall for the builder. The operating subsidy provided the LHA with a parallel bonus, doubly sweetened by the highly desirable characteristics of elderly as tenants—they usually have no young children, they are not prone to vandalism or violence, they pay their rent regularly, and they cause little wear and tear on the premises. Moreover, the elderly are almost universally regarded as worthy of assistance, for with few exceptions they *are* someone's mother or father and that, in the American scheme of things, guarantees virtue and deserving. And to ice the cake, the elderly required small apartments, they lived readily in high-rise buildings, hence they were ideally suited to the kind of housing the industry was tooled up to build in the 1960s. The orgy of construction for the elderly that followed was paralleled by a declining rate of construction of "family" housing.

Although the shift to housing for the elderly is readily explained, it is somewhat less easy to justify. Granted immediately the elderly poor required assistance, it is uncertain that their need was greater than the needs of other poverty-stricken families. In any case, no one bothered to inquire, nationally or locally. The change in clientele was made by substitution and not by addition, by diverting resources from one target population to another and not by increasing the total enough to handle the additional burden. The emphasis on new construction was particularly unfortunate. The bulk of the apartments available in the private sector were small in size, therefore it would have been much more reasonable to try and lease existing smaller apartments for elderly tenants. The result of the shift, intended or not, was a major reward for one class of prospective tenants (the elderly) and a significant reduction in the effort to service another class of tenants (dependent families). In St. Louis, for example, the percentage of elderly families in public housing rose from around 15 percent in 1955 to about 30 percent in 1970 and to more than 55 percent in 1975, while the total number of units available actually declined.

The next major change in the public housing fiscal structure was made in 1969. The Brooke amendment to the housing act of that year limited the rent that could be charged any tenant to 25 percent of adjusted income. The maintenance and operations subsidy needed to compensate the LHAs for lost revenue was added in 1970. Significant and regular payments were not made until 1972. When the operating subsidy finally arrived, it was inadequate! Moreover, the Housing Act of 1968 had already authorized a number of activities that increased the fiscal burden on the LHAs by requiring provision of such tenant services as educational and occupational counseling, additional private security guards and recreational equipment and encouraging development of tenant participation in management through stimulation of tenant organizations. In effect, the "social" dimension of housing operations was very substantially expanded while the sources of future revenue, and the level of resources to be supplied, remained uncertain. The level of support required to operate and maintain its developments proved difficult to estimate; the federal government hedged the commitment and kept the LHAs limping along until HUD, aided by the Urban Institute, generated a subsidy formula. In 1972, a subsidy amounting to 3 percent of development costs was set as a base for operating and maintenance expenses, though HUD's own earlier figures suggested that 7.5 percent of investment was a more appropriate figure. The amount of subsidy was later increased to 5.5 percent of development costs, still not enough by standard calculations even if the deferred maintenance problem was ignored. The transition to operating subsidies was painful for everyone concerned; local authorities were caught between mounting costs, diminishing income, and increasing pressure from tenants. The federal government found itself riding the tiger of escalating subsidy costs. By the end of 1972, the Nixon administration had decided to halt expansion of public housing; a moratorium was announced early in 1973 and maintained until the following autumn. When the program was allowed to resume, it was limited to leasing. The pressure for more operating subsidies continued, however, and in 1975 a special utilities payment was made available to adjust the shortfall between LHA income and expenses. Despite the subsidies, the LHAs continued to receive the equivalent of a starvation diet.

Beginning in 1970, the federal government tried to improve the physical condition of the developments by providing modernization funds that could be used for capital replacement and major repairs. Some of the larger LHAs also received grants to help restore reserve balances badly depleted during the previous decade. Again, the resources available to HUD were nowhere near the level of funds actually needed. Moreover, some funds were earmarked and had to be used for specified purposes that were not necessarily the first priorities of the LHAs. In St. Louis, for example, nearly $2.5 million was used to remove lead-based paint from about half of the apartments in the two older developments though funds for such fundamentals as plumbing, heating, and electrical renovation could not be obtained. Given the immense gap between resources and needs, there was probably no alternative to the use of lotteries, though how the wheel was spun at HUD remained a mystery. In 1974, for example, a few cities shared in the melon known as the Target Projects Program (TPP). St. Louis, one of the lucky winners, received $1.8 million to supplement capital improvements by training staff, developing new procedures, making minor physical improvements, and employing tenants to assist with the work. So important was the last of these functions that TPP was in some quarters identified as the "Tenants Put on the Payroll" program, perhaps with cause. The fact that St. Louis had just begun a tenant management program may have influenced the decision to make the allocation, but that does not suggest that national spending decisions were based on a careful weighing of the potential benefits and costs of the available alternatives. Such special subsidy programs indicate the nature of the fundamental unresolved difficulty underlying the whole public housing effort in the United States: so long as Congress cannot or will not underwrite a serious effort to supply decent housing to all those who need help, one set of random efforts may be just as good as any other.

Privatization

The second major policy change introduced into public housing during the 1960s was increased privatization of various aspects of operations (transfer of some functions to the private sector), usually by authorizing the LHA to contract with private organizations for performance of needed services. The cause of the change was the obviously distressed condition of most large housing authorities; the justification was implicit in the received wisdom of the society, primarily the belief that private organization is prima facie more efficient than public. Until 1974, legislation tended to foster privatization rather than force it; the Housing Act of 1974 and the administrative regulations that accompanied it made privatization the central thrust of federal policy for the immediate future.

Three basic elements in the privatization of public housing appeared first in the Housing Act of 1965. First, the act authorized "turnkey" construction, the development of apartments by private entrepreneurs on their own sites for sale to LHAs. The private developer contracted with the housing authority to provide a completed development. He obtained a site, arranged for architectural and construction services, and delivered the finished product to the LHA, ready for use. Ostensibly a response to complaints about the quality of design and construction of conventional housing, the turnkey development proved very popular and, after 1965, most new construction was done by the turnkey method. How closely the program lived up to expectations is uncertain. Development time was probably reduced, but in St. Louis there was little evidence of significant improvements in design, location, or construction. Although site costs were reduced, the cost of construction remained high. There is no good reason to suppose that the LHAs could not have achieved the same results with even greater economy had they been given a freer hand in operations.

The second form of privatization authorized by the 1965 act was the sale of public housing to tenants. Ordinarily, such sales were limited to detached, semidetached, and row-type housing; high-rise apartments were specifically excluded from the homeownership program. Finally, the 1965 act authorized the sale of public housing to not-for-profit organizations who would provide housing for low-income tenants. Neither procedure was widely used. In St. Louis, one small development served as an experiment in homeownership; none of the housing was actually sold to a nonprofit organization.

In 1967, the federal government authorized contracts between LHAs and private firms for management services. A standard fee was paid for each unit placed under management: if the contract called for "soft" management, the LHA retained responsibility for maintenance; alternatively, a "hard" contract could be negotiated in which the management firm also supplied routine maintenance. In all such cases, responsibility for capital replacement and major repairs remained with the LHA. Contracts were normally written for one year with more or less automatic renewal, though they could be terminated for cause or by consent.

Both turnkey development and contract management have been widely used in public housing, in St. Louis as elsewhere. Their popularity with LHA management is readily accounted for. Private firms have much more latitude in dealing with their employees than do governmental agencies; as legislation against discrimination increased, hard-pressed bureaucrats welcomed the opportunity to escape at least partly from the contradictory pressures. Moreover, private firms do have some genuine operational advantages over public organizations: they can locate and employ needed skills more quickly, purchase with greater facility, experiment more, and cut losses more quickly—there is less inertia effect in private operations, other things equal. But the use of contractual services is not without costs. The LHA can lose much of its control over daily operations. The nature of the contract relation creates a significant lag time between detecting pending trouble and forcing the contractor to produce a solution. The primary weapon available to the LHA is contract termination, and that is not very useful against minor contract infractions such as late reports, modest performance delays, and so on. The development manager who is an employee of a contracting firm is far less accessible to the LHA director than his counterpart who is an employee of the LHA. The most serious fault with contractual management, however, lies in its long-range impact on the quality of governmental services. If it is a fact that governments perform poorly and inefficiently in the managerial arena, then purchasing such services on the private market will only guarantee that the inefficiency is prolonged indefinitely and the long-term cost of operations is increased. If governmental operations were for some reason beyond all hope of improvement, there would be no alternative; otherwise, such a policy of despair is not warranted and short-run contracting merely delays the inevitable. It seems wiser to explore the various means by which governmental performance might be improved before adopting a strategy guaranteed to eliminate future improvements.

Other Changes in Public Housing Policy

Various modifications have been made in the original public housing program over the years, usually in an effort to eliminate observable deficiencies or to respond at least to major complaints. Unfortunately, such changes have all too rarely been grounded in careful study of past experience or parallel operations; most commonly, they have been ad hoc improvisations that rely on current fads in social science or administration, ignoring appropriateness or performance. In 1968, for example, Congress forbade the use of high-rise buildings as family dwellings except in emergency; a careful study of St. Louis public housing indicates that the effect of building height on development performance has been minimal. Again, Congress and HUD have urged the scattering of public housing sites, thus avoiding the large aggregates that characterized building in the 1950s. But a blanket order to scatter all forms of housing is irresponsible and improper, for it ignores the evidence already available about the effects of scattering or concentrating different kinds of populations. Elderly tenants, for example, who formerly lived in scattered (and private) dwellings and now live in relatively small (one hundred to two hundred unit) developments would resist scattering to the death since it would mean the end of valued social services and close association with others. Again, efforts to encourage the development of congregate housing for the elderly without specifying the conditions in which it is most likely to succeed or fail is an invitation to disaster unless they are viewed as deliberate experiments—clearly not the intent of the act. A larger-scale example of the same type of error appears in the housing program for the elderly taken as an entity. The federal government encouraged a vast increase in the number of elderly persons housed in public facilities, but the policies to be followed as elderly tenants lost mobility and required increasing amounts of nursing service were left to be worked out ad hoc between LHAs and state welfare agencies, often at great cost to everyone concerned and without federal fiscal support.

An even more striking example of the wayward character of federal policymaking is found in the field of housing management. In the late 1960s, HUD apparently discovered that the quality of management available in public housing left much to be desired. Substantial sums were set aside for management improvement. Although these expenditures may have been justified, there is little evidence to suggest that the experiments and studies sponsored by HUD have contributed much to operating efficiency. Nevertheless, the Housing Act of 1974 contains a rather pretentious instruction to the HUD secretary to secure "sound management practices" in housing operations. The specifics that flesh out the injunction, however, are less than impressive: LHAs should exercise "good judgment" in tenant selection, collect rent promptly, and evict those who fail to meet their financial obligations. An unkind critic might note that the LHAs did these things very well indeed in the quarter-century before HUD's appearance on the public housing scene.

Having stressed the need for good management and sponsored a special institute devoted to the task (and there is probably no more difficult management problem to be found in the field of rental housing), HUD proceeded to make a mockery of its own arguments. First, it committed the government to a radically new conception of tenant–management relations, and then it accepted and supported the principle of tenant management of public housing facilities. The "expanded social services" conception of housing management began with the Housing Act of 1968; the Housing Act of 1969, doubtless stimulated by tenant disturbances in many of the larger housing authorities, reiterated the need for a new approach to tenant–management relations. The initial watchword was *tenant participation* in operations: new lease and grievance procedures were established, tenant organizations were encouraged, managerial control over the conditions of tenancy was significantly reduced by a combination of statutory changes and court decisions. Courts, federal administration, and legislature, aided and abetted by the youthful lawyers in the legal-aid societies, combined to erode LHA control over the tenant body in the name of tenant participation. Tenants were entitled to adequate counseling, recreational facilities, and, most important of all, a voice in the management of development affairs. Moreover, efforts to organize tenants for such purposes were entitled to formal and financial LHA support. Title II, section 3(4) of the Housing Act of 1974 is quite explicit:

> The term operation also means the financing of tenant programs and services for families residing in low-income housing projects, particularly where there is maximum feasible participation of the tenants in the development and operation of such tenant programs and services. As used in this paragraph, the term "tenant programs and services" includes the development and maintenance of tenant organizations which participate in the management of low-income housing projects; the training of tenants to manage and operate such projects and the utilization of their services in project management and operation.

The act clearly assumes ultimate transfer of management functions to tenant organizations and directs LHAs to take positive and deliberate action to further that outcome.

The HUD commitment to introducing and extending tenant management in public housing is by all odds the most astonishing development in the program's checkered history. Why did it occur? Certainly not by reason of evidence derived from experience. Tenant management was tried on a small scale in Washington, D.C., and Boston in 1971; the first major program began in St. Louis in the spring of 1973. The Housing Act of

1974 was signed in August of that year, long before any conclusive or even indicative evidence had been obtained from the tenant management program. At the end of FY 1976, the value of the tenant management program in St. Louis remained uncertain. Preliminary experience might have justified further trials, particularly of different forms of manager–housing authority relations, but nothing in the St. Louis experiment justified a full-fledged commitment to the principle. Moreover, normal management practice suggests the contrary: given the complexity of the task, the notion that public housing managers could be recruited and trained in a few short weeks from the tenant population bordered on the ludicrous. The decision at best was ideological; more likely, it was merely a resort to current fad as a way out of a nasty situation.

Since the reasons tenant management was promoted in Congress were not included in the official regulations, aside from nominal references to the need for "more participation" by tenants, the point of breakdown in the decisioning apparatus cannot be located and the motives of those involved remain obscure. Cynicism suggests that tenant management is yet another classic example of co-opting the enemy and sharing the prize, thus solving the dilemma posed for the federal administration by potentially unruly tenants. The procedure operated well in colonial empires as a temporary stopgap but failed eventually, as it did on the American Indian reservations. Unfortunately, the legendary cowardice of bureaucrats and legislators tends to make such temporary solutions attractive. On that interpretation, the Housing Act of 1974 appears as a holding action by the federal government, a delaying tactic that will make Indian reservations of the conventional housing facilities. Handing the reservations over to the Indians is the best cheap strategy available for surviving the economic crisis with fewest casualties. Unfortunately, that approach to the problem does nothing either to provide decent housing for low-income populations or to improve the lot of low-income populations to a point where subsidized housing is no longer needed.

Leased Housing

The long-term future of conventional public housing in the United States dimmed unmistakably in the 1970s. Construction, whether conventional or turnkey, came to a halt; an ominous provision for closing out badly damaged developments was added to the housing legislation. By mid-1976, Pruitt and Igoe in St. Louis were being torn down and carted away. Despite such notorious failures, it would be a serious mistake to label all conventional public housing, however developed, a failure. Nevertheless, that attitude is common among legislators, tenants, the general public, academics, and even former supporters of the public housing program. The distinction between the failure of a specific effort (public housing as it was practiced in the United States) and the failure of a general strategy for supplying low income housing has been ignored consistently. Some genuine failures, inadequate treatment in the media, and widespread ignorance of the particulars of program operations have combined to reinforce the belief that abandoning conventional public housing is the course of wisdom.

Official policy in the 1970s clearly accepted these faulty premises. When the moratorium on public housing expansion was lifted in the fall of 1973, only the leased housing program was permitted to resume operations. Section 8 of the Housing Act of 1974, which gave legal form to the leasing commitment, has become the principal focus of federal efforts in the public housing field. The message to the LHAs has been unmistakable: the future lies with leasing and not with conventional development or its variants.[3] Concurrently, the channels through which housing assistance is channeled to the population have been shifted from a federal–city axis to a federal–state axis; a Republican national administration, faced with city governments dominated by the opposition party, had no choice but to alter the resource routes so that funds passed through the state governments where some measure of Republican strength remained. The trend is likely to continue, whatever the short-run outcome of national elections, because of the inertia built into the national administrative machinery and the extent to which the federal–city connections have been dissolved. The overall effect of the change is likely to be a sharp decline in the role of the LHA, an increase in the authority and influence of the local HUD agency, and transfer of some housing operations from city to state administration. Paradoxi-

3. The 1976 housing bill included proposals for allocating new resources for conventional construction, but the amounts involved were small.

cally, an administration dedicated to decentralization of authority and the principle of local autonomy may have created a centralized housing administration with far more power than any of its predecessors managed to exercise and may have done so in the name of small government and decentralization of power.

Leasing of privately owned facilities for use as public housing offers a quick and effective device for transferring public housing into the private sector; the technique has been a rallying point for opponents of public ownership since the mid-1930s. The section 23 leased-housing program was added to the Housing Act of 1965 under cover of the hue and cry raised over the rent-supplement provisions of the housing bill. It was supported by the U.S. Chamber of Commerce, the National Association of Real Estate Boards, and various Republicans in Congress known for their hostility to public housing. Leasing began as a very small-scale program for using housing stock already in existence as a means of supplementing the more conventional developments; the initial quota was a modest 10,000 units per year for a four-year period. It was justified, to Congress and to the public, as a way of reducing costs and making greater use of the existing housing stock, which would enable housing authorities to respond more quickly and efficiently to tenant needs. By limiting the number of units that could be leased in any single facility to 10 percent of the total, the sponsors expected to disperse public housing tenants more widely and thus avoid some of the stigma that had become attached to "the projects." In practice, that limit could be waived by the LHA on its own authority, hence it did not serve as an effective control over concentration or dispersal. Finally, supporters of leasing argued that owners of substandard housing would be encouraged to rehabilitate their holdings in order to qualify for the program, hence leasing would contribute to improvement of neighborhoods and upgrading of the housing stock.

If the LHA could control the quality, location, and price of housing units leased for use by low-income families, the section 23 lease program would be a valuable adjunct to conventional housing, assuming that the purpose of the LHA is to supply as much of the need for housing as resources permit. However, the private housing market would have to provide the LHA with a supply of adequate housing that is acceptable with respect to quality, location, size, availability, and cost. In general, leasing is likely to be more expensive than building or purchasing, particularly in the long run, because rents will include profits, local taxes, and the cost of financing on the private money market. Moreover, a number of factors can disrupt the effectiveness of the leasing program: the supply of housing may be inadequate with respect to quality, size, location, or cost; even if housing is available, owners may not be willing to lease their property to public agencies for use as low-income housing; finally, the tenants themselves may object to certain aspects of the program such as dispersal and separation from neighbors, distance from home neighborhood, church, schools, and so on.

As it turned out, the private market did not supply the housing needed by the LHAs, taking the nation as a whole. That opened the door to a line of activity far removed from what Congress had authorized and much more difficult to justify as an alternative to conventional public housing development. As the president of the Section 23 Leased Housing Association pointed out in July 1971:

> The leased housing program, as originally constituted, did not work because it was premised upon the assumption that there was ample housing available for lease. However, if there was any, very few landlords offered it. Therefore another concept, called "turnkey leasing" was developed. This contemplated leasing of new construction rather than existing units.[4]

What began as a program for leasing existing housing, for which there is ample economic justification, turned very quickly into a program for constructing new housing to be offered for lease, for which little if any real justification can be offered. That required some fundamental changes in the program: The income level of the target population was moved upward, equity funding techniques were applied to public housing, and the state entered the picture as a potential developer and funder. The implications of these changes are uncertain but likely to be very far-reaching indeed!

Lease of Existing Housing

Until 1974, virtually all of the leasing carried out in public housing made use of the section 23 program added to the Housing Act of 1937 by the Housing Act of 1965. An alternative

4. Cited in Charles L. Edson, *A Section 23 Primer*, exhibit 6A, p. 4.

mode of leasing, authorized in section 10(c) of the Housing Act of 1937 was used briefly in the 1960s and then abandoned. Section 10(c), which required exemption from local taxation, a special agreement between local government and LHA, and a payment in lieu of taxes, proved unattractive to both local government and LHA. Only $500,000 worth of annual contract commitments were made under its provisions, all before 1969.

Section 23 leasing required prior approval by local government; it could not be undertaken by the LHA of its own volition. But, since leased property was privately owned and paid full taxes, approval was fairly easy to obtain, other things equal. Of course, some locales would have nothing to do with public housing in any form whether or not taxes were paid, but these were exceptions. Leasing did not require an LHA, but in most cases established housing authorities administered the programs. Leasing authorizations were allocated through the local HUD office. The LHA that received an allocation advertised its readiness to lease and sought owners willing to supply apartments and prospective tenants wishing to rent them. Leases were negotiated for twelve to thirty-six months in the early days of the program, but the time was extended to five years in 1966 and to fifteen years in 1970. While the program was targeted at existing housing, some of the "existing housing" being leased after 1970 was quite new or even built for the occasion.

In most cases, the LHA (or other agency) leased the units from the owner and subleased them to the low-income tenant, but the section 23 program also allowed for a direct lease between owner and tenant. The owner was paid a "fair market rental" set by HUD that included the cost of range, refrigerator, utilities, and management services, less any utilities costs paid directly by the tenant. Rent levels had to be consonant with area rents; the housing had to conform to local standards and building code requirements. Qualitative criteria were minimal: heating, lighting, and cooking facilities had to be provided; the neighborhood had to be free of "characteristics seriously detrimental to family life"; reasonable access to schools, transportation, shopping, churches, and so on was required. Usually the LHA performed simple maintenance leaving all extraordinary repairs and services to the owner.

Ordinarily, the LHA collected rent from each tenant and

paid it to the owner together with an additional subsidy obtained through an "Annual Contributions Contract" with HUD. The amount of the subsidy was calculated using a very complex scheme known as the "flexible formula," intended to ensure that no more was paid for leased housing than would be paid if an LHA had constructed the facility.[5] If the leasing program operated at a deficit, the LHA could also receive subsidies normally provided for very large or elderly families ($120 per year per family). There was understandable concern lest the leasing program drive up the price of existing housing in tight markets, and LHAs were cautioned to proceed carefully if the effects of leasing would drop the local vacancy rate below 3 percent.

Tenant eligibility for leased housing depended on income, and the LHA could apply the standards used in conventional public housing if it chose. However, the "20 percent gap" did not have to be maintained, hence income levels in leased housing could be somewhat higher than in the conventional program. Nevertheless, the 25 percent limit on income instituted by the Housing Act of 1969 applied to leased housing as well. Tenant eligibility was decided by the LHA and in most cases the LHA also selected the tenants. HUD policy allowed the owner to choose the tenants subject to LHA approval or from an LHA-prepared list. Since no rent was paid on vacant units if the owner selected tenants, that method was seldom employed until after 1973, when the rules of selection were changed. Evictions were the prerogative of the LHA alone, though the owner could request eviction of an unruly tenant. Until 1973, the owner could contract with either a private firm or an LHA for maintenance and management services; after 1973, contracts with private firms were no longer permitted.

In 1971 and again in 1973, some major changes were made in the program that controlled lease of existing housing;[6] those changes were consolidated in the Housing and Urban Development Act of 1974. They had the effect of placing complete responsibility for management in the hands of the property owner and significantly reducing the role of the LHA in the lease arrangement. The lease was thereafter made directly between owner and tenant, omitting the LHA. The owner's

5. See Circular FHA 7430.3, *Low Rent Housing: Flexible Formula and Revision of Leased Housing Programs*.
6. Edson, *Section 23 Primer*.

duties and responsibilities were extended to include paying utilities, taxes, and insurance; performing all maintenance functions; processing tenant applications and selecting tenants; collecting rents and accepting what were called "the risks of loss from vacancies," risks that were moderated somewhat by HUD's agreement to continue payments if the tenant violated the lease. Though rent adjustments were made annually, increases were subject to limits established in the Annual Contributions Contract, hence the owner who wished to raise rents had actually to find tenants with higher incomes to occupy his premises. Calculation of subsidies was much simplified: the fair market rent established by HUD was added to the estimated administrative expenses and the estimated family contribution was subtracted from the total.

The changes placed some definite responsibilities on the tenant family, for the first time in the history of the public housing program. In the past, a prospective tenant had only to apply, establish eligibility, and wait for an opening. Now, qualified tenants were given a certificate of eligibility, good for forty-five days (and renewable in the earlier version of the regulations), which committed the LHA to housing assistance payments in the tenant's behalf. Responsibility for finding an apartment, however, lay with the tenant; the LHA could assist only in hardship cases.

The new regulations significantly reduced the role of the LHA in leasing. Although the LHAs determined tenant eligibility and issued certificates, they had little operational responsibility unless they contracted with the owner to perform managerial services. Otherwise, their principal functions were to conduct an initial inspection of the premises and to process the housing assistance payments. Formally, the LHA also had final control over eviction proceedings.

The Housing Act of 1974 made some major additions to the new administrative regulations. "Low" and "very low" incomes were defined for housing purposes as 80 percent and 50 percent of the median income for the area respectively; "large" and "very large" families were similarly defined as containing six and eight minors respectively. These definitions provided a base for determining rent levels. Families that were very large or had very low incomes (or medical expenses equal to 25 percent of income) were required to pay only 15 percent of income *before* deductions for rent; all other families were charged 25 percent of income *after* deductions and no family could pay less than 15 percent of income for rent. The deductions allowed were modest: $300 per minor child, medical expenses in excess of 3 percent of gross income, and "unusual" costs. Each family was given a small utilities allowance. Thirty percent of the families in leased housing were to come from the very-low-income group.

The certificate of eligibility was made valid for a sixty-day period, and an additional sixty days were authorized if the tenant had made a serious effort to locate housing. Each family was to be allowed a "shopping incentive credit," defined in a way calculated to baffle even the most ardent bureaucrat:

> (b) The amount of the monthly Shopping Incentive Credit shall be the dollar amount equal to that percentage of the Gross Family Contribution which the Rent Savings is of the Fair Market Rent. The Rent Savings is the amount by which the Fair Market Rent (1) exceeds the approved Contract Rent (plus any applicable allowance), or (2) exceeds the initially proposed Contract Rent (plus any applicable allowance), if that be higher than the approved Contract Rent (plus any applicable allowance).[7]

The net effect, apparently, was a monthly reduction in rent equal to the percentage of the "fair market rent" saved by the tenant. That is, if the fair market rent was $200 per month and the tenant obtained the unit for $190 per month, the 5 percent saving translated into a $5 per month rent decrease for the tenant.

The 1974 act further increased the owner's control over the leasing program. An owner could now evict tenants with LHA approval, and such approval was apparently contingent only on the legitimacy of the owner's interpretation of the contract. HUD also agreed to pay up to 80 percent of the rent for a period of sixty days if a tenant vacated a leased apartment in violation of the contract, which was a significant reduction of the amount of risk assigned to the owner. Although the full effect of the 1974 Housing Act on the leasing program remains to be seen, some implications of the new regulations are clear. The authority of the LHA is much reduced; the tenant's responsibilities are greater; the owner controls the bulk of the operation. Indeed, the LHA is specifically enjoined from any action that

7. See *Federal Register*, 5 May 1975, Section 8 Leased Housing Assistance Payments Program, Existing Regulations. The regulation was somewhat simplified in March 1976.

would "directly or indirectly reduce the family's opportunity to choose among the available units in the housing market." Yet it seems reasonable to assume that the prime limit on the individual's freedom of choice is likely to be the inability of the LHA to intercede on his behalf. While not quite so serious as refusing to allow a physician to choose his patient's medicine, much the same principle seems involved. The potential bargaining power of the LHA as collective purchaser and government agent is much reduced. Granted the LHA's potential has not been fully exploited, the potential remains important even if unused. Finally, the search and lease arrangements are a virtual invitation to collusion between owner and tenant at the expense of the public treasury. If the fair market rents are high enough so that the owner is adequately rewarded from the subsidy payment alone, as seems the case in practice, then the owner's interests are best served by retaining the tenant regardless of whether the tenant's rent is actually collected (by the owner, under the terms of the act). Such arrangements would be almost impossible to detect. Finally, carelessness or bias in the LHA inspection of units would have the effect of converting the program into a support system for marginal local slums with little possibility of forcing an improvement in quality or terminating the lease.

Construction for Lease

The Housing Act of 1965 clearly intended that leasing would be limited to the existing supply of housing and that it would serve as an adjunct to the conventional housing program. That intention was transposed or transformed by HUD into active support for construction of new housing for lease and for substantial rehabilitation of existing housing. The reasoning used in HUD to justify the change would do credit to a correspondence-school lawyer. HUD argued that as soon as new housing was built it became part of the "existing" stock, hence it could be included in the program. Moreover, since the LHAs were creatures of state law and not federal law, nothing prevented *them* from entering into an agreement with a developer to lease as yet unbuilt property for use in the low-income housing program. Congress, instead of resenting or resisting such blatant flouting of its intentions, changed its legislation in 1970 to legalize the administrative modifications. The LHA was allowed to commit its annual contributions in advance; the developer could use them to obtain financing. The original commitment extended for eight successive five-year periods, a total of forty years; that period was reduced to twenty years by the 1974 Housing Act.

The result of the HUD interpretation was a sharp increase in the amount of new construction for lease as public housing, particularly in states where public housing was difficult to site. Between 1969 and 1974, some 61,000 units of housing were added to the lease program; of that number, more than 75 percent (46,123) were new construction, less than 1 percent (300) were substantially rehabilitated, and 24 percent (14,500) were part of the existing housing stock. This caused some anxiety among program supporters, and an effort was made to maintain an even balance between new construction and lease of existing housing.

Until the Housing Act of 1974, the regulations governing administration of new construction were the same as those applied to lease of existing stock. But the owner of the new apartment complex was in a much stronger position vis-à-vis both tenant and LHA than his counterpart who owned existing housing. Most of the advantages were due to needs arising out of the effort to finance new construction or rehabilitation. The rule that limited the LHA to leasing 10 percent of the units in any one complex was clearly inapplicable to projects built specifically for LHA use. Similarly, new construction financing could not be obtained if HUD gave priority to developments in which fewer than 20 percent of the units were leased by an LHA. Serious financial problems appeared if subsidy payments were stopped during vacancies created by tenant violations of lease provisions. HUD maintained its policies through 1973 in the face of bitter protests from owners, but financing requirements did force some concessions. An automatic inflation adjustment in rent was incorporated into the rules, and further changes were allowed if inflation turned sharply upward— thus nullifying the stabilizing effect of leasing on operating costs. The owner retained total managerial control over newly constructed units and could contract with either an LHA or a private firm for managerial services. In effect, lease of new housing allowed the reintroduction of the traditional landlord system with only minor modifications. The owner paid for taxes, utilities, and other services; was responsible for all maintenance; processed applications; selected tenants; and collected rents. After 1974, he also determined tenant eligibility, verified it periodically, set the amount of each family's contribution and subsidy, and terminated tenancy subject only to delay by the LHA.

The LHA's functions in the new construction-for-lease program were minimal. It could serve as a cosponsor of a development but could then exercise no managerial function over the property. It could manage, but only at the owner's request. HUD regulations made joint sponsorship complex and difficult, and the central administration clearly favored direct applications from developers and individual state agencies. Selection of developers, site and plan approvals, and fiscal arrangements were all made entirely through the local HUD office. The language of the regulations allowed but did not require HUD to notify the LHA when a new construction for lease program was announced in its area—a basic indicator of impotence in the bureaucratic world. While the LHAs retained some broad supervisory functions with respect to lease of existing housing, the April 1975 regulations governing lease of new property did not contain even one numbered paragraph enumerating the LHA's responsibilities within the new program.

The key to a strong construction-for-lease program is the availability of financing and the opportunity for profits it provides. From the point of view of the developer, access to capital at preferred rates or the right to depreciate the investment quickly and thus generate tax losses is essential. Both of these techniques found a place in the construction-for-lease program, often they were combined in the same development. To obtain preferred borrowing rates, the LHA's power to issue tax-free bonds was exploited and the creation of state agencies with similar powers was encouraged by HUD. One common procedure was for the LHA to create a nonprofit corporation that built apartments, then leased them to the LHA under an agreement that transferred ownership to the LHA at the end of a twenty-year period. The corporation could issue tax-exempt bonds because of its special relation to the LHA. Since local corporations pay local taxes, that method of financing proved popular with local governments whose tax bases were declining. The same tax break was obtained if the LHA loaned a developer the capital needed for construction using funds obtained by issuing tax-free bonds. The completed development was then leased to the LHA in the normal manner. More than thirty states created financing agencies with the power to issue tax-exempt bonds for specific purposes; they could provide capital for developers using the LHA's pledge of payment as security for a loan at a favored rate of interest.

Even more spectacular returns to the developer were produced by the technique known as "equity syndication." The key to its success was the Internal Revenue Service's willingness to allow accelerated depreciation on multifamily properties intended for use by low-income families. In effect, the IRS ruling allowed the developer to depreciate the combined value of his "up front" investment *and* his mortgage in a very short time, usually five years. Since this was generally more depreciation credit than one person could use unless his annual income was enormous, a portion of the depreciation credit could be sold or assigned to the members of a limited liability company formed specially for that purpose.

As an example, a developer who invested $500,000 of his own money and borrowed $4,500,000 more to build a $5 million project (a common ratio of investment to borrowing in the industry), could depreciate the property at a rate of $1 million per year for the first five years of operation. In effect, the developer "bought" $500,000 worth of depreciation over a five-year term for only $50,000. He needed only find individuals with large personal incomes and sell them the depreciation cumulated in the development. For the person with a large income, the depreciation would be a good buy; the developer, obviously, could charge rather more than his own investment. At the end of five years, when the property value was reduced to nil, the project could be sold and the return treated as capital gains—taxed at a much lower rate than personal income. The "rollover" provision that allowed developers to defer taxation on profits simply by reinvesting in new construction (as a private homeowner can avoid taxes on profit from sale of a house by purchasing another) was not extended to construction for lease. Nevertheless, it remained a very attractive investment.

III.

Conventional Public Housing in St. Louis, 1943–1969

The St. Louis public housing program is a rich mine of information relating to the effects of almost every major aspect of federal public housing policy. From the opening of the first set of apartments in 1942 through the end of FY 1975, the St. Louis Housing Authority (SLHA) developed 8,055 units of conventional public housing, all new construction, and 1,830 units of turnkey housing. Fifteen units of turnkey housing consisted of rehabilitated dwellings housed in three small buildings on separate sites in the central west end of the city. Nearly 800 units of conventional housing and about 80 percent of all the turnkey units (1,534) were intended for use by the elderly. One 82-unit complex of row houses was used for a tenant homeownership program. Authorization to lease 600 dwelling units was received under the section 23 lease program in 1967; that allocation was increased by 300 units in FY 1976. The developments ranged in size from 16 units of family housing on one site to the 2,870-unit Pruitt–Igoe complex. Construction included two- and three-story row housing and twelve-story high-rise dwellings. The conventional developments were clustered around the rim of the central business district; the others were scattered across the city, mainly along the east–west corridor between downtown St. Louis and Clayton.

Most of the programmatic changes introduced into public housing in an effort to improve performance after 1965 were given an extensive trial in St. Louis. Almost all the turnkey housing was placed under private management shortly after delivery. The city was the site of the first major experiment with tenant management carried out in the country. The 1969 rent strike was the most serious such tenant action in the country. And Pruitt and Igoe, perhaps the best-known disasters in the history of American public housing, were both the first experimental site for using dynamite to raze large buildings and the first major housing developments to be dismantled and carted away.

By the end of FY 1977, the 1315 units of housing completed in 1942 were still operating but were much dilapidated from heavy use and poor maintenance. Of the 5,578 units of conventional housing built between 1953 and 1968, less than half (2,618 units) remained active. The large (1,162 unit) conventional development completed in 1968 was functioning well, though there were already signs of wear in the family units. Pruitt and Igoe were gone. About 200 units had been merged to form larger apartments and some 130 were being used for a variety of communal purposes—church group activities, children's facilities, and so on. The physical structures that remained were relatively unattractive and in some cases uninhabitable.

The scope of the St. Louis experience with public housing provides an opportunity to answer a wide range of questions about federal policy. The scale was large enough and the time period sufficiently long to allow differences in performance to emerge; the significant uniquenesses of the individual projects were not lost in a welter of aggregate figures. The unusually open and cooperative spirit displayed by the staff of the Housing Authority both facilitated use of the program as a test site and guarded against gross misrepresentation of the data. The "real life" character of the test, the fact that federal policy changes had to be integrated into an ongoing operation subject to real-world constraints, avoided the artificiality that so often mars "experimental programs" tentatively intruded into current operations or carried out in an entirely artificial atmosphere—the HUD "Experimental Housing Allowance Program" undertaken at several places in the 1970s is a good example of the genre.[1]

Phase 1: 1943–1953

The enabling legislation required by the Housing Act of 1937 passed the Missouri legislature early in 1939, clearing the way for establishing local housing authorities able to contract with the federal government for development and operation of public housing. The new St. Louis Housing Authority was duly allocated more than 1,300 units of new construction, divided

1. U.S., Department of Housing and Urban Development, *Housing Allowances: The 1976 Report to Congress*, and Tulsa Housing Authority, *Experimental Housing Allowance Program: Final Report*.

between two developments of identical size, design, and construction. They were completed in the summer of 1942 and began operating immediately.

The Developments

The two developments, though identical, were physically separated and racially segregated. Carr Square (1–1), located some fifteen blocks northwest of the central business district, was intended for use by blacks; Clinton Peabody (1–2) was designated for white occupancy and located an equal distance to the southwest. Each comprised fifty-three two- and three-story buildings and a community center, arranged in orderly rows on about twenty-five acres of land. Each building contained between eight and sixteen dwelling units of varying size and organization: some were apartments all on one floor, others were duplexes or townhouses divided between two floors. Most of the apartments were small: in Carr Square, 474 of 658 had only one or two bedrooms; and in Clinton Peabody 433 of 657 units were of that size. About 30 units in each development included four bedrooms. None was larger than that. Several different living arrangements could be obtained, depending on unit size. Basically, the apartments were built around a family-style kitchen of good size and included a kitchen, living room, bath, appropriate number of bedrooms, and small storage space. There were no central laundry facilities.

Compared to some of the later acquisitions, the cost of the two developments was reasonable, about $3.5 million, equal to roughly $5,300 per unit or $1,200 per room (see Table 1). The maximum allowable cost at that time was $1,250 per room in high cost areas such as St. Louis and $1,000 per room elsewhere. Although the legislation said little about construction quality the buildings were apparently well designed and solidly built, for a management review team found the basic structures sound and renewable some thirty years later. About a third of the original price went to purchase and improve the site, a good indication of the cost of the hidden agendas included in the program. Both developments were sited in the midst of an extensive reach of dilapidated commercial and residential structures, some already empty and abandoned. In the area occupied by Carr Square, for example, about 90 percent of the buildings razed to make room for construction dated to the Civil War and beyond. The location seriously disadvantaged the tenants, particularly in later years as deterioration accelerated. The developments were relatively isolated from employment, shopping, recreation, schooling, churches, and other social–economic facilities. Yet they became the core sites around which the additional developments authorized by the Housing Act of 1949 were constructed.

Despite their locations, both Carr Square and Clinton Peabody performed admirably over the next thirty-five years. Occupancy remained very high even in the worst years of the 1960s; at most times, there was a long waiting list for admission. In the 1940s, when there was little if any stigma attached to living in public housing, crime was negligible despite the neighborhood, turnover was low, structures were well maintained, grounds were neat. Until 1950, most heads of household, regardless of race, were employed males. In the 1950s and 1960s, the discrepancies in economic opportunity between races began to appear in the statistics relating to income, employment, and dependence on public assistance. The white tenants in Clinton Peabody were more likely to be employed, have higher wages, and have smaller families than their black counterparts in Carr Square; fewer depended on public assistance for all of their income. For younger white tenants particularly, public housing at that time seemed to be functioning as a way station on the road to homeownership. Turnover rates were highest among the younger, employed white tenants with higher incomes, and "moving to purchased home" was frequently the reason given for leaving the developments.

Public housing was not intended for persons of extremely low income or persons totally dependent on public assistance. The target population of the 1937 Housing Act, to the extent that it can be inferred from legislative and other sources, was the employed worker with a small family and a very low income, too poor to make a down payment on the future family home. The rent levels clearly support that interpretation. In 1942 rents began at $11 per month for a family of two earning less than $780 per year. While that seems low today, it was then much higher than the cost of slum rentals. As Robert Fisher has pointed out, those who moved from slums to public housing often increased their rents by 50 to 100 percent. Doubtless many slum dwellers could not afford such an increase or preferred to pay less for housing of poorer quality. Of course, the tenants were poor, even though they were not part of the lowest income stratum in society. In 1945, a family of two could not be admitted if its income was over $1,425 per year and was forced to leave if income rose beyond $1,800 per year.

Few welfare recipients were admitted to St. Louis public housing before 1954 unless they had additional sources of income and could pay more-than-minimum rent. A quirk in the welfare regulations forced a reduction in welfare payments to families that entered public housing because rents were so low; that reduction then forced the Housing Authority to reduce the family's rent. The Welfare Department then lowered payments still further, and so on. An enforced descending spiral led ultimately to minimum rents for all welfare tenants—the Housing Authority, in effect, subsidized part of the welfare payment. Since the Authority was totally dependent on rental income and required a minimum income to survive, it could not accept every tenant technically eligible but able to pay only minimum rent. The fiscal arrangements made by the Congress literally forced the Authority to use a quota system (maintained until the early 1960s) that limited admission by the prospective tenant's rent level as well as by income. Persons of very low income often had to be refused admission because the quota was already filled, even though the family was eligible and the space was available. Such restrictions were grossly out of keeping with the spirit of the program, of course, but were unavoidable given established fiscal policies.

Program Weakness: Finance and Maintenance

The public housing program incorporated in the 1937 Housing Act was doomed by its fiscal provisions. A program targeted at a very-low-income population yet wholly dependent on rental income was highly vulnerable, particularly to inflationary pressures. If costs rose rapidly, the earnings of low-income tenants were unlikely to keep pace; the low limits placed on reserves increased the long-run pressure on the Authority. Significant short-term increases in Authority costs would force an increase in rents to either cover a resulting deficit or prevent one. That increased both the relative and absolute burden on the tenant, the amount of rent paid, and the ratio of rent to income. Technically, tenants could not be evicted and replaced because they could not afford higher rents, but forced rent increases had precisely that effect. Unfortunately, those fiscal arrangements were reproduced without change in the Housing Act of 1949 and remained in force until 1969/1970.

During the first decade of operations in St. Louis, the incipient rent–income squeeze was delayed by the special circumstances arising out of World War II. The two developments were completed in 1942 just as war industry manpower shifts began putting pressure on the city's dilapidated housing stock. The apartments were opened to war production workers as a matter of course. Since most war workers earned much more than the limits allowed for public housing, they were required to pay premium rents. Housing Authority income was therefore far greater than could normally be expected. There being little need for maintenance and repairs in the new buildings, the fortunes of war generated significant "profits" for the Authority until the late 1940s. Had federal policy allowed hoarding of surpluses against leaner days, the onset of fiscal pressures might have been delayed very considerably by this windfall. The law, however, required that "profits" be used to service bonded indebtedness and to pay lieu of taxes to local government. The record does not show how much income went to pay bonded indebtedness, but the Authority paid the city of St. Louis about $335,000 in lieu of taxes between 1942 and 1953. Although that was only one-fourth of the "normal" tax bill for a private owner, some felt it was still far more than the value of the police, fire, and other services that the city rather grudgingly and sometimes sporadically supplied. When the sum of costs is totaled for 1942–1953, the two developments provided some 5,760,490 days of actual occupancy for their tenants at a total daily cost to government and tenant combined of some $1.973 in Carr Square and $2.098 in Clinton Peabody—roughly $59 and $62 per month respectively. Most of the cost was paid by the tenant: The net federal subsidy was only $0.139 per unit per day. In due course, the government paid the price of its shortsightedness, and savings measured in pennies became dollars in costs—old adages are sometimes worth attending.

The fundamental inadequacy of the fiscal arrangements was revealed starkly and rapidly when the last of the overincome war workers left the developments in the later 1940s. Tenant incomes dropped; Authority costs rose; Authority income fell.

Predictably, there was a quick and very substantial increase in minimum rents—about 80 percent in two years. The $11 per month minimum set in 1942 had been retained until 1950 without change; rents from overincome war workers had more than offset the low minimum. With the high-rent tenants gone, minimum rents were increasingly important to the Authority. The minimum rent was raised to $16 per month in 1950 and to $20 per month the following year. Given the amount of inflation in the economy, the increases were not unreasonable. The consumer price index increased by 53 percent from 1943 to 1953. But the increases were made in real-world dollars and they came in a very short period of time, and that magnified the impact on tenants. Despite the increases, the first deficit appeared on the Authority's books in 1954. The inadequacy of the fiscal policies in periods of normal operation was very quickly made clear.

The weakness of the administrative apparatus in St. Louis, which contributed significantly to the Authority's problems in the late 1950s and 1960s, was of local origin. The operation was highly centralized; the development managers were basically rent collectors at the sites. While this was often assumed to be the prime cause of administrative weakness, the lumping of public housing with land clearance and redevelopment under a single director probably counted more heavily in the result. The failure in maintenance was due to external factors, chiefly the influence of local craft unions. The Authority's approach to tenant affairs was formal, legal, and rather authoritarian, a pattern common to landlord–tenant relations in the 1930s. Procedures were relatively inflexible, the Authority relied heavily on legal actions expensive to tenant and Authority alike. Few social services were provided the tenants; few were expected. Authority recommendations to the regional administration that more services be made available were met with negative and often acidulous responses, perhaps because operating costs in St. Louis tended to be higher than in the rest of the region. As the program expanded in the 1950s, the work of the Land Clearance and Redevelopment Authority also increased; the amount of detail was soon far more than one person could manage well. Moreover, the expansion was handled by simply increasing the scale of the existing administration; no significant reorganization of operations was undertaken until after the rent strike. The result was a predictable slowdown in performance. Of course, some functions continued to operate well, even through the 1960s. Procedures used to admit new tenants, for example, were cumbersome but fair and effective so long as the turnover rates remained low.

The principal operational problem, which plagued the Authority for decades and contributed significantly to its ultimate collapse, was the failure to provide adequate maintenance and repairs. For some reason, the St. Louis Housing Authority could not bring those functions under administrative control. As early as 1943, the auditors complained of the absence of sufficient controls over maintenance, but with little effect. Year after year, the same shortcomings were noted in the audits: daily activities tended to be ad hoc and unsystematic; work controls had not been established; maintenance records were inadequate; there was no inventory of equipment; response time was slow; performance was poor. Labor gangs dominated by union representatives were sufficiently powerful to force uncontrolled and inefficient use of very expensive labor. Work output was often unbelievably low. A report from the 1960s, for example, noted that a full crew of glaziers replaced only eight moderate-size panes of glass in a full working day. Had the work been done quickly and well, the cost might have been bearable. But the delays were unconscionable and the work often slovenly. In 1959, disgusted regional supervisors demanded and got a major reduction in the maintenance staff, but that only complicated the problem. The fact that work was not being done properly and on time did not mean that the maintenance staff was not needed.

Such criticisms notwithstanding, the performance of Carr Square and Clinton Peabody in their first decade of operation deserves its measure of praise. To 1954, the developments had provided excellent service to their tenants. The physical structures remained in good condition, turnover was slow, the waiting list for admission was long, the public image was favorable. Thus far, the burden on the public treasury had been very slight. Those fortunate enough to gain admission were able to purchase more housing per dollar of expenditure than could be obtained anywhere else in the area. To that extent at least, the program was successful. It had performed almost as its designers intended. What is tragic, looking backward, is how little it would have taken to continue that success through succeeding decades. Fiscal weaknesses could have been remedied by a very modest operating subsidy and some changes in policy relating to reserves. Minor administrative adjustments would have produced a more humane and responsive operation. The one intractable area of performance, maintenance and repairs, was dominated by relations with the unions and improved little over time, not until 1969, when the local teamster's union negotiated a settlement that allowed use of unskilled labor in maintenance.

Phase 2: 1953–1969

On the surface, the future of public housing in St. Louis looked better at the beginning of the 1950s than ever before. Nationally, the congressional deadlock that had prevented passage of a housing bill after 1945 was broken by Truman's unexpected victory in 1948. One of the first major pieces of social legislation passed by the new administration was the Housing Act of 1949, hailed as a major victory by prohousing forces. The bill accepted as a national goal development of "a decent home and suitable living environment for every American" and authorized construction of 810,000 units of public housing over the next six years, an estimated 10 percent of total national need. In Missouri, the battle that followed elimination of tax exemptions for public housing from the 1945 state constitution was finally settled by the Missouri Supreme Court in January 1949, when it confirmed a circuit court ruling that local housing authorities were entitled to the exemption regardless of the specific provisions of the state constitution. That cleared the way for participation in the benefits of the 1949 Housing Act, and St. Louis promptly entered a request for 12,000 more units of public housing. The 5,800-unit allocation received in 1950 was warmly welcomed.

Twenty years later, after a long series of financial crises, a major rent strike, and an appalling amount of vandalism, the conventional housing program was an almost total wreck—physically, financially, organizationally, reputationally, and even morally. In retrospect, the outcome was both foreseeable and perhaps avoidable. The disaster was programmed; only the timing was uncertain. The basic weaknesses in the 1937 act were already apparent in 1949 yet were transplanted unchanged into the new legislation. The strength of national and local opposition to public housing ensured that those weaknesses would be exploited as a weapon against the program. The Truman victory in 1948 may have forced the 1949 Housing Act on the Congress, but the opposition in the House of Representatives retained enough power to come within five votes of deleting the public housing provisions of the bill. The outbreak of war in Korea in 1951 provided an opportunity for banking, real estate, and other hostile business interests represented in the United States Chamber of Commerce to pressure Congress into reneging on the authorization for public housing construction made in 1949. Thereafter, additional authorization was yielded grudgingly, usually at the insistence of the Senate. Public housing barely survived the Eisenhower years. Given the hostile climate, particularly in Washington, there was no hope of obtaining either needed improvements in policy or additional financial assistance. Even suggesting the need for more resources might have been suicidal in the 1950s. The mindless ideological warfare carried out by opponents of public housing became a self-fulfilling prophecy; the opposition eliminated the opportunity for policy improvement through operational experience and forced reliance on slogans and folklore.

The lethal weakness remained the fiscal provisions of the 1949 act. So long as local housing authorities were forced to pay operating expenses, utilities, lieu of taxes, and capital replacement costs out of rental income, the program was vulnerable to damage on every side. Either productive inefficiency in the industry or deterioration in the quality of construction could produce a disaster. Lowered productivity would mean higher development costs and less available housing to provide income; a less durable product meant increased operating costs and reduced capacity for repairs and replacement. Severe inflation would produce a rent–income squeeze that would either drive the tenants from the developments or force them to pay an inordinate part of income for housing. Either outcome would be a flagrant violation of the norms that supported the legislation.

The past history of the economy gave ample reason to expect a number of inflationary–deflationary cycles of varying severity in the expected lifetime of the facilities. Since low productivity in the housing industry was one of the major justifications for public housing in the first place, the outlook was hardly sanguine as the 1950s began. Finally, the ideological character of the opposition to public housing meant that modifications and improvements needed to succeed would be opposed on principle and evidence based on past performance would not be considered germane. The failure that shortsightedness ensured was used by the shortsighted as a club for attacking the program. The Congress finally produced a classic political "solution" to the dilemma: the victim was blamed, the program was abandoned to slow extinction, the genuine social problem that public housing was meant to alleviate was increasingly ignored. In 1974, opponents of public housing obtained from Congress what they had failed to obtain in the 1930s; the principal thrust of the program was redirected to support the profitmaking element in the private sector. In the process, publicly owned housing was literally condemned without trial and abandoned. Ironically, the incompetence of some of its supporters supplied the evidence used in the condemnation proceedings. In due course, some former proponents apostatized and joined the attack.

The Second-Generation Developments

Although the danger signals were available for all to see, no one stopped at the beginning of the 1950s to look the public housing gift horse in the mouth, locally or nationally. The Housing Act of 1949 was followed by a rush to the public trough. Local patriotism, growing concern for the economic future of the central cities, increased information about the degree of dilapidation in the central cities (supplied by the 1950 census), and even avarice combined to generate a headlong plunge into the uncertainties of large-scale development of public housing. Without any careful examination of past performance, market research, or concern for long-run implications of participation, local housing authorities pressed for construction authorizations and hurried into production as fast as the bureaucratic machinery allowed, urged on by political supporters and local interests hoping to benefit from the program.

At this time, the federal bureaucracy made a serious error in judgment. Mistakenly believing that efficiency and economy were thereby promoted, they channeled construction into very large complexes made up mostly of high-rise buildings. In St. Louis, plans of long standing for constructing another development identical to Carr Square and Clinton Peabody were scrapped in a matter of weeks in favor of an untried high-rise design. The architectural firm that produced the new plans designed and supervised construction of most of the conventional public housing built in the city from 1950 to 1960. And such is the way of things architectural that its work was highly praised within the guild. In April 1951, for example, *Architectural Forum* published a highly laudatory account of the design of Pruitt and Igoe, duly echoed in the local press.

Most of the public housing produced in St. Louis under the terms of the 1949 Housing Act emerged in one great gush between 1953 and 1957 (see Table 1). In a five-year period, five developments, containing nearly five thousand dwelling units, began functioning in the city. A sixth conventional development was completed in 1961; the last major conventional construction was completed in 1968. A single building for the elderly was added to the Vaughn development in 1963.

Conventional public housing construction in the 1950s reflected then-current trends in the industry. The buildings were steel and concrete structures faced with brick, of medium height, located on flat and relatively featureless areas cleared from the slums adjacent to the two older developments. Cochran Gardens (1953) comprised 704 units of housing contained in two six-story, two seven-story, and four twelve-story buildings clustered a few blocks north of the central business district. Pruitt and Igoe together contained thirty-three eleven-story buildings, each some 170 feet long and containing 80 to 90 dwelling units. Vaughn and Darst were identical, each consisting of four nine-story buildings containing 656 apartments. Webbe included two nine-story buildings, a twelve-story building, and one building for the elderly eight stories tall. Densities were higher than in the two older developments, ranging from about 40 units per acre in Cochran Gardens and Vaughn to about 55 units per acre in Pruitt and Igoe. The relatively high density was a serious problem for tenants because there were a great many children in the apartments and little recreational space in the surrounding area.

Siting

Design, construction, and siting inadequacies in the second generation of conventional developments contributed heavily to their subsequent tribulations. Some errors resulted from simple miscalculations in design or construction, others were clearly a product of selfish pursuit of short-term gain by those involved in development. One great difficulty in housing development is that program beneficiaries receive their rewards before their products are tested in use. Enforcing responsible performance by producers is almost impossible when payment precedes consumption. In housing development, the architects, builders, and site owners take their payments, deserved or not, and depart, leaving the unfortunate owners and tenants to suffer with the consequences of misdeeds and oversights virtually without redress.

The locational shortcomings that marked the first two developments were compounded in the second generation. Carr Square, Vaughn, Pruitt, and Igoe were clustered on a 98-acre tract, a 4,814 dwelling-unit oasis in a sea of decaying and abandoned buildings. To the southwest, Clinton Peabody, Darst, and Webbe formed an 1,893-unit operation in a similarly dismal setting. Empty buildings were an eyesore and a danger to children; recreational facilities were woefully inadequate; access to transportation, shopping, and recreation was severely restricted. The location and design of the site opened the buildings to uncontrolled transient traffic that in time contributed significantly to both crime and vandalism. The developments acted as magnets for those in the surrounding territory whether they sought companionship, partners in crime, or targets for criminal activity.

Less directly, site selection altered the real economic costs of essentials such as police and fire protection, garbage removal, education, and utility services. It also influenced the amount and kind of social services provided for tenants by public and private agencies. Purchase and renovation of slum land, required by national policy, added significantly to development costs. Doubtless some property owners benefitted and others suffered from the siting process. Finally, there were minor cosmetic benefits (keeping abject poverty out of sight), psychic effects for some (there goes the neighborhood!) and minor personal impacts (where can we play baseball now?). Unfortunately, site selection was apparently unaffected by consideration for the long-term impact of location on tenant population or housing administration.

Amount of housing

Not only was the second generation of conventional housing poorly sited, but given the fiscal arrangements designed by Congress, too much was built at the wrong time. St. Louis did not generate enough effective demand for apartments, there was not enough willingness to rent at the price required by federally imposed conditions. The 1940 census of housing revealed a staggering amount of dilapidation within the city and demonstrated that large numbers of persons were living in unspeakable conditions. The 1950 census of housing suggested that little improvement had been made in the previous decade. However, these were indications of need and not of effective demand. Need translates into effective demand or willingness to buy through a network of mediating prices, economic and social conditions, residency requirements, and so on. If goods are free, the translation requires only a simple act of will accompanied by the physical effort needed to take possession. But if goods are very costly, even the most urgent and powerful of needs may remain unfulfilled.

In public housing, neither the tenant's willingness or his ability to pay determined rent. In the long run, the income that the Housing Authority needed to survive had to be obtained from the current tenant population. An inefficient housing industry raised the real cost to occupants by decreasing the supply and increasing required maintenance and repairs. The allowable level of tenant incomes was a function of the rents being charged for housing in the private sector (determined at least partly by local real estate dealers who had a vested interest in minimizing income limits that determined eligibility and thus maximizing the number of families seeking housing in the private sector). In principle, anyone whose income was not sufficient to purchase needed housing on the private market was eligible for public housing; in practice, that amount was calculated by a formula based on rent charges for decent housing of suitable size in the private sector. Of course, individuals whose incomes qualified them for admission to public housing might still prefer to live elsewhere. Private sector rents might be more attractive, the individual might prefer more cash in hand to better living accommodations. Nonmonetary aspects of public housing such as social stigma, lack of access to schools or transportation, social reputation, racial integration, and so on might also lead to rejection. And many prospective tenants, particularly those most highly desired by local housing authorities, were also targets for competing housing subsidy programs. Those leading to homeownership in decent residential areas were much more in line with traditional American family aspirations hence more likely to attract the relatively well-off and stable elements of the working poor.

Design and construction

Demand for public housing was also adversely affected by various design features—very small apartments, skip-stop elevators in medium-rise buildings, lack of playgrounds, poor equipment in the dwelling units, and so on. Inadequate market research, or perhaps the profit potential of various combinations of apartment size, led the designers to grossly overbuild small apartments and to build too few large family units. More than 66 percent of all conventional units built after 1950 contained only one or two bedrooms; in contrast, only 8 percent of them contained four bedrooms and a small handful contained five. Yet there was a pressing need for larger dwellings. Few were available in the private sector and they were proportionately very expensive. That information was readily available. The error was avoidable. Its effects were significant. Some of the one-bedroom units in Pruitt and Igoe remained unoccupied for the life of the development; yet at the very end of the trail, larger families were willing and even eager to remain there because of the acute shortage of large units in the private sector. After 1960, the Housing Authority combined some of the smaller units to form four- and five-bedroom apartments, but the process was expensive and the work was never completed.

Other design and construction inadequacies, notably in Pruitt and Igoe, did much to account for the rapid physical debilitation of the second generation conventional developments in the 1960s. There was nothing intrinsic to public housing that would account for the poor quality. Indeed, Cochran Gardens, which was completed in 1953, provided an interesting contrast to the more conspicuous failures. The buildings at Cochran were of different heights—six, seven, and twelve stories—but uniformly rectangular in shape with a central corridor; an elevator facility was placed at the midpoint of the rectangle. There were usually eight apartments on each floor, fronting on the central corridor. The family-style kitchen used in 1942 was replaced by an open kitchen and a combined living–dining area, separated from the kitchen by a free-standing storage unit. Space within the units was comparable to that provided in Carr Square and Clinton Peabody, adequate but not lavish. Construction was solid, the hardware, windows, and so forth were of good quality, dangerous piping was concealed, and there were no untoward hazards to children. The overall appearance of the buildings was good, though the surrounding area was badly run-down and there was not enough playground space for the children. What happened in the rest of the second-generation developments is perhaps best illustrated by Pruitt and Igoe.

Pruitt–Igoe. The original Pruitt–Igoe specifications called for a mixture of high-rise and row housing, playgrounds and other recreational facilities, and construction standards equivalent to those employed in Cochran Gardens. Those plans foundered on estimated construction costs. The bids on the original specifications were far in excess of statutory limits. The specifications were modified and bid a second time without success. A third set of specifications actually governed construction. In the process of reducing construction costs, conception and execution moved from small and frugal to mean, shoddy, and cheap. Much of the cost paring was done at the points of daily contact between tenant and apartment; such items as the ultraexpensive steam-heating system, which added enormously to initial cost and to subsequent operating expenses, remained intact throughout—a tribute to the power of the local steam fitters.

The end product was an incipient disaster. Living space was niggardly to the point of being unhealthy, perhaps 20 percent less than in Cochran Gardens in some units. The quality of the hardware was so poor that doorknobs and locks were broken on initial use, often before actual occupancy began. Windowpanes were blown from inadequate frames by wind pressure. In the kitchens, cabinets were made of the thinnest plywood possible, counter surfaces originally specified as heat resistant became plain wood, sinks were extremely small, there were no exhaust fans, stoves and refrigerators were of the smallest size and cheapest construction available. Even the bathrooms were slightly smaller than standard.

More generally, hot water pipes were inadequately shielded, places where children might clamber and fall were not screened; both conditions remained until some children had been badly burned and others had taken serious falls. The roof coating was reduced in thickness in successive specifications. Waterproofing was omitted from basement walls. Children's playgrounds disappeared from the plans; landscaping went into the discard. To add insult to injury, elevators were installed on a skip-stop basis that allowed them to take on and discharge passengers only on the first, fourth, seventh, and tenth floors in an eleven-story building. Since some buildings contained as many as 150 dwelling units, and the annual turnover rate was about 20 percent, the amount of frustration and ill-will generated by that one economy alone is beyond calculation. Moreover, the elevators were apparently ill-designed to cope with large families, hordes of children, and constant operation; perhaps no system of elevators can be constructed for that kind of use. Whatever the reasons, the elevators required repairs almost continuously from the first week of occupancy, and one elevator managed to fail on opening day.

The quality of construction and design was only slightly better in the other conventional developments built in the 1950s (Vaughn, Darst, Webbe); had they not suffered slightly less from vandalism in the 1960s, indeed had it not been for the overpowering impact of Pruitt and Igoe on public perceptions, they would have qualified as disasters in their own right by 1970 and been treated accordingly.

The second generation of conventional developments, beginning with Pruitt and Igoe, were victims of a mindless concentration on dollar costs that disregarded the long-run cost of poor quality and of a voracious and inefficient construction industry that fed on the aspirations and fears of the city's political and economic leaders. The result was a classic example of the folly of relying on rigid cost limits and competitive bidding to produce decent performance. The question whether the facilities likely to be produced under existing regulations would fulfill the housing-in-use function of the program effectively was nowhere raised, at least not publicly. Like the famous Russian factory that allegedly fulfilled its annual quota, specified in terms of weight, by building one gigantic bolt, the construction industry provided the Housing Authority with the allotted number of units within the established price limit and then departed.

Cost and quality

The question *why* suitable dwellings of good quality could not have been built within the established cost limits was not raised then and for some reason is seldom if ever raised now in discussions of public housing "failures." In retrospect, the cant phrase *high construction cost area* was used by those involved with the developments as a means of legitimating what was little better than legal larceny. The economies practiced in Pruitt and Igoe and afterward did not produce "cheap" housing in the sense of housing that cost very little, though they did produce "cheap" housing in the sense of housing that was of very poor quality. On the day they were completed, the buildings in Pruitt and Igoe were little more than steel and concrete rabbit warrens, poorly designed, badly equipped, inadequate in size, badly located, unventilated, and virtually impossible to maintain (the walls and floor were plain concrete that too easily crumbled into sand under pressure). The conditions inside unventilated, overcrowded apartments in an eleven-story building on a typically hot and humid summer day in St. Louis defy imagination (the central corridor that made crossventilation possible in other developments was abandoned by the architect).

The cost of these squalid habitations was outrageous. Construction costs in Pruitt and Igoe were about 60 percent above the national average, 40 percent above average cost per unit in New York City, 55 percent higher than the cost of Carr Square and Clinton Peabody, all expressed in deflated 1967 dollars. Only the elderly building in Vaughn, which required an astronomical $60 per square foot (though it was a precise duplicate of the elderly building in Webbe which cost far less) was more expensive. Cost for each square foot was in excess of $30, expressed in standard 1967 dollars; each dwelling unit cost an average of $20,000. That was perhaps 15 percent less than the cost of top-grade luxury apartments in the central city. In 1967, older three-bedroom homes were selling for less than $18,000, and there was an ample supply of new three-bedroom homes available at around $21,000. A luxury home could be built in the suburbs on a wooded lot for much less than $30 per square foot. The assumption that Pruitt–Igoe was too cheaply or inexpensively built, or that the developments were victims of an economy move, is simply ludicrous. And the responsibility of the construction industry for a major part of the debacle cannot be avoided by claiming that high initial costs were accepted in order to shift future maintenance costs to the federal government. Nothing in the architect's specifications or the various modifications introduced into the design suggests a positive relation between durability and cost; the subsequent history of the buildings argues to the contrary. The most expensive of the conventional developments, Pruitt and Igoe, proved least durable, most difficult to maintain, quickest to founder.

The Struggle for Survival

The second generation of conventional developments began operating in St. Louis in April 1953 when Cochran Gardens opened. Within two years, the Authority was in financial difficulty; by the end of the 1950s, it was pinned to the horns of a fearsome dilemma of rising costs and falling income. Escape without national assistance was out of the question: the state was unconcerned and the city lacked resources. Nationally the public housing program was trapped in a hopeless political situation that precluded assistance. Local housing authorities had to attract enough tenants to generate needed income; without income they could not provide the services that would attract tenants; the circle was vicious; the margin for error was too small; the time frame too tight. Fairly small shifts in either costs or demand could produce disaster.

The fiscal crunch

Although the Authority's operations were determined by a complex set of interacting factors, the best indicators of performance are found in the financial condition of the Authority in the 1950s and 1960s. There are two good indicators of basic financial health: in the short run, the relation between current income and expenses; in the long run, the relation between income, expenses, and overall development costs. No housing authority can survive the long haul without performing well by both criteria. The rule of thumb that can be used to judge long-run financial soundness is that yearly rental income must equal at least one-sixth of investment cost. Between 40 and 50 percent of that income, roughly 6.5 percent of development cost, will be needed for maintenance, repairs, and capital replacement and ordinary operating costs. However, local authorities had also to pay for utilities and lieu of tax charges from local governments, therefore a more realistic long-run minimum requirement was that annual income should equal 7.5 to 8 percent of development costs. That assumes, of course, reasonably good construction and normal construction costs. The HUD estimate that $754 should be collected in revenue for each $10,000 in development costs is very close to the rule of thumb used in the private sector. If the ratio holds even approximately, housing authorities whose incomes fall much short of these figures will in due course find themselves in serious financial straits, beginning usually with the second decade of operations.

The St. Louis experience with Carr Square and Clinton Peabody provides a good first test of the ratios. Between 1943 and 1953, when the two developments were functioning well and income was somewhat above normal, cumulated rents averaged about 6.1 percent of development costs per year, suitably deflated. That amount was marginally too low, and in fact deficit operations began in 1954. However, if the large sums used for mortgage payments could have been retained for capital replacement, the fiscal situation in 1953 would have been much stronger. In 1953, the two developments were generating only 5.8 percent of development costs in rent. Revenues declined slowly relative to investment until 1956–1957, when the introduction of rent increases reversed the trend. By 1968, they were earning about 8 percent of investment costs each year.

The other developments, however, fared less well. Cochran Gardens managed to collect about 4 percent of its capital investment annually between 1954 and 1968. But Vaughn could produce no more than 3.5 percent of investment, Darst–Webbe barely reached 3.3 percent, Pruitt achieved 3 percent, and Igoe barely 2.5 percent. Overall, maximum yield from rents was reached in the early 1960s when rents were high and occupancy still good. As the 1960s progressed, increased rents tended to be offset by falling occupancy.

When reserves are very limited, as was the case in public housing, the ratio between current income and expenses becomes increasingly critical. From 1943 to 1953, the income–expense ratio in Carr Square and Clinton Peabody was about 1.43 each year (income = 1.43 x expenses). Carr Square, which housed fewer employed heads of household, had a slightly lower ratio (1.31) than Clinton Peabody (1.55). At the beginning of the 1960s, the ratio of income to expenses was above unity for each of the conventional developments, but just barely: 1.2 in Carr Square, Clinton Peabody, and Darst–Webbe; 1.05 in Pruitt and Igoe. In the first two years of the decade, the ratio fell considerably; only Darst, Webbe, and Vaughn remained above the break-even point (major repairs in Carr Square and Clinton Peabody lowered the ratios there). The ensuing rent increases restored a favorable balance everywhere but at Pruitt and Igoe. After 1960, neither of the two white elephants managed to cover operating costs from rental income. In fact, after depleting their own small reserves, Pruitt and Igoe absorbed the lion's share of the reserves that had been cumulated by the other developments. In the accounting system used by the SLHA, all reserves were pooled. However, separate records were kept and the Authority was eventually reimbursed for the excess absorbed by Pruitt and Igoe. The two projects were an enormous and continuing burden on Authority resources until the mid-1970s when they were destroyed. The two large projects provided less than 70 percent of their own total expenses between 1957 and 1968; the remainder came from the other developments, forcing them to reduce operating expenses and defer maintenance. Had it not been for Pruitt and Igoe, the situation in the other conventional developments would have been far less desperate in the 1960s. Even in the 1970s, they continued to absorb capital replacement funds that were desperately needed and would have produced noticeable, positive improvements elsewhere.

Occupancy

In an ongoing operation such as public housing, the vital signs are as closely related as those that concern the health of the human body. The Authority's financial weakness was mirrored accurately in occupancy statistics—the portion of a full year that the apartments were occupied. Carr Square and Clinton Peabody remained full; occupancy was consistently between 97 and 99 percent in the former and 96 and 99 percent in the latter until the very end of the 1960s. Cochran Gardens was only slightly less effective, averaging from 95 to 98 percent until 1969, when it fell sharply. Vaughn peaked below 94 percent occupancy, averaging between 88 and 93 percent through the 1960s; Darst–Webbe consistently averaged 92 to 95 percent until 1968, when occupancy fell off very drastically. Pruitt and Igoe, comparatively, failed from the outset. Pruitt achieved 95 percent occupancy for the first two years of operation, dropped to 80 percent for 1961, and operated about three-fourths full for most of the 1960s. In 1969, occupancy plummeted to 57.1 percent (and much of the rent was never paid). Igoe did even more poorly in occupancy, peaking at 86 percent its first year of operation and stabilizing at about 65 percent for most of the 1960s. In 1969, occupancy dropped to 48.9 percent, lowest in any of the conventional developments. After 1960, all the conventional developments suffered some loss in both applications and occupancy because of the declining reputation of the developments, spurred by the December 1959 publication of a strong grand-jury attack on the Authority for failing to maintain the safety of the tenants. Low occupancy was not, as legislation seemed to imply, a simple function of tenant dislike for high-rise apartments. Levels of occupancy in the twelve-story buildings at Cochran Gardens, for example, were far better than occupancy in the eight-story buildings at Vaughn; upper levels in the taller buildings often had better occupancy rates than lower floors. There is no consistent pattern linking building height and patterns of occupancy.

Fighting a losing battle

As early as 1954, it was clear that the St. Louis Housing Authority would somehow have to improve its fiscal position, either by reducing costs or by increasing income. The outlook for cost reduction was poor. Major expenses included management, utilities, and maintenance, and only the last of these offered any hope of significant savings. Unfortunately, past experience with maintenance suggested this was an unlikely avenue to improvement. Through the late 1950s, the Authority acted on the assumption that its problems were due to lack of income rather than excessive costs. That is, most of its efforts were aimed at increasing revenue, either by improving occupancy or by increasing rents.

The effort to improve occupancy took several forms. First, the Authority abandoned the so-called interim-redetermination method of calculating rents. That system forced a rent change every time the tenant's income changed and required the tenant to report all income changes to the Authority and accept responsibility for back charges if unreported increases were discovered. Instead, the Authority adopted a "fixed-rent" system in which rents were set annually and changed only after each annual review. Second, the Authority entered into a special agreement with the Missouri Welfare Department calling for *higher than normal* rents (to prevent a reduction in welfare payments). Third, the regulations were changed in 1957 to allow broken families to remain in (but not enter) public housing, a policy that helped swell the ranks of ADC mothers in the developments.

Before these policy changes could produce any significant effect, the impact of the Eisenhower recession began to be felt in St. Louis. In the developments, recession was accompanied by increased amounts of crime, vandalism, larger numbers of apartments vacated without notice, many more delinquent accounts, larger unpaid balances on the books, increased accounts receivable (about $84,000 by 1958, concentrated heavily in Pruitt–Igoe), higher collection losses, more legal actions, more evictions, higher legal costs. There was a steady erosion of the Authority's capacity to attract tenants and deliver services.

Concurrently, the physical deterioration of the conventional developments accelerated very seriously. The 1959 *Audit and Consolidated Management Report* summarized the more ominous trends in the developments very effectively. The buildings were being seriously damaged by vandals—principally transients rather than residents, according to the report. The failures of the maintenance program were both numerous and serious, though costs remained very high—higher than in any other city in the region and three times the level in the private sector. As a result of the evaluation of maintenance made in 1959, the auditors demanded and got a 10 percent reduction in the maintenance force, eliminating about twenty-five positions altogether. The auditors stressed the need for improved maintenance, better management control over all aspects of operation, more tenant education, stricter control over rent collection, tenant payment for damages to apartments, and collection of delinquent accounts. The auditors were rather better at locating deficiencies than at suggesting means of solving Authority problems, of course, but the tone and content of the report and the clear evidence of deterioration were ominous portents for the Authority's future. It is unlikely that the Authority's difficulties were *caused by* the economic recession. The overall weakness of Authority operations, particularly in maintenance and fiscal affairs rendered it unable to cope with the additional stresses produced by the economic downturn. Like a human body seriously weakened by privation, the Authority was highly susceptible to damage and unable to shake off the effects of damage very quickly.

The 1959 audit caused a great deal of internal discomfort for the Authority, and the reduction in maintenance staff was a damaging blow to operations. The effects of a St. Louis grand jury report made public at the end of 1959 were also serious. The very sharp critique of crime in the developments was widely publicized and did more to destroy the public housing image in the area than any other single event of the 1950s. The impact on occupancy was immediate. In the quarter ending March 1959, the Authority received 611 applications; some 525 were received in the following quarter. In the quarter following the grand-jury report, only 295 applications for admission were made to the Authority, and that low level of applications continued until the summer of the following year.

Through the early 1960s, the Authority struggled unsuccessfully to stabilize operations, improve service to tenants, restore the physical state of the buildings and improve public order on the premises, and increase occupancy and revenue. Lack of resources was a constant handicap. Pruitt and Igoe still weighed upon the Authority like old men of the sea, implacably gobbling resources desperately needed for other purposes. The Authority's problems were complex; some had no solutions. The scale of operations was now so large and the rate of change so rapid that minor problems escalated into nightmares virtually overnight. The side effects of action often wiped out the benefits of action leaving a negative balance. Efforts to speed processing of applications lowered the quality of applicant screening, and the Authority found itself evicting, at great cost in money and effort, the very same tenants it tried earlier to attract. A police check was added to the screening process, reducing the need for eviction but slowing admission by days or weeks. Welfare tenants proved a constant source of difficulty. Teen-age children from single-parent households played an important role in the physical deterioration of the premises. More importantly, they had a negative economic impact on the Authority's fiscal position. The special arrangement with the Missouri welfare system had been designed to increase income. But between 1 May 1961 and 31 March 1963 some 322 welfare families left the apartments owing the Authority a total of more than $20,000—an average of about $65 per family, or about two months' rent. Even likely sounding ways of improving living conditions sometimes had strange effects: for example, the Authority agreed to replace all ground-floor windows free of charge in order to improve the appearance of the developments, and window breakage on the ground floors increased by more than 35 percent in the following quarter.

Some of the Authority's efforts to improve operations were substantial and expensive, adding significantly to operating costs. In 1960, mainly as a result of the grand-jury action, the Authority hired private security guards at an annual cost of nearly $70,000; the arrangement continued until 1968 and terminated when the expense was no longer bearable. It was never clear whether the guards were effective, but the psychic benefits could have been substantial given the levels of anxiety common among the tenants. In an effort to improve management at Pruitt–Igoe, the operation was divided among five managers—at considerable expense. That arrangement lasted around two years but produced no improvements of consequence. A home visitor service was created in 1960; it closed in 1967 for lack of funds. Legal actions by the score were undertaken to rid the developments of undesirable tenants and delinquents, but that too created problems. Once a tenant was notified that a suit was pending against him, the Authority could no longer accept rent. The tenant remained on the premises and continued to be billed. If the tenant was evicted, the delinquent rent was generally not collectible; if he remained, the delinquent account was virtually impossible to reduce or liquidate. In either case, the Authority was the loser—and paid the legal fees as well. The welfare offices at Pruitt and Vaughn were enlarged at considerable expense, but the major effect was apparently to reduce the caseload of each social worker to fifty families.

Minor programs for alleviating specific conditions within the developments were tried by the score. A rent incentive plan, offering rebate of one month's rent after one year of occupancy, was established at Pruitt–Igoe. Two months of rent-free occupancy were offered certain incoming tenants as an incentive to living in the developments. Apartments were leased at virtually no cost to all sorts of religious and other organizations to allow them better access to tenants. Tenant councils were established. Free cleaning materials were provided. Prospective tenants were transported to the developments at Authority expense. A program for resident supervisors was established. A local university was hired to provide tenant orientation programs. And the public housing tenants were studied, and restudied, and then studied again. Washington University received $750,000 in one grant alone to study the tenants in Pruitt–Igoe. But the preliminary report issued in 1966 was only a simple summary of some 250 interviews, no final report was received by the Authority, no final report found its way into the university library, and HUD could not supply a copy either. Other governmental agencies joined the fray, trying to put out the fire by the conventional bureaucratic device of flooding it with money. The Office of Economic Opportunity supplied nearly $200,000 to "transform the housing projects into a living community," by unspecified means. A local school district received $100,000 for summer operations intended to change the "attitudes and values and behavior" of the black children in the district, though the evidence clearly indicates this same school had failed to do anything of the sort during the regular school year—had it succeeded then, the special summer sessions would not have been needed. The Human Development Corporation received more than $850,000 in 1964 for educating and training the very poor in the city, many located in the public housing developments.

The pattern of activity, in major and minor programs alike, was the same: a burst of publicity when the grant was received, a set of promises, a perfunctory performance, then silence. The major discernible long-term effect of such programs was to condition the residents to regard all improvement schemes as phony public relations actions and to encourage them to "get theirs." In all honesty, the scale of the need made mock of well-intentioned small-scale efforts. At peak occupancy, there were about 12,000 tenants in Pruitt–Igoe alone; perhaps half of them were minors. A day-care center that served thirty-five children or a kindergarten that took care of thirty others had little serious impact on conditions in the developments. There was no indication that such efforts were meant as "seeding operations" or even experiments. There was simply never enough money; therefore, it was distributed by lottery. The few children who held winning tickets gained minor and temporary benefits from the programs. How the winners were chosen is uncertain. The principal beneficiaries seem to have been those who played the grantsman's game with skill and perseverance or gained some useful publicity through "worthy" associations.

From the point of view of the Authority, nothing worked. Operating costs continued to rise and at an increasing rate. By 1966, the Authority was operating at a deficit. Management costs, which had averaged 8 to 9 percent of operating costs, increased to 18 to 20 percent of much larger operating costs. Ordinary maintenance costs in St. Louis reached $23 per unit per month (PUM) compared to about $15 PUM in most other cities in the country. Routine expenses alone accounted for about 99 percent of income before any provision was made for replacement of capital and nonroutine maintenance. Much of the added maintenance cost was apparently due to vandalism. In 1969, the *Management Report* estimated that some $2 million—about 40 percent of all labor costs and 30 percent of all material costs in the Authority—was needed to repair the effects of vandalism between 1965 and 1969 alone. And conditions worsened steadily. By 1968, the developments resembled a city under siege. Vandalism was rampant, crime commonplace, garbage and refuse everywhere. It is hardly surprising that occupancy declined and new tenants were scarce. In 1966, some 425 tenants were admitted to conventional housing; in 1967, that number shrank to 208; in 1968 it was down to 197; in 1969, only 71 tenants entered the premises, usually to find large apartments. The annual operating deficit reached $2 million by the end of the 1960s, though total income was just over $4 million per year.

Faced with a deteriorating physical environment, decreased occupancy, and rising costs, the Authority had no alternative, given federal policy, to raising its rents still further. Since most of the tenants remaining in the developments were in the lower income brackets—those who could afford to move left quickly as the living conditions worsened—increased rental income had to come from the lower end of the rent scale. Between 1952 and 1968, the rent structure shifted upward notch by notch as the Authority struggled to meet its obligations. The 1952 minimum rent of $20 per month was raised to $32 in 1958, to $43 in 1962, and to $58 in 1968. By 1969, virtually all the tenants were squeezed into the $50 to $80 per month bracket. The burden on the tenants, particularly those with fixed incomes, was unbelievable. More than 20 percent of all families (1,060) were paying more than 45 percent of their income for rent; another 25 percent paid more than 50 percent of income for rent. And some 70 unfortunates actually paid more than 75 percent of their monthly income to the Authority. Such unconscionable rent charges, due mainly to the unavoidable rent increase of 1968, set the stage for the 1969 rent strike and helped pave the way for the Brooke amendments limiting the portion of a tenant's income that could be charged for public housing.

Why?

It would be very improper to assign blame for "the failure" in St. Louis public housing to a limited, specific cause—whether policy, individual, institution, or group. Indeed, even the term *the failure* is misleading. *Disaster* is more appropriate. Program operations produced mixed results; many factors contributed. Some of the developments, notably· Pruitt–Igoe, performed very badly; others, notably Carr Square, Clinton Peabody, and Cochran Gardens, performed well, even extremely well, all things considered. There were errors in the basic statutes, in federal regulations, in local Authority policies, in the work of architects and contractors, in the actions of various interest groups, in the reaction of the general public, and in the behavior and attitudes of the tenants. Some major factors can be identified and their influence traced. That may help to correct the conventional wisdom in those areas where it has done most damage in the past.

The assumption most in need of challenge is that the disaster was due to the characteristics of the resident population. What is often called the "culture of poverty" may have accelerated but certainly did not cause it. And those who hastened to interview and analyze the tenants in Pruitt and Igoe committed the same mistake as the student of prejudice who begins with an examination of the victim. The ADC families headed by younger females with large numbers of children and little discipline certainly helped create a headache for those responsible for the developments. Yet, if the physical structures had been better designed and built, and there are some reasons at least to presume this was not unreasonable to expect, much of the problem could have been avoided. And conversely, given the quality of construction and the policies governing operation, no change in population could have altered the long-run outcome very significantly.

On the other hand, there is a genuine need to call attention to the deficiencies in the fiscal program and the weakness inherent in the construction industry. Relations between costs and benefits, payment and performance, also deserve consideration. One of the truly shocking aspects of this study was the discovery, in 1971, that the basic records of housing operations were still virgin, accessible but unsought and unnoticed.

The housing program launched in the 1950s was a fragile thing. The local housing authority was weakest at precisely those points most likely to be stressed by rapid expansion. The state and city were unconcerned or unhelpful; the federal regional offices had no resources. The Authority's clients were powerless, lacking in resources, unorganized, lacking even in capacity to organize effectively. The expansion of program occurred at precisely the moment that the first signs of fiscal weakness appeared, at least partly masking them. Workers in the Housing Authority were plunged into the most stressful of all work situations: they were forced to learn new modes of operation under extreme time pressure with little margin for error. The cost of failures in foresight and planning escalated with the increased scale of operations. Had the program expanded in tranquil times, or better still on the eve of an economic boom (as the first generation hit the market at the beginning of World War II), some of the initial shock might have been absorbed using surplus resources. But the economic seas were already stormy by 1954 and worsened rapidly thereafter. The enemies of public housing could not have designed a set of operating conditions more likely to ensure failure. The Housing Authority went through a series of *Perils of Pauline* type trials between 1954 and 1970 that would sound contrived in a movie thriller. Unlike Pauline, the Housing Authority was ravaged at every turn. In a world in which survival depended on a balance between income and cost, it must at times have seemed that the very heavens were conspiring to reduce income and increase expenses.

First, effective demand for housing, which had placed unrelenting pressure on the housing stock through the 1940s, receded dramatically in the early 1950s—just as the supply of public housing was beginning to expand vigorously. Out-migration from the central city, begun long before World War II and accelerated by various federal housing-subsidy programs, was one factor in the change. The economic slowdown sent semimigrant workers back to the rural areas to await future employment. There was a steady out-migration of black males of working age. In consequence of these and other trends, Cochran Gardens, which opened in April 1953, soon found itself with excess vacancies, particularly in three-bedroom apartments. By 1954, occupancy was declining but a massive influx of new units was due within months. That provided the impetus for the special agreement between the Authority and the Missouri Welfare Department.

A second major change in the operating environment of the program occurred in 1954 when the U.S. Supreme Court upheld a state court ruling that a housing authority could not deny admission to an applicant on racial grounds—effectively desegregating public housing. Ironically, that decision helped solve the short-run occupancy problem at Cochran Gardens, for there were many black applicants for space in the hitherto all-white development. But in the long run, the effort to desegregate failed dismally and actually contributed to the decline of the developments. Until 1955, all of St. Louis's public housing was segregated. Carr Square housed only blacks; Clinton Peabody and Cochran Gardens were reserved for white occupancy. Pruitt, Igoe, and Vaughn were expected to join Carr Square as part of the black allocation; Darst and Webbe were planned as all-white developments adjoining Clinton Peabody. Following the Supreme Court decision, the Authority decided not to try and integrate Pruitt, which was already partly rented, and concentrated on integration of Igoe.

The effort failed and the conventional developments moved steadily toward racial segregation—and achieved it by the end of the 1960s, for all practical purposes. The effort to integrate Igoe actually worsened conditions there because the Authority shunted prospective black tenants to Pruitt while it sought white applicants willing to live in the integrated development. The causes of the failure of integration efforts seem reasonably clear. St. Louis is a border city that draws much of its population from the rural hinterlands in the Mississippi basin, areas where racial integration had made much less progress by the mid-1950s than in the industrial North or the larger southern cities. Attitudes and behavior antithetical to racial integration were both common and powerful. They very effectively neutralized the Authority's efforts to achieve a racial balance in the developments.

The failure of racial integration did more than reduce demand for apartments in the developments; as might be expected, it altered the character of the overall population in public housing. Black occupancy became the rule; incoming families were larger and more dependent on public assistance; tenant incomes were lower; the number of female heads of household in residence increased. Some of the changes in cultural values and habits that followed contributed to the Authority's management problem: newer tenants displayed lower levels of family discipline, a reduced sense of responsibility for public property, less willingness to cooperate with authority to maintain order, and so on. While such generalizations seem to hold for the larger conventional developments, they should be treated with caution. Carr Square, for example, was entirely populated by blacks from the beginning, and most of the tenants living there received public assistance, yet it remained the most orderly and easily managed complex in St. Louis. Moreover, the popular image of the black ADC mother as an ignorant lout from the backwoods, newly arrived in the city and unfamiliar with most of the trappings of modern society, is grotesquely mistaken. A Missouri Department of Welfare study of 964 ADC mothers in Pruitt–Igoe, carried out in 1962, showed that more than half of them had been born in St. Louis and about 85 percent had lived in the city for at least ten years.[2] Ill-educated they may have been, but they were quite familiar with and adapted to city life.

The large number of juveniles in female-headed families in Pruitt and Igoe probably contributed to the vandalism and order problems facing the Authority, at least to the extent that single-parent families tend to exercise less discipline and con-

2. Division of Welfare, Missouri Department of Public Health and Welfare, *The ADC Families of Pruitt–Igoe: A Descriptive Study.*

trol over children than two-parent families, other things equal. But the racial character of the population would still not have been decisive. Major changes in public attitudes toward society and public property occurred everywhere in American society in the 1950s and not among the black poor alone. It was an era of rising expectations, larger aspirations, stronger demands, increased militancy, greater questioning of authority, rising impatience, and so on. Such attributes were shared by blacks, and particularly by black youth, but were not exclusive or unique to them. The elders of the white community also bewailed the loss of respect for tradition and established institutions, the ill treatment of community property, the decline of the work ethic, and changes in personal morality.

Such changes in attitudes and values tend to influence community affairs indirectly, altering the climate of opinion and with it the norms of acceptability. By doing so, they exert pressure on those who operate established institutions. The housing authority could no more escape the trend than could the local school. And for the Housing Authority in St. Louis, that meant a fundamental change in attitude and performance. For years, it had concentrated on providing housing services, in the very narrow sense of the term—in keeping with the practices of the 1930s. It had been little concerned for the social, psychic, or even economic dimensions of its tenants' lives. In this, it should be said, the Authority was emulated by most other collective institutions in American society and strongly supported by the entrenched political and social authorities. By the late 1960s, that approach to the operation of collective facilities was increasingly regarded as anachronistic. The St. Louis Housing Authority was not unique in its failure to adapt to these changing conditions; like the medical profession, it tended to react strongly and rigidly along traditional lines, and that made the task of adapting more difficult and generated more friction and opposition than might otherwise have been the case. However, given the Authority's lack of resources, it is doubtful that it could have satisfied either critics or tenants even given the best will in the world.

IV.

Conventional Public Housing in St. Louis, 1969–1976

The Rent Strike and its Aftermath

The turning point for the conventional public housing program in St. Louis was the rent strike that began in February 1969 and lasted until October of that year. At the beginning of the strike, the program was highly centralized, very traditional in outlook, somewhat paternalistic or authoritarian in its relations with tenants. The physical conditions in the developments had deteriorated markedly in the past decade; the financial condition of the Authority was desperate. When the strike ended, the program emerged into a new phase of operations, marked by three distinct major trends. First, tenant influence on program operations expanded greatly and rapidly in response to both legislative changes and pressure from local tenants. Second, Housing Authority control over the details of day-to-day operations declined very significantly. The legal relation between landlord and tenant was changing everywhere in society, and those changes were reflected in the public housing program. The practice of contracting with private firms for management and other services required in public housing was being extended rapidly under strong prodding from the federal government. The Authority, under pressure from the committee of local leaders set up to end the rent strike, decentralized much of its operations. The third major trend, in some measure contingent on the others, was toward very rapidly increasing operating costs. New social service costs were added to the regular operating burden; the inflation rate at times reached 10 percent per annum; physical facilities long neglected and badly vandalized had to be repaired before the program could resume. Ultimately, these costs appeared in the federal ledgers, bringing about a moratorium on expansion and leading eventually to a major new emphasis in the public housing program.

The Tenant Rent Strike of 1969

The rent strike should have surprised no one familiar with the recent history of St. Louis public housing. It had long been threatened. And American society in the 1960s provided the frustrated tenants with examples and precedents for refusing legally required payment to authority when it failed to provide services considered theirs by right. The Harlem rent strikes of 1963–1964 were still fresh in memory; university students were wrestling seriously with school authorities about their respective roles in those institutions; militants and liberals were probing deeply into such hitherto sacrosanct areas as police behavior, rights of women, rights of children, and so on. The trend to social concern was even reflected in the Housing and Urban Development Act of 1968, which required local housing authorities to provide their tenants with increased services, improvements in management, and lower rents. At the very least, such legislation tended to provide legitimating support for tenant actions.

The strike was triggered by the rent increase carried out in November 1968. Complaints were loud; revocation was demanded; a strike was threatened. An effort to obtain assistance from the Missouri legislature failed—predictably—and HUD declared the grievance a "local" matter. The tenants were literally forced to look to their own resources. Aided and even prompted by local ministers, the Legal Aid Society, and the more ephemeral good wishes of the newly formed National Tenant's Organization, the tenants in Carr Square, Cochran Gardens, and Vaughn Apartments prepared to strike. Early in February 1969, with some modest local fanfare, the rent strike began. Tenants were urged to pay their rents to the strike leaders instead of the Housing Authority; funds collected were placed in escrow accounts—and in some cases were simply hidden to avoid court action.

In retrospect, the original demands of the strikers were reasonable and amply justified. They asked for rent reductions, improved service (particularly for routine maintenance and such things as garbage collection), rehabilitation of the physical structures, and perhaps most important of all, increased security for person and property in and around the apartments. The demands were moderate, in keeping with the character of those who led the strike in its early phase. The Carr Square tenants who provided the initial backbone for the strike were part of the most stable population in the St. Louis housing program. By no stretch of the imagination could they have been characterized as radical or extreme. But their living conditions had literally become intolerable. In Carr Square, the buildings were old, deferred maintenance was taking its toll. Though vandalism was not serious, plaster fell regularly from the ceiling; electrical wiring and plumbing were old and unreliable. Leaking pipe connections discolored walls and created noisome odors. Broken windows, leaking faucets, uncertain hot water, and other needs that maintenance could not handle had escalated to the point where conditions were barely livable. In many of the other developments, the quality of the environment was far worse; roving gangs stalked the streets, sniping was commonplace, vandalism was rife. And for many tenants, the appalling pressure of rents in excess of 50 to 75 percent of total monthly income created genuine suffering. In brief, the tenants' grievances were serious, genuine, and extensive; if anything, they were stated in overly moderate terms.

Negotiations

Regardless of the facts or merits of the case, the Housing Authority was powerless; it had no resources to give, and the strikers' problems could not be solved without funds. City, state, and federal administration alike turned a deaf ear to pleas for additional funds. The strike dragged on through the spring and summer of 1969. The Authority could do nothing of consequence; the strikers refused to concede. More precisely, those who came to control and direct later stages of the strike refused to concede and in fact tended to escalate demands. The final settlement reached in October far exceeded the original strike goals in both principles and particulars. The *St. Louis Post-Dispatch* (12 October 1969) argued that the strikers had refused in July what was accepted in October. But that missed the central point of the settlement: it was negotiated with an external agency (the Civic Alliance for Housing) able to deal directly with both the federal government and the city and to force changes in the Housing Authority from the outside. The strategy was sound, for neither the city nor the Authority had the resources needed to make the changes that tenants demanded. The only key to the manacles that policy and circumstance had forged was large sums of money and major changes within the Authority; the only route to that set of possibilities lay through local business leaders, union leaders, and other community panjandrums. The Civic Alliance for Housing, formed as a means of ending the strike in the early autumn of 1969, had a powerful union representative as chairman and strong representation from the local community. Although there was probably no alternative available, the dangers implicit in this type of ad hoc arrangement were well illustrated by the Alliance. The members tended to be sympathetic to the strikers and largely ignorant of the long-run costs of technical concessions. They were, moreover, much inclined to "get the matter settled" even at cost, since the costs would, in any event, come from the public treasury. Some of the arrangements made by the Alliance created significant long-term costs for the Housing Authority and introduced major changes in the operation of the conventional housing program without adequate consideration of the consequences.

The Settlement

Perhaps the most striking result of the settlement was the nearly complete turnover of Housing Authority leadership that followed. The Housing Authority was separated from the Land Clearance and Redevelopment Authority; most of the top-level administrators in housing followed the director into the land clearance program. All members of the old board of commissioners were forced to resign. The Authority's affairs were for all practical purposes placed in the hands of the Civic Alliance for the indefinite future. In some respects, the long-run interests of the early strikers coincided with those of the public housing program. But time and achievement expanded the ambitions of the strike leaders. Forcing out the old management and overturning the rules of operations created new opportunities; control was now vested in an external agency friendly to the tenants, unfamiliar with detail, impatient of delays. The result was a major transfer of authority out of the SLHA to newly formed tenant organizations. Indeed, the tenants' operating model of public housing, as it emerged from negotiations, envisioned housing developments that were nearly independent, self-governing communities, banded together for common purposes (and coordinated by the Civic Alliance and not the Housing Authority). Service cooperatives would be formed and a management training enterprise would ready the tenants to control the developments. Unfortunately, the vision stopped short of economic self-sufficiency; the prime employer would be the Housing Authority and the ultimate bill would be presented to the federal treasury. The model remained an Indian reservation, utterly dependent on transfer payments. But in the model, some Indians were more equal than others and there were a few slots for Indian agents to serve as advisors.

The provisions of the settlement that had the greatest long-run impact on the St. Louis housing program spelled out the future role of tenants and their organizations in Authority affairs. A Tenant Affairs Board (TAB) was created, consisting of elected representatives from each development. TAB was given a good deal of authority in operations: two of its members would be included in the new board of commissioners—and it could actually veto proposed appointments of other members; it had to be consulted on all major policy matters. In addition, TAB was to supervise liquidation of tenant indebtedness, serve as an appeal board on eviction cases (subject to final approval by the board), and sponsor actions desired by the tenants. The technical details relating to settlement of differences between Authority and tenants in the period after the strike can be bypassed, but it appears that TAB was to serve as arbiter in the event of disputes.

The Housing Act of 1968 authorized and encouraged tenant participation in management; the Housing Act of 1970 authorized tenant participation in all aspects of operations. The St. Louis settlement went far beyond either set of authorizations. The principle of full tenant control over housing operations was accepted; provision was made for training tenants in management skills; and it assumed formation of tenant-controlled corporations able to contract with the Housing Authority for performance of management functions. The experiment in tenant management was to take place first in Carr Square and Vaughn Apartments. The major innovation was the use of an independent corporation as a contracting agent for the tenants, effectively removing the tenant managers from direct Authority control.

Why did the Authority accept such a drastic settlement? It had little choice. The Civic Alliance forced the issue. HUD, the city, and other interested parties concurred; the Authority could do little but accept. Curiously, the impact of the strike on the Authority tended to be grossly exaggerated by those involved. Strikers were heavily concentrated in Carr Square, Vaughn, and Cochran Gardens; the strike involved only a small part of either total revenue or total tenant population. The strike leaders collected nearly $200,000 during the strike, about 8 percent of the total rent for the period—a significant but not lethal loss. The amounts actually withheld, whether stated in absolute numbers or as a portion of total rent, were small: Carr Square/Vaughn, $114,376 (16 percent); Cochran, $67,325 (20 percent); Clinton Peabody/Darst/Webbe, $19,869 (2 percent); and Blumeyer, $19,697 (3 percent). The total amounted to an income loss equivalent to average rent payments for about 400 tenants—there were about 5,200 tenants in residence in 1969.

The worst fiscal effects of the strike were the result of "freeloading" tenants who simply stopped paying rent altogether and, of course, the vandals. As the strike dragged on, the number of active strikers declined and the number of freeloaders increased. The result was a staggering increase in the Authority's outstanding accounts not covered by escrow funds held by the strikers. At the end of September 1968, the Authority's accounts receivable totaled about $73,000; one year later, the debt had grown to about $730,000. The strike leaders held a little more than $200,000 in their accounts, about 8 percent of one year's rent; the freeloaders "held" more than half a million dollars, nearly 30 percent of annual rent. Moreover, the Authority could expect ultimately to collect the funds withheld by the strikers; the task of collecting overdue individual accounts was impossible. The distinction is well illustrated by rates of repayment after the strike ended. In Carr Square, accounts receivable decreased by 22 percent in the first year after the strike; in Vaughn and Cochran, they dropped 6 percent and 2 percent respectively. But in Igoe, the receivables *increased* by 26 percent, in Darst the increase was 37 percent. By the spring of 1970, more than 20 percent of all tenants with unpaid balances had left the developments.

Aftermath of the Strike

Nationally, public housing entered a holding period in 1970, emerging in 1974 with a new focus and new impetus. In St. Louis, as in other large cities, the conventional developments remained the central concern—if only because of the sheer number of apartments involved. Over 8,000 units of conventional housing had been built in the city; even without Pruitt and Igoe, the 5,000 remaining units made up about two-thirds of the total supply—there were some 1,600 units of turnkey and 600 units of leased housing available at the end of 1975. The struggle to keep the conventional developments alive, or more precisely, to bring them back to life, absorbed most of the energy and resources of the Authority through the early 1970s. In the main, that meant dealing with the direct and indirect effects of the rent strike, for problems the strike did not cause it generally aggravated severely, whether they involved the physical condition of the buildings or the financial condition of the Authority.

A brief survey of the major dimensions of the conventional program at the time of the strike settlement will suggest the nature of the Authority's problems, the extent of its needs, and some of the major impediments to improvement. The survey will concentrate on physical conditions, security, the management–fiscal position, and occupancy. Obviously a whole host of related factors impinged in some way on operations, but they cannot all be considered in a limited space.

Physical conditions

A fairly comprehensive survey of the conventional developments was made in December 1970 by a "Consolidated Management Evaluation team."[1] While physical states varied widely, only the two buildings for the elderly remained in good condition—an indication of the extent to which occupants were involved in the destruction. The complexity of the issues facing the Authority was reflected in the report. The team found gross irresponsibility among the tenants, widespread vandalism, and an urgent need for security and stability. Indeed, they urged against making improvements until security conditions were stabilized. Four levels of disrepair were noted, represented by Carr Square–Clinton Peabody, Cochran Gardens, Vaughn–Darst–Webbe, and the Pruitt–Igoe complex, in order of ascending amounts of damage.

Although Carr Square was the center of the rent strike in its

1. U.S., Department of Housing and Urban Development, "Comprehensive Consolidated Management Review Report of the St. Louis Housing Authority, St. Louis, Missouri," 6 May 1971. The actual review was carried out between 30 November and 11 December 1970.

early days, there was little strike damage to the premises. The sister development, Clinton Peabody, was only slightly damaged through vandalism during the strike. Both developments, however, were in poor physical condition because they were old and had been long neglected. In Carr Square, no painting had been done since 1961; kitchens, baths, entryways, and stairs needed major renovation; plumbing, electrical equipment, baths, stoves, refrigerators, and other basic equipment had to be replaced in most cases. Plastering had deteriorated, doors and windows either needed replacement immediately or would have to be replaced soon if painting was long delayed. In effect, the buildings were structurally sound but needed to be rebuilt from the basic shell. Obviously, this was not the result of strike damage but of over-deferred maintenance and capital replacement.

Cochran Gardens was badly vandalized during the strike. One building was vacant, flooded as a result of burst pipes; the others were structurally sound and well built but in need of repairs. Vandalism had been aimed mainly at the lobbies and entrances, where walls were marked, mailboxes destroyed, lights and switches ruined, and elevators badly mauled, and at the roofs, a prime source of marketable copper—from flashing, downspouts and gutters, pipes, and so on. It was a tribute to the quality of the original construction that the engineers suggested that Cochran be given priority for rehabilitation. By the end of 1970, Cochran was further along the road to recovery than any other conventional development, assisted by its selection as the site of the first major investment in security guards and by development of the "block partnership" concept—involving the tenants in painting, repairs, and other acts of restoration.

Vandalism in Vaughn, Darst, and Webbe was very extensive. One building at Webbe had been flooded and was closed; a loss of 110 dwelling units. The others had been ravaged mercilessly. Roof flashing was torn away, producing serious leakage and extensive water damage inside. Conduits, electrical fixtures, wiring, plumbing, in brief, anything that could be sold, had been taken from the vacant units. Lobbies and public areas had been savaged; the grounds were in disarray; halls and stairwells were filled with rubbish; garbage and glass were strewn everywhere. More than half of all windows in vacant units were broken; in the abandoned units, *all* the windows were gone. Doors and windows, ranges and refrigerators, plastering and piping, electricity and heating, all needed replacement in whole or part. This was not a result of normal wear and tear; the buildings were less than fifteen years old.

Hard though it may be to believe, conditions in Vaughn–Darst–Webbe stood in relation to those in Pruitt and Igoe as the effects of a gentle rain to the impact of a major hurricane. Damage in Pruitt and Igoe, much of it dating to the late 1960s, was nearly unbelievable even when seen. As late as December 1969, some of the buildings still had water flowing freely through the halls and down the stairs. While a few buildings remained in use, the rest made up a strange kind of contemporary nightmare: rows of buildings with their windows and doors hanging loose in their frames, rooms jammed with rubble, walls demolished in the search for valuable wire or pipe, gaping holes everywhere, roofing torn from its base, site littered with garbage and broken glass. Twenty-three of the original thirty-three buildings were closed, a loss of some 1,900 of the original 2,870 units of housing in the two developments.

The engineering report made no estimate of rehabilitation costs for conventional housing, but a gross figure of $30 million was often used as a baseline by those involved with the program. In all likelihood that figure was much too low unless Pruitt and Igoe were excluded. The total cost of the developments, excluding Blumeyer and the two elderly buildings, was just under $90 million in undeflated dollars; a proposal in 1974 to rehabilitate some buildings in Pruitt and Igoe estimated a cost of some $30,000 per unit, substantially more than original cost. But given the basic design and construction of Pruitt–Igoe, and the unfortunate associations it had compiled, expenditures at these levels would have been literally impossible to justify. The point is, however, that the Housing Authority began the 1970s with some 5,000 units of housing in desperate need of major repairs and capital replacement. In those circumstances, sums allowed for rehabilitation that seemed exorbitant on the surface were in fact inadequate given the extent of the need and the nature of the damage.

Security

Those who live through periods of intense disturbance in society, particularly if they are directly in contact with its consequences, tend to come away firmly impressed with the overriding importance of security of person and property for human existence. The engineering report reflected the impact of such direct contact with the results of violence quite accurately. With respect to Cochran Gardens, Vaughn, and Darst–Webbe, the report urged very strongly against any effort to restore or rehabilitate the developments until order and security had been established: "Without this protection and enforcement, any thought of adequately maintaining and rehabilitating this project is meaningless." The chief difficulty with security is that no one knows how to obtain or produce it. The breakdown of social controls in the 1960s demonstrated dramatically the ineffectiveness of such external factors as law, police, or parents for controlling large numbers of people as well as the futility of massive investments in technology. The police are effective for controlling street gangs but not very large populations. In the long run, social controls must be internalized to be effective, and the manner in which this is best done eludes us—socializing control in a manner that destroys the benefits of socialization is a travesty. The Housing Authority's experience with crime and vandalism strongly reinforces these impressions. Until 1967, a small mercenary army was maintained in the developments; when resources failed, the army was disbanded and an increase in crime and vandalism followed. And coincidentally or not, the development in which private police were again introduced (Cochran Gardens) was the development at which order was restored and vandalism eliminated.

The need to restore security ranked very high on the tenants' list of priorities throughout the disorders of the late 1960s; reinstitution of security patrols was urged most strongly during negotiations for a strike settlement. In the first weeks following the settlement, the tenants carried out their own patrols; in 1970, paid guards were installed in Cochran and HUD in due course provided funds to train and operate a security force in the other conventional developments. Curiously enough, the surviving records of the training program are unimpressive. Attendance was modest and often sporadic; only a small handful of people actually completed the training. Complaints about the "bookish" quality of the training were frequent; the tenants clearly regarded the program and the guards with indifference; the guards themselves did not take training seriously and seem not to have made any significant effort to do more than make an appearance. An evaluation of the program made in 1972 by the St. Louis police found performance poor, supervisors ill-trained, employees unconcerned, tenants indifferent or even hostile, favoritism common, and action badly hampered by the power struggle going on between TAB and the Housing Authority.

Yet trends in reported crime indicate that either the guard system was effective or the guards had the good fortune to begin working just as the factors that led to increased crime and vandalism were weakening. Certainly, the official data relating to major crimes against person and against property declined steadily after 1970. Of course, the crime rate had also increased in the 1960s when a security force was guarding the developments. But in a less strained climate, a show of force may suffice to produce tolerable levels of order and reduce uncontrolled street violence and molestation.

Management and finance

The belief that public or private organizations that fall on evil days are in some way paying the price of poor or ineffective management is rarely questioned. But the concept of management covers such a range of organizational features and practices that accusations of "bad management" tend to be uninformative. Moreover, it is increasingly realized that managers who rely too heavily on "management principles," however sound, are likely to breed trouble. What happened to the St. Louis Housing Authority after the rent strike is a good illustration of the dangers of acting on principle in disregard of consequence.

That the management system in St. Louis public housing needed improvement in 1969 was agreed by everyone. The source of the difficulty and the best available solution were uncertain. Some aspects of operations functioned well; others did not. A variety of expedients had been tried in the 1960s; none had produced any major improvement in performance—probably because performance was tied to availability of resources and not management technology alone. Management performance must be measured against genuine possibility; King Canute was not powerless merely because he could not stop the tides—he simply lacked the power to stop tides. In St. Louis, the combination of two large agencies in a single directorate was probably a mistake; the quality of management personnel was low, particularly at the level of the individual development; recording and filing procedures were in some respects inadequate. Such errors, readily altered when resources are available, had little to do with the overall breakdown of operations.

The rent strike settlement produced massive personnel changes at the top. A new board of commissioners, a new acting director (formerly in accounting), and new senior administrators in some departments were appointed more or less concurrently. To add to the uncertainty, outside consultants employed by the Civic Alliance recommended a set of new operating principles, duly adopted by the new board in February 1970, that altered the operating constraints in some very fundamental ways. Most important was acceptance of the presumption that centralization of authority had been a prime managerial error in the past, hence decentralization of operations was essential for improvement. It should be noted that the conception of tenant management based on individual tenant organizations was contingent on acceptance of the principle of decentralization.

Two of the basic operating changes introduced in February 1970 were economy measures. The social services program, nearly moribund in any case, was simply abolished. A major personnel cut, eliminating thirty-six administrative workers and sixty-nine maintenance workers was carried out. An agreement allowing use of general mechanics instead of skilled workers for all ordinary maintenance made that reduction possible—a tribute to the clout exercised by the head of the local teamsters. Understandably, the next management review strongly urged replacement of the maintenance force—adding 130 positions at an annual cost of some $915,000. The third change, a major step in decentralization, transferred the functions of the central housing division to the individual developments. The fourth permitted development of a central accounting system and a centralized, computerized record-keeping system. To some degree, these last two actions pull in opposite directions: computerized records and accounts tend to eliminate the need for decentralization of operations. Moreover, the central housing division had worked well in the past; the individual developments were not staffed to perform the work and were already overloaded because of staff reductions. The computerized records and accounts system provided a means of maintaining central control over decentralized operations. But the wisdom of the change remained uncertain. In retrospect, it seems a dogmatic application of principle carried out for reasons irrelevant to the consequences.

The effects of decentralization were augmented by the introduction of contract management into Authority operations in both the conventional developments (through tenant and private management) and in the turnkey program. The combined effect of the two changes was to create a "holding company" operation at the Housing Authority—the phrase was used frequently by the new director. The Authority continued to operate, of course, and there is no question that decentralization and contract management made the transition easier. But there is little direct evidence to show that the changes produced better service or greater efficiency.

Occupancy

Occupancy statistics are the best available indicator of the operational impact of the rent strike on the conventional developments. They also suggest some basic differences in their survival capacity. The Blumeyer Apartments, which did not open until 1968 and were little affected by the strike, can be left aside. Excepting the buildings designed for elderly tenants, all others were in some measure adversely affected by the strike. Carr Square and Clinton Peabody, the old fortresses of the St. Louis program, survived remarkably well considering the physical effects of past neglect. Occupancy dropped to perhaps 92 percent annually immediately following the strike; but by FY 1976, both were again humming along at better than 98 percent occupancy and applications for admission were plentiful. The other developments were less fortunate, or less deserving. Cochran Gardens, despite a very considerable outlay of funds, recovered slowly. Occupancy in 1970 was only 65 percent; by FY 1976 it was hovering around 82 to 83 percent. Vaughn, Darst, and Webbe fell to 70 percent, 62 percent, and 38 percent respectively in 1970; though Vaughn and Webbe were back at around 85 percent occupancy in FY 1976, Darst remained at 70 percent—again despite very substantial expenditures for capital replacement. Precise calculations are difficult because some apartments were closed semipermanently by heavy damage; others had been combined to form larger units, and so on. But the figures indicate trends reasonably well. In Pruitt and Igoe, which together had only 1,250 apartments rented at the beginning of 1970 (about 44 percent of the original total), occupancy waned steadily in the 1970s as the developments were phased out and ultimately demolished. By 1973, activity at Pruitt had ceased; by the end of 1974, Igoe had also expired.

A footnote on applications for admission will underline the special position of the two older developments in the conventional housing program. Early in 1970, there were nearly 2,100 vacancies in conventional housing and only 155 applications in hand. In Carr Square and Clinton Peabody, there were only 17 vacancies and more than 70 applications for space. In the other conventional developments, there were only 77 applications for over 2,000 vacant apartments—most applications were for apartments with four or more bedrooms, sizes not available at Carr Square or Clinton Peabody.

The Road to the Reservation

From almost any point of view, the outlook for conventional public housing in St. Louis was extremely gloomy in 1970. The physical facilities were damaged, the reputation of the program was ruined, little assistance was available from state or local government. The management, never very strong, had been weakened by the reduction in force and put off balance by major changes in policymaking procedures and substantive policies. An external agency (the Civic Alliance) controlled operations. A newly established tenant organization (TAB), flush with victory and eager to prove its worth, eyed every action with care and suspicion.

Meanwhile, the federal government, finally forced to recognize the need for new fiscal ground rules, moved slowly and very hesitantly to deal with the problem. HUD, caught between local housing authority need and an ungenerous Congress, could do little more than design a holding operation, stall for time, and put out fires when the pressure became too great. What was made available by the legislature was distributed by the administrative agency. Little more could be done. Meanwhile, much emphasis was placed on the development of tenant services and expansion of "tenant participation." Even so, the awesome increase in expenditures soon frightened the administration and led to the 1973 moratorium on expansion.

The grace period was used to develop a new direction and emphasis for the future. The goal was to avoid an infinite expansion of costs yet somehow stabilize operations in conventional developments. The turnkey developments, not yet in the fiscal straits facing the conventional projects and perhaps able to avoid them with modest assistance, had a more promising future, at least in the short run. For the conventional developments, the end of the road seemed likely to be the inner city analog to the Indian reservation, maintained in stable and peaceful condition by extensive service programs and the judicious use of tenant participation.

Costs and Subsidies

No matter how the problems of conventional public housing were approached, the key to maintenance, improvement, and longevity was money, more money by far than the Congress had provided for the program in the past. Capital replacement, maintenance and repairs, security, extension of tenant services, improved management, and the myriad of associated problems depended fundamentally and inescapably on expansion of staff and purchase of more goods and services. To complicate the local authority's problems, increases in tenant rents, the traditional source of additional income, could not be made. The 1969 Brooke amendment limited rent charges to 25 percent of the tenant's net income and specifically forbade rent increases between annual reviews. In one stroke, the local housing authorities were made totally dependent on the federal government. The allowed rent–income ratios would certainly reduce the income of the housing authorities; there was no alternative source of revenue. Needed assistance could come only from the federal government. How expensive the new policy was likely to be its supporters had not calculated and probably did not care. The side effects of the Brooke amendment were likewise ignored. Rigidly applied, the new policy not only lowered tenant rents, it altered the character of the tenant population by penalizing the employed tenant. The penalty was incorporated into the definition of "income" used in the Housing Act of 1970. The method of calculation ignored the difference between a worker's gross pay and his take-home pay; there was no parallel difference in the income of the tenant dependent on public assistance. The net effect was relatively higher rent charges for employed workers.[2]

Given the federal government's track record in public housing, introduction of a new policy intended to subsidize operating expenses could reasonably be expected to generate a subsidy that was (1) insufficient for the purpose intended and (2) late in arriving, leading to very substantial privation. That expectation would not have been disappointed. First, LHA income was actually decreased. Then, after considerable delay, Congress provided a bare subsistence diet for a program just emerging from a prolonged bout with acute starvation. There were never enough resources to do the needed job properly, either in daily operations or in capital replacement. The formula for calculating the subsidy, developed by HUD with the assistance of the Urban Institute, virtually ruled out a serious attack on the problem of maintaining and improving program performance. Inflation eroded the value of resources made available, and rising utility costs consumed so much of the subsidy that in St. Louis it could have been called the "Utility Company Charity Fund" without too much exaggeration. Support for capital replacement was sporadic, and in some cases funds were tied to designated purposes that corresponded poorly with local priorities. In the long run, the resources made available simply were not large enough to do a thorough job of rehabilitation within a reasonable time frame. And, despite the promise of the 1969 and 1970 housing acts, the fiscal crunch worsened for most large housing authorities in the early 1970s. A brief look at some of the details of operating expenses and income of the St. Louis Housing Authority will suggest the factors that led to the ongoing financial pressure (see Table 2).

Even in 1969, when rent levels were at an all-time high, the conventional developments in St. Louis did not collect enough rent to cover operating costs—despite the absence of capital replacement or adequate maintenance. In FY 1969, the rent from the developments amounted to about $4.3 million; total expenses were just under $4.8 million, leaving a shortfall of some $450,000 for the year. About $360,000 of the deficit occurred in Pruitt–Igoe; Blumeyer, on the other hand, contributed some $425,000 in "profits" that helped balance the books. In 1970, the required reduction in rents occurred and income dropped just over $600,000 for the year. It dropped still further

2. Analysis by John Stevenson, St. Louis Housing Authority.

in 1971 and 1972. Anticipating the crunch, the Authority had introduced a range of economy measures, including a reduction in personnel. Expenses in FY 1970 were therefore some $380,000 below the FY 1969 level. Yet the shortfall remained significant—just over $680,000 for the year. Pruitt–Igoe played a major part in the change: in 1970, rent fell off by nearly $670,000 yet expenses dropped by only $200,000, producing nearly half a million dollars in additional shortfall for the year. In 1971, annual income at Pruitt–Igoe fell to about $370,000, while expenses were over $1,250,000, a loss of about $880,000 from that source alone. Even Blumeyer lost its capacity to generate profits by 1971—rent exceeded expenses by only $40,000 that year.

Though rents were declining, expenses soared, particularly after 1970. Excluding both Pruitt–Igoe and Blumeyer, expenses increased from $2.6 million in 1969 to over $4.8 million in 1975; the annual subsidy rose from $341,000 to $2,870,000 in the same period. Compared to the U.S. averages in the mid-1970s, the conventional developments in St. Louis were earning less and spending more. The average rent PUM in St. Louis was just over $26; the national average was nearly $32 PUM. Expenses in St. Louis were nearly 50 percent more than the $49 PUM national average. The subsidy needed to maintain operations in St. Louis was nearly double the national average of $17.88 PUM. Between 1970 and 1975, the conventional developments received some $16,152,331 in federal operating subsidy, an average of about $2.7 million per year. Even these figures are somewhat misleading, for the distribution among the conventional developments was highly skewed (see Table 2). Pruitt–Igoe, for example, accounted for $5,692,013 of the total subsidy (about 35.2 percent); only 59.3 percent of the subsidy went to the viable conventional developments. In 1974, the subsidy was so divided that Carr Square and Clinton Peabody received $17 PUM and $19 PUM respectively, Vaughn and Darst–Webbe received $32 and $37 PUM, and Cochran Gardens was allotted $48 PUM for the fiscal year. That pattern tended to hold throughout the 1970s, though Darst–Webbe increased its share radically in FY 1975 and FY 1976.

To put rents, operating expenses, and subsidies in their proper perspective, several aberrant influences on the figures need to be corrected. The impact of Pruitt–Igoe on Authority finances was obvious. More than one-third of the total operating subsidy went to support it (nearly 77 percent of the whole year's allocation in 1973 when the tenants were being resettled). Until the complex was closed and demolished, it was literally impossible for the Authority to put its financial house in order. Inflation was also a consistent enemy of fiscal stability in the 1970s. If total expenses in conventional housing, excluding Pruitt–Igoe and Blumeyer, are expressed in standard 1967 dollars, the increase between 1968 and 1975 amounts to just over 10 percent. If all of the conventional developments are counted, there was actually a small decrease in the total spent for operations—from $4,359,317 in 1968 to $3,824,536 in 1975. Moreover, when operating expenses are deflated, the amount spent each year from 1968 to 1975 in no case reached 6 percent of total investment—what would normally be considered an adequate expenditure to operate and maintain the property. To put the effects of inflation in another context, the total Authority income for conventional housing (minus Pruitt–Igoe) in FY 1969 was $3,938,177; that is the sum of rent, subsidy, and incidental income. If that amount is inflated to its 1975 equivalent, it amounts to $5,662,030. In effect, to receive an amount *equal to* its 1969 income (which was clearly inadequate for operations) the St. Louis Authority would have had to receive $5.6 million in FY 1975. Its actual income in that fiscal year, counting rent and federal subsidy, was only $5,221,572. The 1969 income level was not maintained, let alone surpassed.

A third factor influencing the Authority's financial position was an astonishing increase in utility costs. Between 1969 and 1975, total expenses in the conventional developments increased by $2.8 million; utilities accounted for nearly 42 percent of the total increase ($1.15 million). If the loss of rent between 1969 and 1975 is added to the increase in utility costs, only three of the developments (Cochran, Vaughn, and Darst–Webbe) received enough subsidy to cover the resulting deficit. Carr Square and Clinton Peabody had a net loss of about $20,000 each; in Blumeyer the shortfall was over $170,000. Cost increases and revenue losses ate up about three-fourths of the subsidy in Cochran Gardens and Vaughn and more than 60 percent of the total in Darst–Webbe. The variation in utility costs among projects is puzzling. Between 1965 and 1969, the PUM average for all conventional developments ranged from about $15 to about $18. From 1970 to 1975, the average ranged from $25 to $28 in Carr Square and Clinton Peabody, through $35 to $37 in Vaughn and Darst–Webbe, to $43 PUM in Cochran Gardens. Part of the high cost in Cochran was due to the very high price paid for steam heat purchased from the local utility company, but the range of costs suggests a serious engineering–management problem in the developments. If inflation effects are removed, the variance remains and Cochran's monthly utility cost per unit is some 60 percent higher than the others.

Finally, some portion of the subsidy received after 1970 was needed to pay for the additional programs authorized or required by housing legislation. In particular, payment for tenant services and security programs ate heavily into the subsidies received by the Authority. In 1975, for example, slightly more than $3 million was received in subsidies; more than $550,000, about 18 percent of the total, was spent on these two programs. Such directed services clearly were intended to benefit the tenants, but the effect was to impose a federal priority on the local housing authority. While local administrators might be no better than national administrators at getting value for money, local inefficiency might be preferable to national inefficiency. Other things equal, in those cases where considerable variation in need could be expected from one city to another, local control would make intelligent adaptation at least possible in principle.

Calculating the operating subsidy

By the late 1960s, the need for an operating subsidy was unmistakably clear. The Brooke amendment to the 1969 Housing Act reduced the resources available to local housing authorities below the survival level. However, no subsidy was authorized until the Housing Act of 1970; even then, no rules were provided governing either the amount of subsidy or the method for calculating it. As an interim measure, HUD simply used the local housing authority's approved operating budget and provided a subsidy equal to the expected deficit—within the limits of available funds.[3] As the rising cost of the operating subsidy began to disturb the Congress, another interim policy was produced and distributed in November 1972.[4] Receipts and

3. Circular HM G 7475.1, *Low Rent Housing: Financial Management Guide*, para. 6.
4. Circular HM 7475.12, *Subsidies for Operations: Low Rent Public Housing*.

expenditures for FY 1970 (or 1971, depending on the calendar dates used by the local housing authority) were used as a base; adjustments were made to reflect income changes due to the third Brooke amendment (1971), the effects of inflation, and the allowed operating reserve. A 3 percent increase in scale was added to the total, and the difference between adjusted receipts and expenditures became the amount of the projected subsidy. The procedure adopted was to begin with a base year in the local authority's records (usually FY 1970) and adjust for obvious changes in activity level—incrementalism of the simplest kind.

As subsidy costs continued to rise sharply, HUD, acting on the presumption that costs were too high rather than subsidies too low—a point of view likely to be most attractive to congressmen—established a task force to develop a formula for calculating the operating subsidy. The group, which included HUD officials, representatives from the Urban Institute, and unspecified "other" organizations, apparently decided to create a prototype that could serve as a baseline for such calculations, since the 1974 Housing Act (section 9) instructed the secretary to

> establish standards for costs of operation and reasonable projections of income, taking into account the character and location of the project and characteristics of the families served, or the costs of providing compara- ble services as determined in accordance with criteria or a formula representing the operations of a prototype well-managed project.

The danger in any prototype development of this kind, obvi- ously, is that the generalized structure created by averaging data will fit none of the particulars, even for the developments included in the averages. Moreover, by introducing different constraints into the prototype, it can be made to serve any agenda the central administration chooses to follow while maintaining the appearance of numerical objectivity. The HUD prototype illustrated the dangers exceptionally well.

The Urban Institute developed the prototype costs for HUD, using survey data taken from 120 local housing authorities: 40 of small size, 40 of medium size, and 40 of large size.[5] Each group was divided into "effective" and "ineffective" performers using four criteria: management appraisals, degree of tenant satisfaction, basic operating data such as vacancy rates, and

5. Circular HM 75-20 (LHA), appendix 1, subpart A, "Performance Funding Sys- tem."

HUD field-office ratings. Operating expenses were excluded from the calculations, though HUD found, expectably, given the criteria, that "effective" authorities were cheaper to operate. A formula was then developed that could predict the expenses of high performance authorities using five factors: area population, average number of bedrooms (in each development), average age of project buildings, average number of stories in project buildings, and relative average operating costs of a sample of authorities from each of HUD's ten national regions. The formula is simply a statistical pattern that will yield actual operating expenses for the "high-performance authorities" when the required data are supplied.

To see how this statistical monster, known as the "performance funding system," actually worked, it is necessary to go to the individual housing authority and follow the sequence of calculations needed to apply it. The authority began with its previous year's operating expenses, excluding utility costs, audits, and certain other minor items. The formula was then applied to the authority's data (area population, average number of bedrooms, and so forth) to generate what was called a "formula expense level" for the authority. The computations involved make the "shopping incentive credit" produced for the leased housing program sound lucid:

> (i) the square root of the population (in thousands) of the area served by the PHA, multiplied by the weight .4196; (ii) the average number of bedrooms per Project Unit, multiplied by the weight 7.7058; (iii) the square root of the average age of the oldest building of each project (weighted by the relative proportion of Project Units) multiplied by the weight 1.9530; (iv) the average height of the tallest building of each Project (weighted by relative proportion of project Units in each Project) in stories, including only stories containing dwelling units or community facilities not in a basement, multiplied by the weight 1.2149; (v) the HUD-supplied index figure for the relative operations costs of a sample of PHA's in the HUD region, multiplied by the weight .3727. The formula constant of $25.2018 is subtracted from the sum of (i) through (v). The resulting amount is increased by the Local Government Wages Inflation Factor supplied by HUD.[6]

The local authority's "range" extends from $10.31 above to $10.31 below the formula expense level for the base year.

These figures in hand, the authority could begin to calculate its "allowable expense level." If actual expenses in the base year did not exceed the top of the "range," allowances by HUD

6. Ibid., para. 890.105(b).

were added to the expenses in the base year and adjusted for inflation effect using a formula supplied by HUD. If the base year expenses were above the "range," the same calculations were made, but they were added to the top of the "range" and not to the base year. In effect, the "range" was an absolute base for calculating the subsidy. If the base year expenses were above the "range" by a significant amount, the authority could qualify for "transition funding," which provided an increased subsidy. In subsequent years, the housing authority adjusted its allowable expenses by adding the change in the formula expense level and adjusting for inflation.

A utilities subsidy was provided separately, probably in an effort to squeeze authorities into reduced usage. The utility cost was added to allowable expenses to produce the "total expense" calculation for the authority for the year. The authority subtracted its anticipated income from total expenses to determine the amount of subsidy to be received. Anticipated income was calculated by determining average rent per unit for the previous year, augmenting it by 3 percent, and multiplying it by the number of units expected to be rented (97 percent occupancy had to be assumed unless another level was authorized by HUD).

The performance funding system did not begin operating until FY 1976, and there are not enough data available relating to its impact on local housing authority finances for adequate evaluation. But there are good reasons to believe it merely continued the holding operation in public housing, minimizing federal outlays for the program while giving the appearance of objectivity and impartiality. The fact is, the system was neither objective nor impartial. It was simply a well-calculated device for holding costs within foreseeable limits. Development of the device *began* with a conception of the limits to be maintained and not with an approximation or estimate, however rough, of the resources actually needed to provide an adequate housing program.

There are two basic reasons for asserting this position. First, the target of the statistical rigamarole is the quality of *management* and not the quality of the services that management provides. The basic measure of effectiveness is capacity to bring operating costs within prescribed limits. The regulations are quite clear on the purpose: "PFS [performance funding system] is intended to recognize and give an incentive for good management and to avoid the expenditure of public funds to compensate for excessive costs attributable to poor or inefficient management. PFS is intended to provide the incentive and financial discipline for excessively high-cost PHA's to improve their management inefficiency." Now, that may sound admirable at first reading, particularly to a taxpayer. But that is the case only if cost reduction, not program performance, is the primary goal of administration. The PFS is a classic example of one-dimensional bureaucratic response to one-dimensional political criticism. The congressional harpoon calls forth the bureaucratic meat-ax. Congressman X says "the local authority has oversize feet"; HUD allows a fixed time for shortening, then cuts the feet off. Such reasoning has nothing whatever to do with performance improvement.

The second cause for concern is the number of points in the apparatus at which subsidy payments can be controlled. Behind the confusing clutter of numbers required to generate the regression equations is a relatively simple device for allocating the funds that Congress provides each year. Performance funding could be expected to bring "high-cost" authorities within specified cost limits very quickly. The implicit learning theory in PFS is interesting if unacceptable: those who are inefficient in the use of resources will increase their efficiency if their tasks are expanded and their resources are reduced. Clearly, that is not necessarily true in the real world, whatever the assumptions that HUD econometricians can conjure from imagination. The inefficient may simply remain inefficient, but on a smaller scale, especially where their task is very loosely defined. Moreover, the ultimate loser is clearly the tenant, and perhaps in the long run the society as a whole.

If the cost limits developed by the Urban Institute and HUD could be accepted with confidence, if some relation could be assumed between "high performance" as identified by their analysis and the quality of services supplied by the authority, the procedures, though grotesque, might be reasonable. But the criteria used—buildings in good condition, satisfied tenants, low vacancy rates, high collection rates, and good HUD field-office ratings—ensure selection of authorities whose costs are low and whose physical plant has not been damaged very seriously in the past. At the very least, that procedure penalizes those unfortunate enough to inherit a local authority that had been through bad times—St. Louis, for example. No authority with a great deal of older conventional housing could possibly score as well, other things equal, as an authority whose holdings are mainly or entirely turnkey and therefore newer and more likely to house elderly tenants. The formula thus serves to constrain the flow of resources to the older developments. That tendency is reinforced by the use of per-unit-per-month (PUM) data for calculations. In a new complex where all units are operating and contributing to both income and cost, deciding what units to count is no problem. But what happens in an older development with units, whole floors, and even whole buildings out of commission, temporarily or semipermanently? The balance of costs and income will certainly work against rehabilitation of lost units and thereby contribute to the long run attrition of the program.

Finally, any incrementalized subsidy program that makes no reference to any external criteria of adequate funding or required performance (costs in the private sector, in Canadian or European public housing, and so on) is automatically suspect—a potential self-fulfilling ordinance. Subsidizing public housing by reference to a base year is equivalent to picking a "base year" in the life of a human being who has been starved systematically since birth and then using the consumption patterns in that year as a base for calculating required nutritional intake. The base year may be relatively superior yet absolutely bad. There is in any case no way to extrapolate to successful performance from a record of failures without introducing external points of reference for measuring and evaluating progress. No amount of statistical manipulation can get past the logical impossibility. The question, "What constitutes an *adequate* level of operating expenses for different kinds of public housing in various situations?" was not answered and could not be answered from the kinds of information employed in developing the formula. In all likelihood, it was not even asked.

Capital replacement

By 1970, the physical structures in the conventional developments in St. Louis, excepting Blumeyer and the two buildings for the elderly, were in very poor condition—little better than shells of uncertain quality in some cases. With reserves virtually exhausted and a substantial operating deficit, there was no possibility of rehabilitating and refurbishing them without large-scale federal assistance. Beginning in 1972, special modernization funds were supplied for that purpose. The amounts are superficially impressive: by the end of FY 1976, St. Louis had received more than $28 million, perhaps one-third of the original cost of the dwellings. The developments, though much improved, were still in many respects inadequate, and two buildings remained untouched and empty, victims of flooding during the rent strike.

Evaluation of such modernization efforts, and particularly of the adequacy of resources supplied through HUD, is virtually impossible. Initial conditions in the buildings were so poor, and in some cases the original design was so faulty, that no one can say with confidence what a "reasonable" rehabilitation cost would be. As in the case of operating subsidies, the Housing Authority lost part of the purchasing power of the grants to the effects of "double-digit" inflation in the mid-1970s. And Pruitt–Igoe continued to impose a drain on resources, even though it was clear by 1970 that at least part of the developments would have to be abandoned. Nevertheless, nearly $1 million was spent on improvements to buildings and grounds in the 1970s, mainly in Igoe where most tenants from Pruitt were transferred after 1971. Another $.5 million was spent to relocate the tenants in Igoe when that development was finally abandoned. The cost of demolishing and carting away the remains was just over $3.5 million more. If the $5 million "juvenation" program in the late 1960s is included, more than $10.2 million in special rehabilitation subsidies was poured into Pruitt–Igoe in the last eight years of their lives, almost 30 percent of all such funds received by the Housing Authority. The end result was a bare patch of ground, perhaps fifty-seven acres altogether, in downtown St. Louis. Many considered this a great improvement, but the fact remains that enormous sums were spent, from sheer necessity, on two developments that contributed little to operations in the 1970s. That certainly penalized the Authority if only because the funds supplied by the federal government were made to seem larger than they really were. The situation provides yet another example of the kinds of errors that can be made by aggregations and simple projections from past performance.

The size, timing, and purposes of the modernization grants received in St. Louis also influenced their value to the Authority in important ways. Between 1972 and 1976, St. Louis received two separate batches of funds, one concentrated in 1972 and the other coming late in 1975. The first batch comprised two grants. One, totaling just over $5 million, was intended for high-priority emergency repairs to restore operations as soon as possible in the badly damaged buildings. It was used to repair boilers and hot-water systems, replace plumbing fixtures and electrical systems, rehabilitate elevators, replace stoves and refrigerators, provide essential small pieces of equipment, and so on. Spread over some three thousand dwelling units in six developments, the $5 million did no more than finance an initial attack on the problem of rehabilitation.

The second large grant received in 1972 provides a good example of the dangers involved in central control over the purposes for which resources are spent. One of the then-current political "hot potatoes" was the presence of lead-based paint in the developments and the acknowledged danger it posed to young children. Some $2.4 million was provided to replace the lead-based paint in the two older developments. The program proved expensive and only 60 percent of the units were treated from that grant—the work was completed later from another allocation. Had the St. Louis Authority been able to direct the allocation of funds, other purposes would have ranked much higher on its priority list—basic heating, plumbing, wiring, bath and kitchen equipment, for example. Nevertheless, the resources were employed for the designated purpose, suitably interpreted to maximize local benefits—doors and windows were replaced; radiators were disconnected, stripped of paint, and repainted; and so on.

From 1972 to 1975, no major grant of modernizing funds was received by the Authority. The second large allocation came late in FY 1975 and was divided into two grants totaling just over $13.8 million. Again, the grants were meant to restore basic operating systems, still uncorrected six years after the rent strike: heating, hot water, baths and kitchens, and electrical service. Some of the 1975 grants, however, were used to modernize the lobbies of the buildings and to improve tenant security by reducing access to the developments from the streets.

Between the two major batches of resources, the Authority did receive a number of smaller grants for a variety of purposes. Just over $800,000 was provided to remodel apartments, mainly by consolidating one- and two-bedroom units to form desperately needed larger units. A small grant of $120,000 was used for small amounts of specialized equipment needed in operations. About $340,000 was spent for refrigerators, boiler-room equipment, and small electrical equipment for the apartments. Another $190,000 went to eliminate lead-based paint from porch supports and install nonslip stripping in the public stairwells. Over $800,000 was made available for garbage compactors in three of the medium-rise developments. About $150,000 was spent on prototype welfare offices. Nearly $800,000 was intended for developing commercial facilities within the projects but had not yet been expended by the end of the time period included in this study.

Two additional points need to be made with respect to the first five years of modernization activity. First, most of the resources were used for really basic refurbishing of such fundamentals as roofs, heating, electricity, plumbing, elevators, baths, and kitchens. The grounds were cleared of glass and other debris, vandalized walls were repaired, and an effort was made to improve the overall physical appearance. The external physical change in the developments did not reflect the amounts spent, taken as a whole or in terms of the individual apartments. Such factors may have played an important part in tenant satisfaction, or the lack of it. Attractiveness and desirability cannot be ignored if they contribute in significant ways to occupancy levels.

Second, the timing and rate of expenditures were unfortunate. It was very unlikely, of course, that the federal government could have provided all the resources needed to complete the rehabilitation of the conventional developments. But the rate of improvement undertaken in 1972, if continued, would have required fifteen years or more for completion. A modernization program that took so long would lose much of its effect. The amount of damage sustained during modernization might even be greater than the improvement, as actually occurred in Pruitt and Igoe in the 1960s. The lessons of the 1960s had still not been learned where they count most—by those authorizing the program. Meanwhile, local housing authorities were forced into an untenable position: their tenants continued to live in unattractive and incomplete facilities and were blaming the authorities; meanwhile, very large sums were being spent on rehabilitation and more were being demanded, and that at-

tracted criticism from above for mismanagement and inefficiency. Of course, proceeding too rapidly may simply increase
costs, and there is no measure of local capacity to absorb and
use funds effectively. But the government's patent failure to
work out an honest approximation of need and a schedule for
rehabilitation that would carry out the required work seems a
good indication of the government's attitude toward the program. At best, the delays were likely to be costly; at worst, the
whole program was put in jeopardy.

Tenant Management

Among the fundable "services" included in the Housing Act
of 1970 was specific support for tenant participation in all
aspects of administration, maintenance, and management of
public housing. Why that provision was added, what purposes
it was expected to further, is nowhere made clear. Most likely,
the authorization was simply a knee-jerk reaction by Congress
to external criticism based on currently accepted rhetoric
about the virtues of participation. It is unlikely that anyone
familiar with the history of public housing seriously believed
that any of the major difficulties in the program would not have
occurred had the tenants been more influential in policymaking. The act produced little change in the tenants' role in
management across the country. But the legislation did create
an opportunity to work out a new set of relations between the
public housing tenant and the management, to develop a larger
role for tenant organizations. The value of experimentation in
this area need not be questioned. What is most interesting here
is the behavior of HUD, which supported a nationwide demonstration of tenant management in five major cities at a cost
in excess of $20 million, presumably on the basis of evidence
provided by the St. Louis experience.

The principle of tenant participation in housing affairs, including management of developments, cannot be judged by the
particular effort carried out in St. Louis. There are many different modes of tenant participation, many different ways for
tenants to take part in housing management. A variety of
organizational structures can be employed for either purpose.
The viability of the particular experiment carried out in St.
Louis may have little bearing on other efforts in other places.
American experience with overseas development has de-

monstrated time and again the dangers of overhasty generalization from particular cases. Haste may lead to unwarranted expansion of what turns out to be only a local success or to costly suppression of generally useful ideas that fail in particular surroundings. Both errors are very common in efforts to provide assistance to the poor and disadvantaged efficiently and effectively.

Background

Tenant management in St. Louis was a child of the 1969 rent strike and very much influenced by the personalities, ambitions, aspirations, and organizations thrown into prominence by the strike action. As the legal consultant to the tenants wrote in 1975:

> A principal goal in designing the TMC [tenant management corporation] program was the preservation of the different social and political relationships which had developed over the years in each of the public housing developments. A distinctive feature of each of the TMC areas, as well as in public housing committees generally, is the existence of a leader or group of leaders who may function differently but who operate within the framework of a subtle, and often very effective political structure.[7]

The author of this extraordinary rationale apparently meant the passage as a justification for tenant management on the St. Louis pattern. It serves better, however, as an indication of the considerations that most influenced those who set up the program.

The two primary elements in the development of tenant management were the tenant leaders and their organization, the Tenant Affairs Board (TAB), and the consulting firm spun off from the Civic Alliance for Housing that became the tenants' principal advisor and agent. Tenant organizations had functioned sporadically in St. Louis for many years; the rent strike elevated some leaders to prominence, helped create an ongoing organization, and provided it with official status. More, the Civic Alliance agreed to provide TAB members with a monthly salary of $500 for assisting with operations—otherwise, the new tenant movement would probably have died peacefully and quickly. The effort to get monetary support from the tenants was not very successful, even in the heated condi-

7. Richard D. Baron, *Tenant Management: A Rationale for a National Demonstration of Management Innovation.*

tions of 1969; amounts collected by the Housing Authority for TAB after 1969 rarely exceeded $1,500 in one year, even in the larger developments. When the Civic Alliance ceased paying TAB members in 1972, the burden was transferred to the Authority with HUD concurrence.

In return for their salaries, TAB members were expected to represent the tenants' interests, to relay tenant demands and reactions to the Authority, and to assist the Authority with its tenant problems—rent collection, evictions, and so on. Through the end of 1972, TAB performance was so poor generally that the auditors recommended that the Authority terminate the contract unless TAB members (1) settled their own very substantial delinquent rents and (2) provided some concrete assistance with rent collections and disciplinary problems. Unfortunately, the audit was less influential than other factors in the situation; payments continued though there is little hard evidence of improved TAB performance.

In other times and circumstances, the tenant leaders' demand for a voice in management would almost certainly have been channeled into an in-house training program operated by the Authority. But conditions in St. Louis were ripe for an escalation of tenant influence: there was much confusion and inexperience within the Housing Authority; the tenants and their advisors had a clearly formed objective and pursued it with great determination. In confusion, as someone once wrote, there is opportunity. The board of commissioners was new and inexperienced; the Authority director was temporary; the Civic Alliance was apparently committed to furthering the tenant management program—the terms of the agreement that concluded the strike were construed as more than a pro forma commitment. Indeed, the director of the Alliance and the former Legal Aid Society attorney who had served as advisor to the strikers formed a consulting firm to guide and assist the tenant organization.

The basic structure in the tenant management program was a not-for-profit corporation, or tenant management corporation (TMC), with a five-person board of directors elected by the tenants of the development every three years. The TMC board contracted with the Authority to manage the development; it also appointed the tenant manager. The chairman of the TMC board and the tenant manager became the TMC's representatives on the Tenant Affairs Board. Formally, policies originated in the TMC board, and the connection between Authority and tenant manager lay through the board. Since the TMCs were also represented on the board of commissioners by two TAB members, their position in the program was far stronger than that of a contract manager. In practice, a strong tenant manager able to act without worrying about TMC board support was almost wholly unfettered within the development. The mode of organization, in other words, maximized the tenant manager's independence of the Authority, particularly in those cases where the TMC board turned out to be ineffectual or indecisive.

The tenant management program was launched in 1972 with the assistance of a Ford Foundation grant of $130,000—to be used to train and install tenant managers in Carr Square and Darst. Technically, the program was an experiment, but it was treated as fait accompli by the tenants and their advisors; before the first two tenant managers were well established, preparations began for introducing tenant managers in two more conventional developments. The attitude of those in the tenant organization toward the program was most clearly stated in article II of the TAB bylaws dated May 1975:

> The purpose of this organization is to improve the living conditions of both conventional and turnkey public housing residents in St. Louis by coordinating the efforts of tenant management corporations and tenant associations to enable them to take concerted action on issues and problems effecting [sic] public housing residents, and to support and assist tenant organizations in carrying out programs which will eventually lead to the formation of tenant management corporations in each of the turnkey and conventional public housing developments in the City of St. Louis, Missouri.

The intent is clear enough.

Tenant managers took control of Carr Square and Darst in March 1973 and of Clinton Peabody and Webbe in June 1974. Efforts to begin tenant management in Blumeyer foundered on the hard rock of tenant disagreement. No further changes were made until 1976 when Cochran Gardens, which had been operated by a private organization known as TAMBO (created under the auspices of the Inner City Missions of the United Church of Christ), was converted to tenant management. The change at Cochran was slight, for TAMBO was based on the principle of strong tenant participation in development affairs. Indeed, it is likely that the tenants at Cochran had more voice

in management under TAMBO than they had under the new
tenant management program.

As might be expected, the tenants selected for management
jobs were the same persons who appeared as strike leaders in
the later stages of the rent strike and as TAB representatives
when that organization was formed. They were trained by the
consulting firm that arranged the Ford Foundation grant—
with a great deal of assistance from Housing Authority personnel. A large part of the two Ford grants was used to load the
dice in favor of the tenant managers in a very interesting
manner. Once installed, the tenant managers put into operation the system of "block control" common in China and the
Soviet Union. The population of the development was divided
geographically into units of about 125 families. Each unit was
made the responsibility of a building manager or "lane" manager who was paid from the Ford grant. They in turn were
encouraged to form suborganizations within their respective
areas. Some $66,000 of the first grant was used to pay these
management assistants. In Darst, which housed some 350
families in 1973, that amounted to an additional hidden administrative cost of $7.14 PUM. Since the *total* cost of ad-
ministration in Darst in 1971 was only $6.41 PUM, these
personnel changes more than doubled real administrative
costs. Yet, since payments from the grants did not show on the
Authority's records, they also did not appear in evaluations
based on those records. In 1974, the Housing Authority was
persuaded to underwite the cost of continuing these positions
permanently. Part of the second Ford grant was then used to
establish another management assistant position, the "social
service director." Such assistance was invaluable, since the
Housing Authority scored its members in terms of rent collection, record maintenance, and production of required reports.

Claims and evaluations

How well has tenant management functioned? The claims
are impressive. By the summer of 1974, after one year of operation, the tenants' legal counsel had published extensive claims
for the technique in the *Journal of Housing* under the impressive if misleading title "St. Louis Tenant Management Corporations Bringing Major Transformation of Public Housing." A
Ford Foundation letter, cited by the *St. Louis Post-Dispatch* (12
April 1976), called tenant management "one of the brightest

hopes for revitalizing the nation's problem-ridden public housing system." And in a proposal for a national demonstration of tenant management prepared in 1975, Attorney Richard Baron asserted that it "offers the promise that the chronic problems of management and welfare dependency which persist throughout urban public housing communities can be solved." Such claims are very striking. The supporting evidence, however, cannot withstand close and careful scrutiny. Discussions of the effect of tenant management on the conventional developments tend to be vague or ambiguous, referring primarily to improvements in physical conditions and allegedly superior performance of tenant managers in not very precisely specified areas. The individual tenant in the developments, when he appears at all, is a shadowy figure who pays rent, cooperates, participates, and supports the management. The published evaluations did not make a systematic inquiry into tenant reaction to the new program. Some negative reactions from tenants have found their way into the Housing Authority files, but there is little hard evidence on which to base a judgment. Costs have been ignored entirely.

The St. Louis University studies. The Center for Urban Programs at St. Louis University prepared three reports on tenant management in St. Louis between 1973 and 1975.[8] The first report, issued in December 1973 after only a few months of program operation, was admittedly partial and tentative. The overall judgment, based on rough comparisons of TMC-managed developments with a counterpart managed by an Authority employee, was mildly favorable with reservations. The report asserted that the physical appearance of tenant-managed apartments was much improved but attributed the change to the employment of youth for summer work. Rents were being collected fairly well and the required annual review of tenant records was improving, but the maintenance program was performing very poorly indeed. Tenant participation in management was allegedly improving, though no evidence was cited; the turnout for the TAB board election, however, reportedly involved no more than 5 to 6 percent of the eligible

8. Center for Urban Programs, St. Louis University, *Interim Tenant Management Corporation Evaluation Report; Tenant Management Corporations in St. Louis: Final Report*; and *Tenant Management Corporations in St. Louis Public Housing: The Status After Two Years.*

tenants. Security had improved, but that was not attributed to the actions of tenant management. Administrative performance generally was held acceptable, but credit was given mainly to the work of building and lane managers. The principal negative finding was a warning against allowing the tenant manager to dominate the TMC board, with the implication that trends in that direction were apparent. The research for the report was apparently limited to interviews with the managers (not the tenants, unfortunately) and informal observations. There was no reference to management records, reporting systems, processing of paperwork, or any related activity, and perhaps most indicative of all, there was no reference whatever to costs.

A "Final Report" published in July 1974 covered the first full year of operations, concentrating on five areas: maintenance, rent collection and occupancy, security, administration, and social services. The latter was a curious selection since there was no activity to report; it was probably included because it occupied a position well up on the priority list of proponents of tenant administration—this was one area in which the TMCs were expected to outperform regular Authority managers. Again, judgment was guarded though favorable. Striking achievements were claimed with respect to the physical conditions of buildings and grounds, tenant morale, and the sense of community among tenants. Security was better, but not because of the work of the TMCs. Maintenance remained inadequate though improving. Rent collection and review of tenant records were considered average, though that judgment is not consistent with Authority records—they show significant weakness in both areas. Very little advantage was claimed for the TMCs with respect to the standard criteria of managerial performance.

In one area, however, the "Final Report" claimed significantly better performance from tenant managers than could be expected from Authority managers, "a higher level of tenant participation in project governance and activities, greater tenant cooperation and acceptance of management function, and an increased sense of community and pride within the projects." Such claims are extremely difficult to support by evidence, obviously. In this case, the only sources employed were persons for whom a favorable opinion in these areas was decidedly self-serving. And the claim is inconsistent with evidence offered elsewhere in the report. For example, the report states with respect to participation, "While precise data on tenant participation and attendance at project meetings is unavailable, it is the impression of the TMC staff and the evaluators that both . . . have increased during the period of TMC management" (p. 34). Two paragraphs later, the judgment is reversed: "Overall tenant participation has not improved to the level envisaged by many with TMC. It is true that tenant access has expanded but there is little indication that tenants take advantage of that access to influence overall policy directions." Similar vacillation appears with respect to other claims. Increased contact between tenants and managers is first stated as fact then qualified as an "impression" gained from discussions with managers. In view of the centrality of the issue to the claims made on behalf of the TMCs, it is very curious indeed that no effort was made to interview tenants and report the results. Instead, the report uses circular reasoning such as the following: "While contradictory opinions can be found, in the opinion of the evaluators, substantial improvements in the mood and sense of participation (if not the practice) have occurred since TMC takeover. Moreover, the fact that people in authority positions are also tenants contributes to the sense of participation and is to be preferred to the absentee manager." What is at issue in the "experiment" is here simply assumed as a premise in the argument.

Like its predecessor, the "Final Report" included no data on costs. The section on the "social services" program simply enumerated the various services available to the tenants from different organizations. There were no conclusions, and the summary of findings did no more than claim "moderate" success in the first year, primarily with respect to tenant attitudes.

At the end of 1975, the St. Louis University center published yet another report. Though no additional data had been gathered, the conclusions were much altered. It was now held that the TMCs had "experienced notable success in a number of areas. These include maintenance, security, social service delivery, rate of rent reviews, rent collection, and occupancy." Neither the earlier St. Louis University surveys nor the Housing Authority's records provided justification for such extended conclusions.

The Baron article. The most influential of the materials on tenant management has been an article by Richard Baron published in 1974 in the *Journal of Housing*, the official journal of the National Association of Housing and Redevelopment Officials (NAHRO).[9] The crux of Baron's claim is that tenant managers have performed as well as others with respect to "hard" indicators of good management and much better with respect to "soft" dimensions of management. While that argument is at least partly testable from existing records, the evidence included in the article is both insufficient and misleading. Of course, the *Journal of Housing* prints only relatively short essays, and much of the article is taken up with historical description of the program's evolution. Nevertheless, both the mode of reasoning employed and the quality of the data offered in evidence are suspect. Basically, Baron proceeds by assertion rather than argument; data are treated both selectively and pejoratively.

For example, the inadequacy of TMC maintenance operations, noted clearly in both St. Louis University studies, is simply ignored. An increase in the average PUM rent at Carr Square of $6 and at Darst of $3 is asserted as evidence of superior performance; but the facts are that rent increased by an average of $4.63 PUM for the whole Authority, and in Authority-managed Webbe, the increase amounted to $6.28 PUM. Similarly, a decrease in vacancies at tenant-managed Darst (from 280 to 218) is cited as a "gain of 62 tenants." In fact, the management had eliminated thirty-two units of housing from service and the actual number of new tenants was only twenty-three—a valuable increase but not outstanding by any means. Again, the article claimed, "Rent collections, which before the rent strike had dropped to less than 80 percent throughout the Authority, have exceeded 100 percent under tenant-enforced rules to pay up delinquencies as well as current rents." Brave words, but mistaken. Before the rent strike, and even during the strike, rent collections were well above 80 percent. Before 1969, they were very close to 100 percent in most cases. Strong tenant enforcement of the "pay up" rule was belied by the steady and significant increase in accounts receivable within tenant-managed developments—an increase of 10 percent in delinquent accounts at the end of one year's

9. Richard D. Baron, "St. Louis Tenant Management Corporations Bringing Major Transformation of Public Housing."

operations. Moreover, both Clinton Peabody and Blumeyer, two of the Authority-managed developments, collected 100 percent of their rent during the period, and the others were very close to that figure. In the Authority-managed developments, increases in accounts receivable rose at about the same level as in tenant-managed developments. The performance of tenant-managed projects, measured in those terms, was routine or less.

Moreover, despite the findings of the St. Louis University studies, Baron gives the TMCs credit for a "reduced crime rate throughout the Authority" and a "much more vigorous . . . tenant participation and support for their program." The only concrete reference to participation in the St. Louis University reports notes an *increase* in attendance *to* 5 to 6 percent of those eligible. And where the university reports deplored the lack of resources that prevented delivery of more social services, the article claims that "residents are much more adept than anyone else at isolating and resolving 'soft management' problems that have traditionally undermined management programs." But, if the TMCs did not have the resources, they could not have been supplying social services, hence they could hardly have engaged in isolating and resolving "soft management" problems—that is what the phrase means. Baron's assertion is an article of faith and not an evidentially warranted statement. Similarly, the claim is made that "the progress and improvements made by the tenant management program suggest that there are viable, inexpensive management alternatives for conventional public housing." Viability remained problematic, even in 1977; how expensive the program has been will be examined briefly below.

Claims and conclusions

On the basis of this kind of evidence and reasoning, more than $20 million was committed by HUD for a national demonstration of tenant management. If the reasoning is allowed to continue unchallenged and the evidence is not contradicted—and perhaps even if it is—the enterprise will turn into another self-fulfilling prophecy, floated on a sea of rhetoric. The tenant management program in St. Louis was not carried out as an experiment, and in consequence very little has been or can be learned from it. That seems a shame, for the site is ideal for an extremely good, controlled study of the effects of management innovation. Carr Square and Clinton Peabody, for example, offered an unparalleled opportunity to compare effects in almost identical physical structures, using one as a control. All that potential was lost in the headlong rush to broaden and expand an unknown—unknown, at least, with respect to performance, if not to benefits. What followed was an exercise in grantsmanship and not an experiment in management.

Had the nature and purposes of the experiment been worked out more competently, the expected benefits identified, and actions taken duly and carefully logged, it would have been possible to develop suitable indicators of achievement and to learn a lot from the effort, whether or not it "failed." The indicators that have been used by those who support or oppose tenant management are virtually useless. When the performance of Carr Square and Darst, both tenant-managed, is measured against the performance of Authority-managed Webbe using the indicators employed by both Baron and the St. Louis University studies, Webbe clearly outperformed either of the TMC-managed developments by a wide margin between March 1973 and June 1974. There was a greater increase in the rent-rolls, in the number of occupied units, in occupancy (ratio of time available to time occupied), and so on. Do the data show that Webbe was the better managed of the three developments? Not necessarily! And the converse is equally true. Management is only one factor in a complex set that determines changes in this particular set of indicators. Occupancy may have increased in Webbe because elderly tenants leaving Pruitt and Igoe wished to stay close to their friends or church, and such things have nothing to do with management quality. Indicators of management performance need to be handled with great care, whether they are used to laud or to criticize.

The fact is, none of the evidence produced by those concerned with the effectiveness of tenant management is very convincing. Data relating to monthly rent collections for TMC-managed developments show remarkably little change over a three-year period. They differ very little from collections made in the one conventional development not under tenant management. Rent-rolls and collections go through regular cycles; those seasonal cycles are far more useful for predicting rent levels than any change in administrative structure. And if the total observed difference in rent levels is only 1.5 percent, how much difference can it make anyhow? Similarly, both evaluators and tenant managers tend to use increases in average monthly rent collected as an indicator of the zeal with which the TMCs sought out undeclared income and imposed a rent on the earner. But when all of the developments are arrayed over time, there is little to choose among them. From April 1973 to April 1974 when Carr Square and Darst were tenant-managed and the other developments were not, only Webbe did as well as the overall Authority averages, and tenant-managed Darst had the poorest collection record of all the conventional developments save Cochran Gardens, the development whose management system most closely approximated tenant management. Between 1974 and 1975, Webbe came under tenant management and also had the greatest increase in PUM rent of all conventional developments. Should that increase be ascribed to the mysterious benefits of tenant management? Clearly not! By selecting dates judiciously, or more often, by listing part of a data set and referring to the rest by implication, it is easy to convey an impression of outstanding performance. The antidote to such intellectual chicanery is a close look at the theoretical structures that link the indicators to performance and a comparison of performances that takes into account *all* of the relevant data.

To continue the comparisons, TMC-managed developments made little use of eviction proceedings. Soft on tenants? Perhaps. But, after 1969, the other conventional developments also made little use of the procedure. After 1969, the flow of new tenants into TMC-managed developments was slow in comparison to the pre-1969 period. Implication? Nothing, for the same holds true for the other developments. Accounts receivable increased steadily in the TMC-managed developments in 1974 and 1975; they increased at about the same rate elsewhere in the Authority. The ratio between units available and units occupied improved slowly and somewhat erratically in all of the conventional developments after the rent strike; no clear pattern differentiates them on the basis of management. The number of days per year for which units were actually occupied by paying tenants, which is an excellent indicator of turnover time and a measure of the housing-in-use actually supplied to tenants, tell the same story. Even such figures as the number of tenants who vote in TAB elections, though they might seem a good measure of "tenant participation," tell a strange story, for they suggest that Blumeyer, where the tenants were so badly divided that they could not begin a tenant management program, had the highest level of participation in the entire Authority. Is too much participation self-defeating? Or should the conclusion be "Scotch verdict?" And where would that leave tenant management?

Taking into account everything that seems germane to the program, most of the testable claims made on behalf of tenant management are simply mistaken. The "hard" data, which very effectively rebut the claims made with respect to the quality of tenant management, also call into question the frequent claims about attitudinal changes among the tenants. If such changes did occur, and if they were as powerful as proponents claim, they ought surely to translate into observable differences among the developments that in turn would appear somewhere in the records. If the "soft" effects are so weak that they generate no second-order effects, why should they be considered important? Strong tenant support for management should surface in maintenance costs, security, number of complaints, occupancy, or some such measure of performance. The overall evidence supports the judgment that TMC-managed developments were in no respect superior and in some respects inferior to other developments managed by private contractors or by Housing Authority managers.

The differences that matter

Leaving aside methods of management, some very striking changes did occur in the conventional housing developments in St. Louis in the 1970s. They affected tenant, management, Authority, and even the general public, often in significant if indirect ways. However, these changes did not differentiate the developments and they cannot be inferred from cross-sectional analysis of the apartments or their occupants. The significant differences lie between all of the developments, taken collectively, as they appeared in 1970 and all of the developments, still taken collectively, as they appeared in 1976. The tenant who lived in *any* of the conventional developments in 1976 would have found himself in a dwelling unit significantly better than that same unit, or any other unit in the development, as it was in 1970, with respect to (1) physical appearance of site and apartment; (2) operating characteristics of plumbing, electrical systems, heating, and hot water; (3) quality and performance of structure, that is, roof, windows and doors, locks, porches, and so on; (4) quality and condition of stove, refrigerator, and other equipment; (5) adequacy of elevator service, where applicable; (6) safety of person and property; (7) quality of support services such as garbage collection; (8) attitudes of management and other employees of the Authority; (9) accuracy of records, and so forth, relating to tenant; (10) cost as a portion of total income. The list could be extended almost indefinitely by breaking these general categories apart. And the changes are common to *all* of the conventional developments.

How to account for the change? MONEY!!! (see Table 2). Very large amounts of resources were spent in the conventional developments in the first half of the 1970s. If an index of comparative efficiency in expenditures could be produced, it would be simple to adduce from the data the relative costs and benefits of different forms of management. No such index is available or likely to be produced. Worse, there is no accurate account of the physical condition of the apartments that could be used as a baseline for measuring change and comparing costs. When due allowance is made for the differences in physical condition among the apartments at the beginning of the 1970s, the differences in allocations are likely to seem minor. In general, Cochran Gardens and Darst received far more rehabilitation funds than any other developments, but that followed from the decision to rehabilitate them first. The extent to which they have been refurbished, as compared to the other developments, is beyond estimation. Similarly, the damage to Vaughn during the rent strike was apparently much worse than the damage to Darst, but without accurate summaries of present and past conditions, no comparisons can be made. In general, the amount of improvement is proportional to the amount of money spent. The world, as may be suspected, operates on the principle that it is very difficult to get something for nothing that is worth more than nothing.

In the context of Authority-wide income and expenditure, those who touted the virtues of tenant management simply tried to take credit for changes that occurred in all of the developments as a result of heavy expenditures. They argued by focusing on changes in the tenant-managed developments and ignoring what happened elsewhere. Whether the funds were more wisely expended by tenant managers or by employees of the Authority, the records do not suffice to show—and that is to some extent a criticism of the adequacy of the records. A comparison of St. Louis expenditures with national averages is worthless so long as the results of differential expenditure cannot be specified. A combination of lower rents, very high utility costs, and higher maintenance costs produced very high overall operating costs and therefore higher subsidies in Cochran Gardens and Darst. Since those figures do not include the cost of special programs such as the Target Projects Program (TPP), Law Enforcement Assistance Administration support for security programs, modernization, related manpower training, and so on, expenditures in 1974 and 1975, when tenant management was operating in these develop ments, must have been four or five times as large as the national average. In calendar year 1976, to illustrate the magnitudes involved, the six older conventional developments housed 3,200 families. An identifiable total of some $4.5 million was spent in those developments during the year from outside sources—city, state, federal, and private. In addition, at least $1.1 million in TPP funds, $5.5 million in public assistance, $3.0 million in operating subsidies, $3.0 million in rehabilitation funds, and $2.7 million in annual contract cost was expended in or on behalf of these developments. The total is in excess of $20 million, an average of some $6,250 per family in that one year alone.[10] Again, if administrative costs, tenant service costs, and security service costs are aggregated for the years in which tenant management was functioning in the developments, the grand total for these three functions alone was over $4.7 million between 1972 and 1975. In 1970, only $381,000 was spent for these combined purposes. No management system could have an impact on operations equal to the effect of expenditure changes of this order.

Reprise

If resources are adequate, the conclusion is inescapable that the differences in conditions of life among the developments are hardly worth discussing. Can it be argued that the absence of difference is actually a reason for preferring tenant management? Aside from the ignorance fallacy involved, there are some fairly strong reasons for regarding tenant management

10. Data compiled by Barbara Freeland, financial analyst, St. Louis Housing Authority.

with extreme caution in the absence of reliable supporting data—that is what makes support for the experiment with tenant management so peculiar. First, the quality of the records and information flowing from tenant-managed developments declined markedly and seriously after tenant management began, and there is little evidence of significant improvement later. The TMC's administrative performance has been characterized by a "roller-coaster" effect common in administrative systems that are not self-energizing, that is, that depend on external stimulation. In such conditions, an external stimulus (usually a kick in the behind from the central administration) is followed by an upswing in performance that dampens quickly, requiring further stimulation. Moreover, the stimulus is effective only in the area of activity for which it is administered; an improvement in reporting is not accompanied by an improvement in processing of applications. Each activity requires independent stimulation, a good indicator of ineffective managerial control. In St. Louis, the very effective accounting and record-keeping system developed and computerized in the early 1970s has served as administrative surrogate to the TMCs for much of their lifetime, supplying periodic stimuli, identifying failures to perform as well as failures in performance. The records suggest very strongly that if the TMCs had been left solely to their own resources, required to operate their own records and accounts systems with only the same supervision accorded private, contract managers, administrative chaos would have ensued in a very few months.

Second, the actual responsiveness of tenant managers to tenant concerns is a matter on which there is virtually no evidence. The system created in St. Louis is peculiarly liable to abuse by strong-willed managers who can profit from the apathy common to all collective operations where benefits to be obtained from participation are slight. The earliest of the St. Louis University reports strongly implied the growth of this tendency in the first months of operation. That should have been sufficient to justify an examination, by some neutral agency, of the actual state of affairs within the developments. The Housing Authority has not received from the TMCs the kind of information it would need to provide effective supervision of TMC operations and effective protection of tenants. Yet the Authority's responsibilities to its tenants are not abrogated merely by allowing a tenant to assume the manager's role in a development. Data that might be considered "internal" to the TMC or the TAB board are often extremely important to the Authority as well. Too little such information has been transmitted to the Authority from the tenant organizations. To take an example, when the Authority was responsible for TAB elections, they were supervised by the American Arbitration Association and the records were clear, accurate, and reliable. In more recent years, only the results of elections have been supplied the Authority, and even with respect to results, the information is not always clear. Since 1974, election to the TMC boards has apparently been regarded as a matter of no concern to the Authority.

In sum, the TMC conception of the relation between Housing Authority and tenant manager is at times badly out of touch with administrative and legal reality. Technically, the TMCs may be legally independent entities related to the Authority by contract. Yet the relation is not simply legal; those who staff the TMC are also tenants, and both sides recognize the special relation and depend on it. The Authority in fact adopts a double standard toward its contract managers and is expected to do so. Treated as purely private contractors, the TMCs at Darst and Carr Square would have been discharged for incompetence in the first six months of operation. The justification for the special consideration expected and granted need not be questioned. But the obligations that justified that special consideration cannot be brushed aside by either side when they are inconvenient. Whatever the locus of fault, the relation needs rethinking and rearticulation in the light of operating experience.

A Last Look at Conventional Housing

By the end of 1976, conditions in the conventional developments were greatly improved over 1969–1970. Subsidies for operations, though still below the level needed for sound operation, were sufficient to allow for modest expansions and improvements in services. Capital replacement programs, long delayed by lack of resources, were under way; and if funds were supplied sporadically and sometimes misdirected, the fundamentals were gradually being rehabilitated. It remained to be seen whether financial support would remain strong enough and consistent enough to complete the job and allow a return to something approximating normal operations.

In all of the developments, occupancy was stable, though at very different levels. The buildings for elderly tenants were everywhere full—in Blumeyer, Vaughn, and Webbe. The family units at Blumeyer, though less than ten years old, were in some cases showing signs of wear, though HUD was reluctant to approve any significant rehabilitation so early in their lives. Despite age and long neglect, Carr Square and Clinton Peabody were once again operating at peak capacity—a fitting tribute to good design and sound construction. Pruitt and Igoe were in their death throes, only some part buildings still awaiting the headache ball—an equally fitting tribute to bad design and poor construction, though an expensive lesson considering how little was learned. Cochran Gardens, one building still out of commission by reason of water damage, stabilized at 65 to 60 percent occupancy, measured against original construction. Vaughn apartments were about three-fourths full; Darst and Webbe (also missing one building from water damage) were about two-thirds occupied. Of the original 6,893 units (excluding Blumeyer), 3,038 were occupied and 445 were available but vacant as of 1 June 1976. Some 191 units had been combined into larger apartments; 75 had been made into public space. Most of the remaining vacancies were one- and two-bedroom units, and some experimentation with admitting single persons to those units was under way.

The population had shrunk but changed little in aggregate characteristics from 1969. The remaining families were mainly black, largely matriarchal, and desperately poor. The more than 3,000 families, a total population of some 13,000 persons, were in three cases out of four headed by a female, and in ninety-six cases of each one hundred, by a black—the 114 white families were located almost entirely in the buildings for the elderly. Families tended to be smaller in 1976 than in the 1960s, and that produced a slight reduction in the number of minors in the developments. Only Cochran Gardens and Vaughn contained more minor children in 1975 than in 1969. Whether that reduction influenced the amount of vandalism in the developments, however, was uncertain.[11]

On the average, the population was considerably older in

11. See, for example, some of the essays in Colin Ward, ed., *Vandalism*.

1975 than in the 1960s. Between 1965 and 1969, about 25 percent of all heads of household were under twenty-five and another 29 percent of the total were between twenty-five and thirty-five years of age. Only 20 percent were more than sixty-five. In 1975, only 5 percent of all heads of household were under twenty-five, another 16 percent were between twenty-five and thirty-five years of age, and about 54 percent of the households were headed by an elderly person (over sixty-five). In consequence, the population in 1975 was not a mixture of young and older persons but a population age-segregated by development: the elderly were concentrated in Carr Square, Blumeyer, and in separate buildings at Vaughn and Webbe; the younger families were most numerous in Clinton Peabody, Cochran Gardens, and Darst.

Whatever the changes in age and family composition, the desperate poverty remained. The rapid inflation of the mid-1970s tended to wipe out the moderate advantage enjoyed by the aged and retired in the late 1960s. By the end of 1975, about 75 percent of all families in conventional housing were below the official poverty level for a family of four. Granting that rent was limited to one-fourth of income, a major improvement over 1969, the amount of hardship within the developments remained substantial. Moreover, there was little change in income levels in the 1970s, despite the at-times fierce inflation; the little change that does appear was actually a retrogression—the desperately poor replaced the very poor. The authority tried to maintain a mixture of incomes in the developments, but with little success.

The 1975 population was marked by even heavier dependence on public assistance than before: from 1965 to 1969, about 52 percent of the total population was dependent on public aid; by 1975, between 82 and 84 percent of the families relied mainly or entirely on public assistance payments. Although 30 to 40 percent of the tenant families contained one or more worker in 1975, the number of families that obtained *all* of their income from employment was very small. In Carr Square, Clinton Peabody, and Blumeyer, some 20 to 25 percent of the families obtained all of their income from employment; in the other developments, the average was about 10 percent. The out-migration of employed persons was not large, taken as a whole. From 1972 to 1975, for example, a net of fifty fully employed heads of household left the conventional develop-

ments. The losses were concentrated, however, in Clinton Peabody (twenty-four families) and Darst (forty-seven families).
The imbalance was compensated by gains in other developments. The ADC mothers were concentrated fairly heavily in
Cochran Gardens, Vaughn Apartments, and Darst; the elderly
in Carr Square.

Finally, a look at performance and price, those last desperate
measures of the economics of housing. Nothing offers better
evidence of the wisdom of building well than the consistent
performance of Carr Square and Clinton Peabody; only
Blumeyer, some twenty-six years their junior, approached
either their levels of occupancy or their low per diem cost.
When operating expenses and annual contributions are
summed, the gross cost for each day of occupancy actually
provided the tenants in Carr Square and Clinton Peabody
ranged from about $2.50 to $3.00 per day per unit in the 1960s
and from $3.00 to slightly more than $4.00 in the 1970s. By
comparison, Cochran Gardens, which matched costs with the
two older developments in the 1960s, soared to between $8 and
$10 per day in the 1970s. Vaughn's daily cost rose from slightly
over $5 in the 1960s to nearly $8 in the 1970s. Darst–Webbe
remained between $4.50 and $6 per day in the 1960s and
reached an astronomical $10 for each day's occupancy in FY
1975. When the inflation effect is removed, the daily cost for
Carr Square and Clinton Peabody was under $2.50 for the
1970s; Blumeyer's costs stabilized at just over $4 per day; the
cost for the others was between $5 and $6 per day, expressed in
standard 1967 dollars. The two older developments, and to a
lesser extent Cochran Gardens, have been a genuine bargain.
All of the gimmicks and gadgets, the ideologically induced
changes, the privatization, have been no match for a combination of sound design, solid construction, and straightforward,
"old-fashioned" management.

1. *Slum area cleared to make way for Pruitt–Igoe, 1954*

2. Site to be cleared for Pruitt–Igoe, looking southeast, 1948

3. Pruitt–Igoe under construction, looking north, 1953

4. Aerial view of Pruitt–Igoe completed, looking southeast, 1955

5. Pruitt–Igoe completed, late 1950s

6. *Apartment interior, 1957*

7. *Apartment interior, 1956*

8. *Nursery-school children in Pruitt, late 1960s*

9. *Thanksgiving dinner in the community center, 1963*

10. *Elderly public housing tenants, early 1970s*

11. *Nursery-school children in Pruitt, early 1970s*

12. Cochran Gardens, early 1970s

13. Signs of neglect, 1968

14. Neglected litter, 1967

15. Child in flooded apartment, 1970

16. *Flooding from broken pipes, winter 1970*

17. *Pruitt–Igoe abandoned and vandalized, 1975*

18. *Interior vandalism, early 1970s*

19. *Interior vandalism, early 1970s*

20. Abandoned buildings, 1974

21. *Experimental demolition, 1972*

22. *Pruitt–Igoe site after demolition, looking northwest, 1976*

V.

Privatization: Turnkey Development, Contract Management, Homeownership

If operation under stress provides the acid test of social institutions and capacity to rescue failure from disaster is a measure of their strength and viability, then American society needs to reexamine its policymaking apparatus from top to bottom. Neither the national nor the local administrative agencies responsible for public housing, neither the legislative bodies and their advisors nor the academic and quasi-academic agencies that might reasonably be expected to contribute to improved performance were able to produce so much as an adequate analysis of the cause of the difficulty in conventional public housing. At best, studies of aggregate data charted the dimensions of the forthcoming disaster; they were intrinsically incapable of suggesting reasoned means of avoiding it. The absence of any compelling diagnosis or reasoned program of action, which might at least have served as a launch point for experiments designed to move society closer to understanding and solving the problem, forced reliance on folklore and re-ceived opinion. Ignorance opened the door to the ideologue, the patent remedy, the self-serving special interest. The result was futile and expensive cosmetic treatment of terminal illness and actions whose latent benefits were far more important to their proponents than were their manifest consequences for the ten-ants of public housing. Many blamed the victim, pointing to racial segregation, juvenile populations, and concentrations of ADC mothers as the root of the problem. Others attacked the physical characteristics of the developments: they were too large, too high, too isolated, too bleak, too badly designed (meaning unspecified), and so on. And some attacked the local housing authorities: they were lacking in managerial skill and foresight, overly bureaucratic, authoritarian, and even lacking in concern for their tenants. The prescriptions tended to be equally simplistic, relying on single-factor accounts of trends in public housing: private development, private management, decentralization, tenant participation, or the use of cash payments to tenants. Privatization of operations was the basic solution most frequently proposed.

Three policy decisions in the 1960s had an especially profound and lasting impact on the public housing program. First, a premium was placed on the development and operation of housing for the elderly. Second, no operating subsidy was authorized for conventional housing. Third, privatization of all aspects of the housing program—development, management, and ownership—was accepted as the best available solution to the problems that plagued the conventional developments. Why a transfer of control over development or operations from a public employee to a private entrepreneur was expected to lead to significant improvements in performance is uncertain. Some proponents of privatization simply opposed public ownership on ideological grounds and took the "failure" of public housing as evidence favorable to their position. Others accepted the popular belief in the superiority of private enterprise (as opposed to the intrinsic evil of public ownership). In most cases, supporters of privatization apparently had only the vaguest notion of how and why it would improve the housing program.

Nevertheless, pressure for privatization continued. It achieved its first major success in the Housing Act of 1965; that statute authorized lease of privately owned facilities for use as public housing (in addition to an abortive rent-supplement program) and the sale of public housing to either individual tenants or to not-for-profit corporations that would continue to operate them as low-income housing. In the next two years, private development of apartments on privately owned sites for sale to local housing authorities and private management of public housing under contract with local housing authorities were authorized by administrative action. All of the programs save leasing were technically part of the "turnkey" program, but to avoid confusion the name *turnkey* will be reserved for private development of housing facilities for sale to local authorities (the name derives from the act of "turning over the key" to the authority after purchase). Private management and tenant ownership will be discussed under their nontechnical labels. No St. Louis public housing was sold to a private organization.

Turnkey Development

For the local housing authority, turnkey development offered the quickest and simplest way of obtaining physical
facilities because it shifted most of the responsibility to a private developer. The local authority had only to obtain an authorization to build and to solicit bids. The contractors located
and purchased the site, employed an architect to produce approved plans, obtained bids on the job, arranged financing,
supervised construction, and so on. Except for one small project
involving rehabilitation of fifteen dwelling units in three small
buildings, all the public housing constructed in St. Louis after
1968 was developed under the turnkey program. Since most of
the turnkey projects were commissioned between 1967 and
1969, they were designed without knowledge of forthcoming
operating subsidies; at that time, only the construction and
operation of facilities for the elderly were being subsidized. Not
surprisingly, about 85 percent of the 1,665 dwelling units constructed in St. Louis by the turnkey method were intended for
the elderly. Only five of the fifteen developments were designed for family occupancy, a total of 242 units, mostly of large
size (six or more rooms). Two turnkey developments combined
a single high-rise building for the elderly with a cluster of row
housing for family occupancy. One of those two combination
developments was used as a site for the homeownership experiment (Euclid Plaza, comprising 1–13A and 1–13B).

Development: Cost and Quality

Did the change to private development of public housing lead
to facilities that were significantly better than those that conventional development could have produced? There were differences, of course, in both structure and location, between the
older conventional developments and the new turnkey housing. But, given the changes that occurred between the 1950s
and the late 1960s in both the housing industry and the federal
regulations governing development, it is unlikely that the end
product would have been very different had the Housing Authority served as developer. In some cases, reliance on private
developers probably reduced local opposition to siting public
housing in the neighborhood. But in most cases, the turnkey

projects were located in areas equally accessible to public authority. Other aspects of the development process were about as expected. The time between authorization of development and project completion was much shorter under the turnkey program than with earlier conventional development. The administrative burden on the Authority was reduced, and since the period of intensive turnkey development coincided with the St. Louis rent strike and its aftermath, that respite was most welcome. On the other hand, the experience that might have been gained in development was forgone, along with the opportunity to test improvements in design and construction suggested by operating experience. The fundamentals that determine development quality were little affected by the change: the landowners faced the same market, the architects were trained in the same schools, the construction practices were incorporated into the same industry. Unless the members of the industry enforced a dual standard depending on whether the purchaser was private citizen or public agency, there was little reason to expect major differences in quality or siting between public and private development.

Location

The conventional developments had been sited in two major clusters on the periphery of the central business district on cleared slum land. The turnkey developments were more widely scattered but located principally on the northern edge of the east–west corridor connecting the downtown area with the new commercial center in Clayton. The quality of the sites varied greatly. Some turnkey projects were located in physically attractive areas (1–17, 1–19, and 1–28); others were built in run-down neighborhoods surrounded by decay and dilapidation (1–16, 1–18, and 1–29). The sites were scattered and the "visibility" of the developments was reduced along with the heavy concentrations of public housing tenants that characterized the conventional sites. How scattering affected the quality of life in the sites—access, facilities available, security, and so on—is uncertain, but it probably varied a good deal.

In general, turnkey development produced little significant improvement in tenant access to public transportation, shopping, and educational, religious, or recreational facilities. Indeed, the decision to scatter the sites and reduce scale, taken in conjunction with the increased emphasis on housing the elderly, may actually have aggravated access problems. Certainly it forced much greater dependence than before on individual transportation, such as minibuses, for each development. None of the turnkey projects was located within five or six blocks of a shopping center that included a grocery, a pharmacy, and cleaning facilities. Most of the apartments were some blocks away from the arterial roads that carry public transportation into the commercial centers. In most cases, the nature of the neighborhood made it unlikely that needed services would be established for the development—the scale was too small, some areas were zoned for residence, the tenants were too poor to generate very much demand for goods and services.

Further, most of the turnkey apartments were located in areas with significant levels of reported crime, and six of them (1–16, 1–17, 1–18, 1–19, 1–20, and 1–29) were placed in locations characterized by the worst crime rates in the city. Conditions in these areas were improving somewhat by 1974, in keeping with the overall trend in the city, and the introduction of public housing had little if any effect on the crime rate. Siting housing for the elderly in such areas suggests the kinds of considerations that a public developer might be expected to honor more readily than would a private developer tied primarily to the profit motive.

The inadequacy of some sites used for turnkey housing was among the side effects of reduced scale and scattered sites that were not as fully considered as they might have been. Market logic suggests that the best way to obtain facilities for low-income families at least public cost is to concentrate the populations to a level where it becomes commercially feasible to provide goods and services directly and intentionally for tenants. In principle, site scattering and reductions in concentration will either reduce the likelihood that private entrepreneurs will supply goods and services or vastly increase costs—as in smaller "neighborhood" and specialty shops. The effect of scatter-siting is to force tenants to rely almost exclusively on nearby facilities. Moreover, the consumer protection a housing authority might provide for a concentrated population must also be forgone. Scattering the lambs through the wolves' home territory is probably too strong a metaphor for the policy, but something along those lines clearly occurred in St. Louis. The principal argument against population concentrations is past experience with public housing. But the evidence in St. Louis indicates that the difficulties were not a function of scale. In the circumstances, the wisdom of scatter-siting remains undecided.

Physical structures

In most cases, the change to turnkey development produced no major improvements in either design or construction of public housing. Indeed, what stands out clearly in St. Louis, and seems to hold for other large cities, is that public housing design and construction simply reflect current trends in the housing industry. The housing authority, like the private purchaser, gets the going product at the going cost . . . plus! Special design and construction features that might improve the capacity to withstand rough treatment by large juvenile populations or otherwise fit the apartments to their intended use are rare. Even such things as the change from high-rise construction to townhouses seem more a reflection of changing consumer tastes or changing production techniques (and their resulting economies) in the industry than of governmental standards for public housing construction. The turnkey developments differ from one another as much as they differ from housing developments in the private sector.

Evaluation of the physical products of the housing industry is much complicated by the absence of a qualitative baseline. There is no "standard" unit of housing, and comparisons of cost and product keyed to number of rooms, area, or even construction materials and techniques can be quite misleading. Design, materials, and construction can be combined to produce housing that varies enormously in durability, replacement cost, and maintenance. For the same reasons, comparisons of construction costs should also be treated with caution. However, the subsidy system embedded in federal legislation rewards those who produce housing by the unit and not those who operate and maintain it—the developer, banker, and construction firm rather than the owner or development manager. Most administrative evaluations therefore concentrate on the cost of producing each unit rather than the cost of using the unit over time. Noneconomic costs are almost universally ignored, even by the tenants! Design and construction features that minimize the cost of producing a marketable unit are therefore much more important to those who control the development process than those features that add to durability and lower operating costs, particularly if the latter reduce profits to the builder. The result has been a marked tendency for the housing industry to move toward the "throwaway" products established long ago in the automobile industry. In an area where technological change is rapid and new innovations have considerable value to the user, there is much to be said for producing and replacing on a short time cycle unless initial investment is very large. But with respect to housing, and perhaps to automobiles as well, that approach to production increases cost through time very substantially, and neither industry shows signs of the frequent technological breakthroughs that would be required to justify the production strategy in real economic terms.

Few of the policies incorporated into the public housing program refer to the quality of the physical product—most limitations refer to costs. It is a commonplace that the quality and durability of multifamily housing have declined markedly since World War II, as might be expected in a production-rewarding subsidized industry. Interestingly enough, the financial industry remains tied to a forty-year bonding cycle that was appropriate to the structures produced in the 1930s. If the expected life of new apartments is now well below that figure, which seems at least possible, mortgage payments will continue long after the useful life of the apartments has ended, as in Pruitt and Igoe, or the consumer will be faced with rapidly rising maintenance and replacement costs. In either case, the overall cost of any given period of occupancy will rise. Since the federal government in effect guarantees both mortgage payments and operating expenses, that could lead to a very high drain on public funds in the relatively near future.

Some of the differences between conventional developments and turnkey apartments seem likely to make the latter more livable, if not more durable. The amenities supplied the tenant are superior: kitchens are better equipped, external appearance is more attractive, surfaces are better protected and easier to clean. Generally, the amount of space available in the family units is slightly larger in turnkey than in conventional, though some of the apartments designed for the elderly are very small. In James House (1–10) and University House (1–20) the efficiency apartments contain about 300 square feet of usable space and the one-bedroom apartments about 450 square feet; that is perhaps 50 square feet below "normal" and more than

100 square feet less than the space available in the more comfortable efficiency apartments and one-bedroom units. Population densities in the developments for the elderly tend to be very high, reaching 400 units per acre in University House (1–20). But turnkey family housing compares very favorably with conventional housing so far as density is concerned, ranging between 15 and 35 units per acre as compared to 40 to 50 units per acre in conventional developments. Such improvements can be considered benefits of turnkey development, of course, but there is no good reason local housing authorities could not achieve the same results either by avoiding the ultraparsimonious approach to development that characterized the 1950s or by simply adopting industry standards.

Housing design, like other aspects of development, tends to reflect current industry practice fairly consistently. In turnkey housing, and indeed in the private sector as well, design tends to the routine, a relatively unimaginative, cost-effective solution to problems. Variations on standard solutions are usually expensive. In turnkey, two basic designs predominated. The elderly were concentrated in rectangular high-rise buildings with elevator facilities in the center, a corridor running the length of the building, and rows of identical cubicles on either side of the corridor. Most of the family dwellings were designed as duplexes or townhouses with living facilities (kitchen, living–dining room) on the ground floor and one or two floors above containing bedrooms, bathroom, and some storage space. Townhouses usually provide slightly more space for the tenant than a one-floor apartment, though they also include more wasted areas and passageways—the economic benefits of enclosing three floors with the same roof are always partially lost. Large families probably find the respite from children that floor separation makes possible a welcome relief, at least until the time comes to clean and make beds.

The exceptions. Most of the apartments produced by the turnkey method were as "conventional" as any conventional development, and some were genuinely drab and depressing, even when new. But in public housing, as in the private sector, rare occasions arise in which a combination of good design, decent construction, and an appropriate site provides a visible object lesson in how good such housing can be and how far from the mark most efforts fall. In St. Louis, the crowning gem in the Authority's tiara is Badenhaus (1–28). It consists of fifty-two efficiency apartments and forty-eight one-bedroom apartments, spread among nine two- and three-story buildings connected by covered and enclosed walkways. The buildings are located on a five-acre site situated atop a knoll with a good view of the central city, several miles to the south. The units are among the largest in the Authority, each apartment has its own outlook onto the grounds or the surrounding area, there is ample community space, and the lounges are located at the intersections of the building—and come with a spectacular view. The covered walks allow freedom of movement without concern for weather or security; the five-acre tract provides room for short walks and minor gardening—which is encouraged. The social atmosphere is open, friendly, and decidedly active. And development costs were reasonable, just over $1,000 per unit more than the national average (see Table 1). What particular alchemy accounts for the social environment that has been created at the development is unknown, but good design and construction and a fine location must certainly have contributed. Perhaps the only weakness attached to the site is its separation from shopping and other facilities; the tenants are heavily dependent on minibus service for shopping, churchgoing, and so on. All things considered, the additional cost of such service is a minor price to pay for the extra benefits it provides the tenants. While the scale at Badenhaus is small, there seems no good reason it could not be expanded substantially, provided operations were managed in ways that would not destroy the social atmosphere.

Could conventional development produce a Badenhaus? That it did not is not evidence that it could not. At the time when conventional development was the accepted mode, developments like Badenhaus were not being constructed anywhere. If the Authority had been serving as its own developer in the 1970s, would Badenhaus have made an appearance? In all honesty, I think the answer must be "no," though I should add that it would not come out of regular commercial development either. Badenhaus was produced by a church group and not a regular developer, and there may be a lesson in that. In any case, little can be said about the best way of *producing* Badenhaus-type innovations; the important thing is to improve our capacity to use or apply innovations and improvements incorporated into them. In that respect, public and private sector alike have fared badly.

Development costs

Is turnkey development a more cost-effective way of obtaining public housing than conventional development? Again, comparisons are difficult because costs vary with the site, unit size, construction, facilities provided, heating, local labor and materials costs, and so on. Further, low initial costs may be offset by the long-run costs of maintenance and replacement. Hence comparisons, whether in terms of units, rooms, or square footage, are liable to be misleading. So much said, some useful comparisons can be made if two points are borne in mind: first, the conventional developments were all sited, for political reasons, in slum areas, and the cost of clearing and preparing the sites was included in overall development costs; second, the bulk of the turnkey housing was designed for occupancy by elderly individuals and families, hence they were smaller in size, on the average, and less liable to the destructive effects of young children and juveniles.

When total development cost per unit is broken down, the most striking difference between conventional and turnkey housing lies in the portion of cost spent for the site and for construction. In the conventional developments, site costs absorbed about 19 percent of the total, ranging from 14 to 15 percent in Pruitt, Igoe, and Webbe to about 25 percent in Carr Square, Clinton Peabody, Vaughn, and Blumeyer. In the turnkey developments, site costs averaged only 10 percent of total cost, and ranged from a high of about 15 percent to a low of less than 1 percent—in 1–20, 1–24, and 1–28. Dwelling construction, on the other hand, accounted for only 66 percent of total cost in the conventional apartments, ranging from about 65 percent to 75 percent; in the turnkey apartments, over 80 percent of the total went for construction, and in some developments (1–24 and 1–28) it absorbed over 95 percent of all development expenses.

If the developments are arrayed in order of total unit cost, expressed in deflated dollars, turnkey construction has a decided advantage. Eight of the nine most expensive units, each costing more than $19,000 in standard 1967 dollars, were developed by the conventional method; only one turnkey development (1–29) cost in excess of $20,000 per unit in deflated currency. On the other hand, thirteen of the fifteen cheapest developments, each costing $18,000 per unit or less deflated, were developed by the turnkey method. All but two of the conventional developments cost more per unit than the average cost in New York City; only one turnkey development exceeded the New York City average cost.

Much the same result is obtained if the developments are ranked according to either construction cost per unit or site cost per unit. Eight of the ten most expensive units, measured in terms of construction cost, were developed conventionally; twelve of the fourteen cheapest units, measured in the same terms, were turnkey developments. However, all but two of the developments cost more per unit to construct than the New York City average.

However, if the developments are arrayed again, this time to show total development cost per *room*, expressed in 1967 dollars, the figures show a slightly different result. Seven of the ten most expensive developments, measured in terms of total cost per room, were turnkey developments. Moreover, all seven were designed for use by the elderly and not as family dwelling units. Eight of the fifteen cheapest developments, using the same measure, were produced by the conventional method. Construction costs per room indicate an even more striking turnaround. Nine of the ten most expensive developments, measured in terms of construction costs per room, were turnkey developed, and again all nine were intended for the elderly. Nine of the fourteen cheapest developments were conventionally developed. Site costs per room, however, continued to favor the turnkey developments. Seven of the ten most expensive projects in terms of site cost per room were conventional; twelve of the fifteen cheapest developments were turnkey.

Turnkey development is not always the least expensive way of acquiring sites. When the cost of purchasing and readying each acre of land is calculated, it turns out that three of the turnkey developers (1–17, 1–18, 1–19) charged more than $315,000 per acre for their sites and a fourth (1–10) spent more than $250,000 for each acre of ground, measured in current dollars. In deflated dollars, each of the four turnkey developments cost more than $200,000 per acre for land; the only conventional development with such expensive sites was the building for the elderly in Vaughn, and that involved a "rounding out" of land holdings in the area that did not accurately reflect the cost of the land on which the building was sited. On the average, conventional sites were more expensive than turnkey sites, but that is to be expected given their location.

How to interpret the data? Other things equal, the cost of developing by the turnkey method is lower than the cost of conventional development, in St. Louis at least. The principal advantage seems to lie in the lower cost of the site; far more of the cost of development is spent on construction in turnkey. That does not settle the issue very firmly, however, because of the great difference in the conditions in which development occurred. Would conventional development have produced the same results in the 1960s? Would turnkey development have operated as well in the 1950s? How do the units compare qualitatively, with respect to durability, cost of replacement, and so on? These are imponderables, given the evidence available, and they suggest that inferences from the data be handled with some caution.

Turnkey Operations

The evidence provided by turnkey operations is subject to many of the same limitations raised by comparisons of development costs. Most of the turnkey apartments were completed after the rent strike; few were beyond the preliminary stages of operation, the "breaking-in" period, by the mid-1970s. Some useful differences can be drawn among the developments in the turnkey program, and some interesting comparisons can be made between turnkey and conventional housing, so long as they are understood to be preliminary and tentative.

The most striking point to emerge from a study of turnkey operations is the overwhelming importance of the distinction between family housing and housing for the elderly. The same difference emerges with respect to conventional developments, but since most of those apartments are intended for family use, there is a tendency to regard it as peripheral. *The fate of housing developments tends to be worked out in the nexus of daily interactions between a set of tenants and a set of physical structures, barring extraordinary occasions, and differential outcomes can be accounted for primarily by the difference between families as tenants and the elderly as tenants.* By comparison, the differences between turnkey and conventional development, between private, public, or tenant management, or between medium-rise and row housing are minor. With respect to operating costs, maintenance, occupancy, and every other basic dimension of housing operations, family housing follows a common pattern however it has been developed, and housing for the elderly does the same.

Occupancy

From initial rent-up through the middle of 1977, the turnkey developments were full to capacity—and in most cases would not accept further applications for admission because the backlog could not be handled in the foreseeable future. Clearly, there was no shortage of effective demand for public housing. Minor weaknesses in occupancy, where they did appear, were in the family developments. The only building for the elderly where occupancy tended to be weak (under 90 percent in this case) was University House (1–20). It was occupied by very elderly tenants, and its occupants were required to participate in a congregate dining program. For some, that was a serious financial burden and for others, a potentially irksome limit on the cost and content of their diet. By 1977, most of the problems had been ironed out and occupancy was above 90 percent.

The rate of turnover in the turnkey apartments differed little from rates in conventional housing. In the apartments for the elderly, 5 to 10 percent of the total changed hands each year; in the family developments, the turnover rate was about twice that large, ranging from 12 percent to 20 percent per year. Experience in conventional housing indicates that the turnover rate is not critical so long as occupancy remains high and very high turnover does not continue indefinitely. More generally, a higher turnover rate will mean slightly lower cost effectiveness because some time is lost moving tenants in and out, even though the waiting list is long. Moreover, management usually takes advantage of a turnover to carry out routine refurbishing of the apartments, and that both consumes time and adds to maintenance costs.

Tenant characteristics

With only one major exception, elderly tenants in both turnkey apartments and conventional housing shared the same characteristics; family tenants in turnkey differed substantially from elderly tenants in turnkey but were very similar to families in conventional developments. The principal difference between the turnkey and conventional populations was the absence of ultralow income tenants in the turnkey developments. Otherwise, the two populations were about the same in age structure, income spread, family size and composition, number of workers in the family, size of family, number of persons receiving public assistance, racial distribution, and number of minor children. There would be little discernible difference between a cross section from either the elderly or family apartments in the conventional developments and a similar cross section from the turnkey developments.

Taken in the aggregate, the tenants of turnkey housing were overwhelmingly black. But the racial distribution within the individual developments was quite varied. Of the six developments occupied solely by black tenants, one housed the elderly (1–10) while the other five were family developments (1–11, 1–15, 1–16, 1–24, and 1–29). In two other developments, one for elderly (1–13) and one for families (1–18), more than 95 percent of all tenants were black. In the remaining two family developments (1–21 and 1–22), about three-fourths of the population was black. In two larger turnkey apartments for the elderly (1–17 and 1–19), the racial distribution was about equal. Finally, the tenants in three of the developments for elderly were over 90 percent white (1–20, 1–23, and 1–28).

Was the racial distribution in some sense an indication of a "racist" administration? Appearances notwithstanding, it was not. Three mutually supporting factors interacted to produce the skewed distribution. First, the turnkey program introduced public housing into areas of the city that were not racially integrated. Second, housing policy gave preference to area residents in the initial rent-up of the apartments, particularly those who had been displaced by public action. Third, area residents who were eligible for occupancy in fact tended to remain in the neighborhood when they could, retaining contacts with friends, churches, and other organizations; using familiar shopping facilities; and so on. In consequence, the racial distribution in turnkey housing tended to mirror city patterns. In any case, a decentralized Housing Authority that requires the tenant to apply directly to the development in which he prefers to live, tends to maintain and reinforce existing racial and other population distributions—the same conditions appear in the leased housing program. The Authority actually has little opportunity to serve as either an integrating or segregating influence on the tenant populations when the intake is controlled by a semiautonomous management in each individual complex.

The differences between elderly and family housing were reflected in tenant characteristics in predictable ways. The head of household in a family development was more likely to be male (one of two) than was the head of household either in a mixed elderly–family complex (four of ten) or in apartments for the elderly (one of three). The exception was Badenhaus (1–28), where nearly half of the households were headed by a male, but that was due to the large percentage of apartments in the development designed for family occupancy—usually by a retired couple. Age patterns also produced no surprises. The elderly tended to be old, with a median age well in excess of sixty-two; in family housing, 40 to 50 percent of the heads of household were under thirty-five and 80 to 90 percent of the total population were under sixty-five. Mean family size among the elderly was barely greater than 1.0 if the special case in Badenhaus is omitted. In the family apartments, the average family size was 4.8 in 1975; and since most of the families had a single parent, that meant a relatively large minor population. Indeed, between 35 and 45 percent of the total population of the family apartments was comprised of children under twelve, and another 35 to 45 percent was made up of children between the ages of twelve and eighteen.

Understandably, the physical condition of the apartments tended to reflect the relative size of the juvenile population. An inspection of turnkey developments in 1975 rated all of the developments for elderly in excellent condition, but conditions in most of the family housing were poor and in three family developments (1–15, 1–21, and 1–29) they were exceptionally bad. Turnkey housing has not solved the problem of developing apartments that can handle large families effectively. In part, that may have been a function of development size; most of the family developments were too small to justify resident full-time management, and managerial "presence" is apparently an important factor in maintaining the physical appearance and condition of the buildings.

Employment, public assistance, and income. Elderly public housing tenants, whether they live in conventional or turnkey apartments, are almost universally dependent on public assistance for the bulk of their income. Those who are employed seldom earn much more than those who receive only public assistance, suggesting that the work is supplementary or part-time and not very well paid. Tenants of family housing are employed more often, depend more heavily on earnings from employment, and earn more than the elderly. There are, however, some important differences in these respects between families in conventional and turnkey developments.

In conventional family housing, not more than one unit in three will contain at least one worker; in turnkey housing, at least three families of every four will include one person whose income is derived solely from employment. Obviously, such income will be much higher than income obtained from public assistance, hence earnings in the turnkey developments—and rents—will usually be higher than in the conventional projects. In the family developments, average income in FY 1975, for example, was around $7,500 per year; the average income of tenants dependent on assistance ranged from $2,500 to about $3,000. Badenhaus was again the exception, largely because of the number of two-person families in residence; there, average income was just over $4,000 per year. In general, earnings of families in turnkey apartments averaged above $1,000 per year more than earnings of families in the conventional developments. Among the elderly, the most common form of public assistance was, of course, social security. In the family apartments, ADC recipients were more common: fourteen of thirty-six families in 1–15 received ADC, twelve of thirty-four families in 1–16, and nineteen of forty-six families in 1–29. Income levels in these developments were among the lowest in the turnkey program—barely $2,600 per year in 1–15 and 1–29 and only slightly higher in 1–16. Public assistance payments in Missouri were, and are, among the lowest in the nation.

Fiscal indicators

Through the early 1970s, the primary fiscal indicators of turnkey housing operations remained at about the levels to be expected of new developments that were fully occupied and operating in a relatively stable social and administrative environment. Rent levels and occupancy remained high, expenses were relatively moderate, there was no need for extraordinary maintenance, reserves were building steadily, and subsidies were low. In fact, there were some unexpected profits from interest on general funds when interest rates soared in 1973–1974. In 1974 alone, interest earnings amounted to about 50 percent of a full year's rental income in five turnkey developments (1–10, 1–11, 1–17, 1–18, and 1–23) and to between 30 and 50 percent of a year's rent in six others (1–15, 1–16, 1–19, 1–21, 1–22, and 1–29). Returns from interest in 1973 and 1975 were less spectacular but still a significant addition to income and very useful for new developments still building reserves. In general, turnkey developments spent little or nothing for tenant services, for extraordinary maintenance, or for security. Collection losses were virtually zero, particularly in the elderly housing. In the first five years of operation, public housing tends to be relatively free of major fiscal problems.

Such distinctions as have appeared among the turnkey developments serve to separate family housing from the elderly housing along familiar lines. In the early 1970s, the rent-rolls for the elderly averaged just over $54 PUM, substantially higher than the national average of $45 PUM and higher still than the $34 to $37 average in the conventional developments that housed most of the very-low-income tenants, usually ADC mothers (Cochran Gardens, Darst, and Webbe). The average rent at Carr Square, Clinton Peabody, and Blumeyer was about the same as the average rent in the turnkey developments for the elderly. In the family turnkey apartments, an average rent of more than $90 PUM reflected the high percentage of employed tenants and relatively high average earnings.

The differences in operating costs between family and elderly housing were also to be expected. In general, overall operating expenses in family housing were about 50 percent higher than in elderly-occupied units, about $90 PUM compared to about $60 PUM. The principal difference was in utility costs (which reflected the size of the units and of the families) and in the cost of ordinary maintenance. Utilities in family housing cost about 50 percent more than in elderly housing, averaging about $50 per month as compared to $25 PUM. Ordinary maintenance averaged about $25 PUM in family and

$16 PUM in elderly apartments. Administrative costs were the same in both types of dwellings because they were administered under contract at a standard monthly rate.

Despite the relatively high overall cost of operations, the family turnkey apartments obtained little or no subsidy between 1970 and 1975. In fact, even the apartments for the elderly got relatively small subsidies in those first years of operations. In FY 1975, for example, a subsidy of about $16 PUM was provided for five developments, 1–10, 1–13, 1–17, 1–18, and 1–20, a modest amount compared to the $40 PUM required in Darst–Webbe or the $50 PUM allotted to Cochran Gardens.

The few signs of weakness in the turnkey developments in the mid-1970s were confined to family housing. The physical structures began to show signs of wear and tear. Accounts receivable were found only in the family dwellings, as were collection losses. Finally, though only seven landlord suits were filed against elderly tenants in a three-year period (October 1973 to August 1976), nearly three hundred suits were filed against residents of family apartments in turnkey. The development with the largest proportion of ADC mothers (1–16) had the worst record with reference to both delinquency in rent and suits for recovery—sixty-two suits filed in three years in a development that contained only thirty-four family units.

Taken in the aggregate, the turnkey developments in St. Louis were in good condition and performing well at the midpoint of the 1970s. But when housing for the elderly is separated from the family dwellings, there were already signs of future trouble among the latter. Physical conditions had undoubtedly deteriorated fairly rapidly in some of the family turnkey apartments, and in several cases the external appearance of the buildings was far from satisfactory. Second, the gross cost per unit day of occupancy (operating expenses plus annual contributions from the federal government) was already equal to the overall cost of operating the much older conventional developments. Part of the added cost was due to higher financing charges, of course, but in FY 1975, the gross cost per unit day of occupancy was around $7 for all of the family units and nearly $8 in 1–21 and 1–29—only Darst–Webbe among the conventional developments was costing more. If past experience holds, operating expenses in the turnkey developments will double in the second decade of operations, allowing for inflation. If that occurs, as seems likely, the first generation of family housing developed under the turnkey program will be far more expensive than any other housing the St. Louis Authority has owned, including Pruitt and Igoe.

Private Contract Management

In the fairly extended period of administrative upheaval that followed the 1969 rent strike, public housing operations in St. Louis were very largely under the control of the Civic Alliance for Housing. Decentralization of operations and the "holding company" concept of the central administration were accepted as basic long-run policy at the Housing Authority. Contract management by private firms and, of course, tenant management were to be the principal instruments for conducting regular management operations. The first contract was drawn during the rent strike for management of James House (1–10); the St. James A.M.E. Church, which had developed the project, agreed to provide management services. Thereafter, turnkey developments were placed under contract management as they became available for occupancy. Usually, central-office personnel conducted the initial rent-up then turned over the management to a private organization. By the end of 1975, only the leased-housing program and one small (82 unit) homeownership project remained under Housing Authority management.

Three different types of organizations were involved with contract management. First, over 2,700 units of conventional housing were placed under tenant management: Carr Square (656 units), Clinton Peabody (654 units), Cochran Gardens (560 units as of 7 July 1976), Darst (562 units) and Webbe (277 units). Second, management was provided by private, secular management firms, usually associated with a regular real estate operation. In 1976, group "A" managed Vaughn Apartments (500 units) and the family dwellings in Blumeyer (574 units). Group "B" managed only 94 units, comprised in three small developments: 1–11 (15 units of rehabilitated housing on three small plots); 1–16, a family turnkey development containing 34 units; and 1–29, another family development in the turnkey program containing 45 units. Group "C" managed two developments: 1–15, containing 36 units of family housing, and 1–18, a medium-rise apartment building for the elderly. Finally, one private management firm formed especially for the purpose was contracted to manage a total of 866 units for the elderly (140 units in 1–13, 128 units in 1–24, 397 units in 1–19, and 201 units in 1–20).

A third group involved in public housing management in St. Louis was made up of religious organizations. They concentrated on housing for the elderly. A Catholic organization operated five developments, totaling 884 units of elderly housing: Webbe Elderly building, Blumeyer, 1–22, 1–23, and the portion of 1–24 assigned to the elderly. The St. James A.M.E. Church managed James House (1–10). Another religious organization managed the buildings for the elderly at Vaughn (112 units). Finally, Badenhaus (1–28) was operated by the Lutheran group responsible for its development.

Most management contracts were for "soft" management services, that is, the contractor was paid a standard fee for each unit managed ($6.87 PUM until the autumn of 1975, when the fee increased to $7.21 PUM). Custodial and maintenance services were provided by the Authority. A few management contracts included "hard" management services, that is, custodial work and routine maintenance. At the end of FY 1975, there were only two such contracts in force. One provided payment of $15 PUM for combined services in the family development 1–29; the other covered facilities for the elderly in 1–13B and 1–17 at $11.51 PUM, 1–19 at $10.29 PUM, and 1–20 at $16.17 PUM. In addition to these regular contracts, special arrangements were required in some other developments: the authority paid part of the cost of a resident custodian, supplied an apartment at low rent for a custodian or manager, and so on. The fiscal impact of these arrangements was trivial, a minor addition to the cost of scatter-siting.

The principal weakness in contract management, as in so many other aspects of public housing, has been the inadequacy of the authorized payments. The Housing Authority has had to rely heavily on humane agencies such as churches for assistance with management, and generally they have confined their activities to elderly tenants. The Authority has often found it very difficult to obtain needed management services through contract, particularly for the small and relatively isolated turnkey developments. Many of them are not large enough to justify a manager or even a resident custodian, yet they contain large juvenile populations—1–16 is a good example, as is 1–29. The Authority has tried to combine them into a single contract, but by mid-1977 it seemed clear that these small developments were among the weakest elements in the turnkey program, not because they were "turnkey" and the manager was under contract, but simply because these are very difficult managerial problems in public (and private) housing.

Private contract management in St. Louis operated mainly in new turnkey housing under conditions in which demand pressure remained strong, income was relatively high, maintenance requirements were limited. The most effective form of tenant criticism, moving out of the development, was seriously inhibited by the absence of comparable facilities in the private market. Much of the contract management dealt with apartments for the elderly, notably easier to manage than family units. Since private contract management was used in all of the turnkey developments, comparison with developments of equal age and similar construction is not possible. Comparison with earlier conventional developments, except in the roughest terms, is likely to be seriously misleading. For one thing, the computerized records and accounts system introduced in the early 1970s profoundly altered management requirements in all developments. The computer's capacity to monitor and direct daily operations and pinpoint problems as they arise effectively relieved management of the need to develop and operate individual control systems and significantly decreased the amount of routine error in performance.

Very roughly, and to some extent impressionistically, the public-versus-private character of management is far less important to the quality of operations than the amount of resources available, the quality of the initial design and construction, and, of course, the type of tenant occupying the unit—whether elderly or family. Most of the indicators of managerial performance commonly used in public (and private) housing—occupancy, administrative cost, maintenance effectiveness, collection losses, accounts receivable, tenant complaints, and so on—seem most influenced by the elderly-versus-family character of the occupants. Strong support for this point of view is supplied by the results of the management-incentive program developed by the Housing Authority for use with contract management. Under the plan, payments for management services increased or decreased by up to 5 percent per month depending on performance. Management performance was measured by six basic factors: percentage of rent collected monthly, percentage of units occupied, rent-roll, number of annual reviews (required by law, hence the standard number was one-twelfth of the total population), ratio of expenditures for ordinary maintenance to budgeted amount (a bonus for staying within the budget), and portion of maintenance time spent at productive work (allowing 15 percent of total for transportation, and so forth). Positive and negative points could be earned in each area; payment was based on the balance of points.

A shortened version of the performance assessment for the period from 1 October 1975 to 30 June 1976, based on collections, rent-rolls, and occupancy, and adjusted to eliminate extraordinary gains and losses in a single month, clearly sustains the importance of the family–elderly distinction. Seven of the fourteen developments rated had positive total scores; seven had negative scores. The average for all fourteen was −188. The average for the eight developments for the elderly was +82. The average for the four family developments was −503. Individual scores for family developments were −218, −638, −664, and −490.

Moreover, the management changes made by the authority because performance was below standard all occurred in the family developments: 1–11, 1–15, 1–16, 1–21, 1–24, and 1–29 all had management contracts terminated for cause in the 1970s. Some contracts in housing for the elderly were terminated, but not because of poor performance: one firm went out of business, another found it uneconomical to continue, and so on.

Clearly, other factors besides the form of management or mode of development account for the relative success or failure of public housing developments. The distinction between family and elderly tenants is one of the more significant of those factors. So much can be said, but a stronger demonstration of the point is literally ruled out by a most unusual circumstance. The peculiarities of public housing operations in St. Louis after the 1969 rent strike eliminated any systematic trial of what was hitherto the only form of public housing management—centralized administration by the Housing Authority. The evidence available does not supply grounds for preferring contract management to tenant management or vice versa. What is curious is that there is no evidence about the effectiveness of Housing Authority management because it was not tried under the operating conditions of the 1970s—with centralized and computerized accounts and records, new turnkey developments, large elderly populations, large operating subsidies, special capital replacement funds, outside support from a variety of public and private sources, a relatively stable and peaceful atmosphere in the developments, and so on. The frequently suppressed assumption that management by local housing authorities has been tried and found wanting is as false as the equally common assumption that conventional housing development has been given a fair trial and failed. In both cases, the data indicate conviction without trial.

Homeownership

Owning the family home is an aspiration almost as firmly entrenched in the pantheon of American values as free enterprise and the independent family. Indeed, when homeownership is tried and fails to produce expected results—better care of property or more stable family behavior—the impulse is to query the training, motives, or competence of the persons involved rather than question the value of the institution. Such beliefs played an important part in shaping the original conception of public housing as a way station between leaving the family in which one was raised and locating one's own family in an individual home. They also account for the addition of tenant ownership of housing units to the list of devices expected to privatize and thus improve the public housing program. The nature of the expectations associated with homeownership are best reflected in such homilies as "what's everyone's property is no one's property" and the quite illegitimate inversion, also widely accepted, that what *is* someone's property will automatically be someone's concern and will receive proper treatment.

In St. Louis, the family portion of a mixed family–elderly turnkey development, comprising eighty-two units of three-, four-, and five-bedroom townhouses and a small but well-designed community building, was set aside for the homeownership program. Operations began in the autumn of 1969. Until the spring of 1973, the homeownership program, in development 1–13A, was managed by the Housing Authority. There followed two years of contract management, including "hard" maintenance, but the contract was cancelled for cause and the Authority resumed management. That arrangement continued through the summer of 1977.

In terms of the ordinary criteria used to evaluate public housing performance—occupancy, operating costs, reserves, expenses, and so on—the homeowner program has performed as well as, or somewhat better than, most family housing. But the other expectations associated with ownership—better care of individual and collective property, pride in appearance, stable residential patterns, orderly environment, self-discipline, and even higher levels of individual savings—have all been disappointed. If anything, the physical structures in 1–13A have been more heavily abused than those in any other family development. A small and attractive community building was literally destroyed and had to be boarded up after it was gutted and burned. The tenants, to put the matter succinctly, continued to behave like tenants, and very unruly tenants at that. There has been no sign of the tenant initiative expected to develop in the program. Indeed, eight years after operations began, the tenant organization expected to do so much had not yet been put into operation. Initiative has been supplied by the Housing Authority. In fact, the tenants have generally responded poorly to prodding, particularly with respect to property maintenance and payment of fiscal obligations. In terms of the accepted stereotype, the project has had many tenants and no homeowners.

Program Design

At least part of the disappointment is traceable to the program design.[1] First, the physical structures, produced by the turnkey method, were unimaginative in design and unimpressive in construction. The walls were thin, the construction shoddy, the equipment poor. Yet the cost per unit was around $27,000. The tenants may well have felt they were a poor bargain. Second, the program was financed by the same methods used elsewhere in public housing. Capital costs were defrayed by the sale of federally guaranteed bonds, paid off through annual contributions over a twenty-five-year period. In St. Louis, the annual payment per unit was about $1,700 per

1. *Federal Register*, 9 October 1973, "Low-Rent Housing Homeownership Opportunities," and circular HUD 7495.3, *Low-Rent Housing Homeownership Opportunities*.

year. No operating subsidy was included in the program. The monthly payments were based on a combination of tenant income and estimated cost of maintenance. The way they were determined literally forced admission of the upper stratum of the low-income population to the program. While a few very low-income families might afford to purchase, relatively high rents were needed to meet the maintenance cost. The rent computation involved (1) determination of the tenant's average monthly income, (2) subtraction of allowable deductions, and (3) calculation of 20 percent of adjusted monthly income. That became the basic payment. Utilities payments made directly by the tenant were deducted from the basic payment according to the HUD schedule of allowances. In all cases, however, the monthly payment had to be large enough to cover basic operating costs as determined by the local housing authority (set at $41 per month in St. Louis) plus the minimum outlay for property care.

The monthly payment was divided among four separate accounts by the local housing authority, each intended to serve a different function. First, $24 per month was set aside (in St. Louis) for operating costs, including administration, utilities used on the common property, common-property maintenance, a common-property reserve, and general expenses such as insurance. Second, $5 per month was placed in a nonroutine maintenance reserve for future major repairs such as roof replacement or furnace replacement. This reserve was attached *to the unit* and not the tenant. If the tenant left, the reserve remained behind. If the tenant purchased the unit, any funds in this reserve could be used to help finance the purchase. Third, $12 per month went to a homebuyer's account or homeowner's reserve. This reserve accrued *to the tenant* and was intended for purchase of the unit. The tenant was expected to accumulate at least $350 in this reserve to consummate his purchase and was encouraged to accumulate much more. However, funds in this reserve could be used for any needed maintenance the homeowner did not provide, for delinquent rents, or for damages, therefore cumulation was not automatic and was invariably slow.

The first three accounts were meant to cover basic operating costs, and each tenant had to make a payment large enough to cover them. However, the fiscal arrangements clearly implied that the tenant would be able to afford larger monthly payments, even though no tenant could be asked to pay in excess of 20 percent of income. A fourth account was therefore set up for each tenant to handle the excess payment, the difference between "rent" paid and actual expenses. These "profits" were used to pay lieu of taxes to local government if required and to reduce annual contributions payments by the federal government. Through 1975, excess payments in St. Louis were used to build a development reserve that by 1977 amounted to more than two years of normal operating costs.

In addition to making the monthly payment, the homebuyer was bound to maintain the unit and the area assigned to it and to pay utility costs (aided by the HUD utility allocation). If the homebuyer failed to meet those obligations, the Authority could have the maintenance performed and charge the cost against the homeowner's reserve, subject to consultation with the not-yet-activated tenant association.

Ownership: Costs and Value

The homebuyer and the Housing Authority were not related by the normal buyer–seller relationship. Until the tenant accumulated $200 in the homebuyer's reserve, he remained a "tenant." Once the reserve reached $200 (expected within two years) the tenant became a "homebuyer." If the reserve was not accumulated in two years, the Housing Authority and tenant association would decide what action to take—presumably either evict the tenant or allow more time. The tenant who became a "homebuyer" need only cumulate another $150 in the reserve and wait—maintaining the reserve constant. When the cumulated reserve equaled the principle remaining on the debt, the sum was transferred to the Authority and the tenant became the "owner." Though tenants were urged to make extra payments and speed acquisition of title, it was not required and none did.

Given the terms of the settlement and the nature of the legal title, the prospective homebuyer's indifference to the rate of acquisition was perfectly reasonable—it was a bad bargain. If the reserve was maintained at exactly $350, ownership was acquired when the debt was equal to $350; at the rate of repayment employed, that would occur in 24.8 years. Nothing was gained by investing more. For example, if the tenant paid in an additional $150 per year, ownership was acquired sooner, but the tenant was better off to place the $150 per year in a savings account, if only because of greater flexibility.

The reason for not seeking more rapid ownership lay in the restriction imposed on profiting from resale. If the tenant bought the apartment early, the Housing Authority could restrict the title so that the owner could not recover more than the original cost, the forgone interest, the value of improvements, and any expenses connected with the sale. In effect, windfall profits from the effects of inflation were eliminated for the first decade.

The first occupant of a homeowner's unit could gain title by cumulating the $350 reserve, making regular payments, maintaining the unit, and living long enough to collect. So long as he did his part, the federal government paid off the mortgage. If the first tenant left the apartment, subsequent tenants were charged either the fair market value of the unit or the amount of the remaining debt, whichever was greater. If the new tenant accepted the existing debt, he followed the same procedure as the previous tenant. If the new tenant was charged the fair market price, the amount was again amortized over a twenty-five-year period, and the entire procedure began anew.

A second major departure from the conventional meaning of "owning" allowed the purchaser to simply vacate the apartment without cause on thirty days notice. The Authority could also terminate occupancy if illegal use of the apartment could be shown. The homeowner was bound for the cost of restoring the apartment to good condition—if necessary, the homeowner's reserve could be used. That settled, the remaining balance belonged to the tenant. The unused balance of either the maintenance or the operating reserve remained with the apartment. The tenant had no more liability than a month-to-month renter and much less than the tenant who signs a standard one-year lease. The arrangement had very little "stick" attached.

Of course, it did not contain very much carrot either. The "ownership" carrot was both distant in time and problematic in value. The tenant was promised a distant reward contingent on regular monthly payments. The amount of the reward was unknown, but clearly it depended on such things as the quality of construction, the behavior of neighbors, trends in property values over time, and so on. The monthly payments were also flexible and could be expected to increase as the apartments aged and became less attractive and desirable, in other words, had less marketable value. Under some (not unlikely) circumstances, the tenant could be asked to pay more and more each month for a future property worth less and less. A close analog would be a long-time employee of a nearly defunct business seeking to last out the time required to secure a dwindling pension in a rapidly inflating economy and wondering if he should seek employment elsewhere.

In the circumstances, the best strategy for the tenant was clearly to regard the property as a simple rental arrangement, discount the alleged long-run benefits, and move out if the short-run alternatives elsewhere became more advantageous. There were no valid incentives for taking the long view unless the property was exceptional in design, location, construction, and future marketability. None of these conditions was satisfied in St. Louis. The greatest benficiary of the program was the tenant with a large family whose income fell into the upper levels of eligibility and whose housing requirements on the private market were very expensive. For him, the 20 percent maximum was likely to be a bargain, and under some conditions he could pay much less than 20 percent of income for rent. So long as the apartments were new and in good condition, he could remain and pay as little as possible. As the apartments aged and costs began to rise, he should prepare to move, once he had extracted maximum benefits from the program.

Operations

The course of operations between 1970 and 1976 suggests that this perception of program benefits was widely understood and acted upon by the tenants. Whether by intent or accident, tenants in the homeowner program had the highest average income per unit, the highest average wage per worker, and the highest ratio of income from employment to total income of any development in the city. Average homeowner's income in August 1976 was $9,483 per year; in leased housing, average income was only $5,139; and in the other turnkey developments, it was lower by several hundred dollars per year— between $7,500 and $8,500 in most cases. The average wage for an employed worker in 1–13A was $11,203, compared to $10,508 in the next highest complex. In the homeowner program, 45 percent of the tenants received all of their income from employment; in the other developments, the average was between 15 and 18 percent. Of course, income levels in 1-13A were high only in relation to those of other tenants in public housing, and even in that context, the large average family size (5.2 as against 4.8 for other family housing) somewhat reduced the economic significance of the difference. By the HUD standards set for section 8 leasing in 1976, forty-six of the tenants were classed as families with "very low incomes," another twenty-seven had "low incomes," and only nine were actually overincome. In fact, twenty-four of the eighty-two families in residence in August 1976 were below the Labor Department poverty level, and the number was increasing—there had been twenty-three families in 1975, seventeen in 1974, and eleven in 1973.

The advantage of the homeowner program to the "higher income" poor is demonstrated by a comparison of rent levels and average incomes. In the homeowner group, the average income of $9,483 produced a top rent of $117 and an average rent of $77. In leased housing, the average income was $5,193, the top rent $175, and the average rent $59. In 1–15, average income was $7,978, top rent $151, average rent $101. In 1–24, average income was $8,606, top rent $121, average rent $87. The value of living in a development that limited rent to 20 percent of income is obvious; the Brooke amendment limit of 25 percent of income is much less advantageous. Moreover, fairly substantial changes in tenant income produced relatively small rent increases. Two cases involving an increase of more than $4,000 between 1973 and 1976 produced rent increases of $18 and $33; three others involving income increases of $3,000 or more produced monthly rent increases of less than $20. Various factors influenced the way in which increased income was counted for rent determination, of course, and these are specific cases and not averages. Nevertheless, for the employed tenant earning most of his income, the homeowner program provided a good base from which income could be increased enough to keep pace with inflation without generating major rent increases.

The assumption that it was good strategy for upper-income eligibles to regard the homeowner program as short-run housing also accounts for the occupancy patterns in the development. By 1976, only forty-six of the original tenants remained in residence. Seven units had changed hands twice; one had been occupied by three different families. Between 1972 and 1975, about half of the units were vacated and reoccupied. The reasons offered for leaving suggest the extent to which short-run advantages of the program were being exploited by tenants with no intention of becoming owners. Of the forty-five tenants who left between 1971 and 1976, three moved from the city, two left because the rent was too high. Sixteen, however, claimed they were moving to a newly purchased home. They could not be located, but in some cases it was known that the tenants had left to purchase section 236 homes that were later lost as the economic situation in St. Louis worsened. Leaving a homebuyers' program in order to purchase a home is an interesting commentary on program effectiveness. Another "action commentary" from the tenants is found in the number of forced departures from the development. In five years, two tenants were evicted by legal action, nine more left while under suit, five left without notice—one pausing to strip the apartment of the refrigerator and other movables—and eight more left under strong pressure from the management. Their reserves covered only a small part of delinquent maintenance and apartment damage.

The nature of the criticism should be kept clear. The homeowner program supplied housing in use as well as or better than other family developments in turnkey. Occupancy was excellent, collection losses relatively small, accounts receivable minor. At the end of FY 1976, only three tenants owed more than thirty days back rent. But as a *homeowner's* program, it failed almost totally. The overwhelming evidence conveyed by the data is of tenants concentrating on short-run benefits, perceiving themselves as tenants and nothing more. Unfortunately, the policies developed for the program seemed to reinforce and justify such behavior.

VI.

Privatization: The Leasing Program

The first important step toward privatization of public housing in the United States was the inclusion of leasing in the Housing Act of 1965. For the first time, privately owned housing was made part of the public housing program, and that opened the door to incremental modification of the portion of the program allotted to public and private facilities. Second, the owner of the leased housing became a third party to the Authority–tenant relationship, again opening the door to incremental modification in their respective roles. By reducing the role of the local housing authority while increasing the authority of the private owner, it was possible to return to something very close to the traditional landlord–tenant relation without any further changes in operating principle. Leasing allowed the conversion of public housing to a rent-subsidy program. The stages by which the change was brought about can be documented quite accurately, though the full effect, particularly on the established conventional and turnkey programs, remained uncertain at time of writing.

The Leased-Housing Program

Leasing of privately owned facilities for use as low-income housing was authorized by the addition of section 23 to the Housing Act of 1937. The purpose as stated was modest, and the initial scope of the program was very small—a few thousand units for the entire country:

> For the purpose of providing a supplementary form of low-rent housing which will aid in assuring a decent place to live for every citizen and promote efficiency and economy in the program under this Act by taking full advantage of vacancies or potential vacancies in the private housing market, each public housing agency shall, to the maximum extent consistent with the achievement of the objectives of this Act, provide low-rent housing . . . in private accommodations . . . where such housing . . . can be provided at a cost equal to or less than in housing in projects assisted under other provisions of this Act. (section 23 [a] 1)

The 1965 act specifically authorized lease of *existing* housing;

HUD interpreted the act as authorization for supporting both rehabilitation and new construction of housing intended for lease. The Congress validated that interpretation in the Housing Act of 1970.

The leasing program expanded rapidly, particularly after the election of 1968. In 1968, it accounted for less than 6 percent of the total public housing program; by 1974, more than 13 percent of all public housing units were leased— 169,000 of 1.3 million. The major expansion occurred in new construction for lease and in the lease of existing facilities; rehabilitation stalled in 1969, and the procedure was not much used for the next seven years. Of the 61,000 plus units added to the lease program between 1969 and 1974, about 75 percent (46,000) were new construction, and 24 percent (15,000) were existing housing. HUD data beyond FY 1974 were not available at the time of writing, but presumably future expansion will be divided more or less equally between new construction and existing housing.

The policies governing the leasing program developed in two fairly distinct phases, marked by radically different approaches to public housing.[1] The section 23 program that began in 1965 lasted until the freeze on public housing in the spring of 1973; the second phase of the program began in the autumn of 1973 when the freeze was lifted from the leasing program and a new set of regulations governing lease operations was published. The new regulations were the precursor of the more elaborate policies incorporated into section 8 of the Housing and Urban Development Act of 1974. Their combined effect was to convert a portion of the public housing program to a rent-subsidy program.

1. For a sequential view of the evolution of regulations governing leasing, see: circular RHA 7430.1, *Low Rent Housing: Leased Housing Handbook*; circular FHA 7430.3, *Low Rent Housing: Flexible Formula and Revision of Leased Housing Programs*; *Federal Register*, 11 November 1973, Section 23 Leased Housing; *Federal Register*, 22 April 1974, Section 23 Leased Housing; *Federal Register*, 23 May 1974, Section 23 Leased Housing; *Federal Register*, 29 April 1975, New Construction for Lease; *Federal Register*, 5 May 1975, Existing Lease; *Federal Register*, 7 August 1975, Lease and Grievance Procedure; *Federal Register*, 8 March 1976, Housing Assistance Payments Program—Existing Housing. In addition, two very useful volumes were produced by the Section 23 Leased Housing Association (name changed to National Leased Housing Association after the 1974 Housing Act): Charles L. Edson, *A Section 23 Primer*, and Charles L. Edson, *1975 Supplement to the Leased Housing Primer*. Finally, the National Association of Home Builders, the National Association of Housing and Redevelopment Officials, and the Council of State Housing Agencies produced the *Section 8 Workbook: 1974 Housing Act* in February 1975, which is quite useful.

Phase 1: 1965–1973

Leasing was authorized first as an auxiliary to the regular housing program, a flexible way of enlarging the local housing authority's capacity to provide service. The scale was small: HUD approval was required to lease more than twenty-five units in any one site. Leases were short, one to three years. The sites were to be scattered. Such limits were clearly incompatible with development of leasing as a major public housing program—construction for lease would be impossible, for example, unless the local housing authority could lease a large cluster of units for a long period of time. In 1966, the time limit for lease was extended to five years, but commitments for up to forty years (HUD's limit on annual contributions) could be made by sequential extensions of five-year leases. For existing housing, however, a limit of fifteen years was established in the Housing Act of 1970.

Those responsible for policymaking in the late 1960s were much concerned with the impact of leasing on local housing markets and with the quality of the housing obtained by local authorities. If leasing was expected to drop the local vacancy rate in rental housing below 3 percent, local authorities were directed to (1) urge landlords to rehabilitate substandard housing, (2) seek to lease units hitherto offered for sale, (3) lease long-vacant units, (4) combine smaller units into large apartments, (5) underwrite housing already rented by low-income families, and (6) lease new housing constructed in response to the leasing program. The value of some of the recommendations was at best marginal, but the direction of concern was clear—memories of the 1940s were still strong.

The minimum standards to be applied to leased units were vague and minimal. The exterior and interior should be in "good" condition; the sanitary facilities "adequate"; light, heat, and ventilation "satisfactory"; cooking facilities "adequate"; living space "adequate"; the neighborhood free of "characteristics seriously detrimental to family life" (which included substandard dwellings or other undesirable elements); and the location should provide reasonable access to public transport, schools, churches, and stores. The meaning of "adequate" and "satisfactory" were very uncertain in the context of the housing market, hence the standards produced a wide range of results depending on local interpretations and local conditions.

Control over operations was retained firmly in the hands of

the local housing authority or other public agency administering the housing program. The local authority located the units to be leased, made the initial inspection, located the tenants, determined eligibility for admission, set rent levels, negotiated the lease of the property, controlled the movement of tenants in and out of the leased apartments, and provided needed custodial and maintenance services. Curiously, no annual inspection of leased property was required. It was not forbidden, but the lack of authorization would have made it difficult to find the resources to carry it out.

The apartment lease could be negotiated between local housing authority and owner or between tenant and owner with the local authority as guarantor. The procedures used to select tenants were flexible: the owner could select with local authority approval, the owner could select from a local authority list, the authority could select with owner approval, or, finally, the authority could make all selections without reference to the owner. The owner preferred tenant selection by the authority in most cases, because it required the authority to pay for each day of the lease, whether or not the apartment was occupied. Under the other forms of tenant selection, the owner was paid only for days when the unit was occupied.

Fiscal arrangements

Since the lease program did not require the "20 percent gap" between the level of income at which tenants might be admitted to public housing and the income needed to afford housing on the private market at a five-to-one ratio, it tended to attract tenants with somewhat higher incomes than those who entered conventional and turnkey housing. Rent levels were set by a complicated method known as the "flexible formula." It calculated the development cost of an equivalent set of premises constructed by the local housing authority, adjusted costs to local standards, and calculated the annual contribution that HUD would make for those premises using the current federal bond rate. That contribution was set as the limit on the subsidy payment that could be made for the whole apartment complex. Subdividing the total produced the maximum allowable subsidy for each unit. If the program operated at a loss, the $10 per month subsidy allowed for the elderly, for very large families, or for very-low-income families could be used to finance the deficit. A reserve of $25 per unit could be cumulated by the authority if all routine maintenance was supplied by the owner; if the local authority divided maintenance responsibility with the owner, it could build a reserve equal to 50 percent of one year's rent. If the authority supplied all routine maintenance, the reserve limit was 75 percent of the annual rent. All costs to the authority, plus routine administrative costs and incidental expenses, were reimbursed by HUD through the annual contributions contract.

Phase 2: 1973 and Beyond

By 1970, expansion of the public housing program through conventional development had virtually stopped and new turnkey authorizations were growing increasingly rare. The central thrust of the leasing program had shifted to the construction of new facilities for lease. Meanwhile, costs to the federal government began to soar under the impact of the Brooke amendment and the effort to rehabilitate the badly neglected conventional developments. The Nixon administration, searching for an approach to public housing that would be more financially acceptable and philosophically congenial (Republicans had consistently supported direct rent subsidies rather than public ownership of housing facilities), froze public housing operations very shortly after the 1972 election. When operations resumed in the fall of 1973, the new emphasis was clear: A holding operation at minimal cost would be carried out in conventional facilities; the leasing program would become the primary future thrust in public housing.

Interim regulations

The new policies guiding the leasing program were published in the *Federal Register* on 9 November 1973. They clearly anticipated the changed roles of private owner, tenant, and local housing authority spelled out in the Housing Act of 1974 and its supporting regulations. In general, there was a major reduction in the amount of control over leasing exercised by the local housing authority, a considerable enhancement of the influence of the apartment owner, and a cut in the nonfinancial assistance provided to the tenant—particularly by the local authority. Further, the direct influence exerted by HUD on daily operations increased greatly, especially after the creation of local HUD offices.

Under the new regulations, the owner of leased property was

given responsibility for "complete and total management, maintenance, and operation of the dwelling unit." He paid the utilities not paid directly by the tenant, provided insurance for the property, paid the taxes, performed all maintenance, took applications from prospective tenants, selected families for residence, collected rents, accepted (grudgingly?) the losses from vacancies and from unpaid rents, and made required reports to HUD.

The local housing authority was left with little to do. It determined the eligibility of applicants and issued a certificate good for forty-five days and renewable. Beyond that, the local authority inspected the premises, reexamined each tenant annually for eligibility, approved the lease, and executed the contract, but such actions were merely pro forma. Even responsibility for locating apartments was transferred to the tenant by what was called a "finders-keepers" policy. The local authorities could assist the elderly and some few others to locate an apartment. The regulations clearly envisioned a return to the "normal" relationship between owner and renter found in the private housing market—the local authority merely served as banker, within narrow limits, for the prospective tenant. The basic rents were actually set by HUD through so-called fair market rentals, determined annually and including all utility costs.

The interim regulations also underscored the importance then attached to scatter-siting and physical conditions by the national administration. The requirement that fewer than 10 percent of the units in any one building should be leased for low-income housing was reinforced by allowing HUD to give priority to requests for authorization that proposed to lease fewer than 20 percent of the units in any one dwelling. The standards to be met by leased dwellings were augmented by requiring one official certificate of compliance with local building codes and another guaranteeing the absence of lead-based paint in the apartments. However, an effort to place full responsibility for vacancies on the owner by limiting rent payments to occupied units failed in the face of powerful real estate interests. In January 1974 the regulations were altered to allow payment by HUD of 80 percent of the rent on vacant apartments for a period of sixty days if a tenant had violated the lease when he vacated.

Section 8

The Housing and Community Development Act of 1974 elaborated and solidified the new approach to public housing. A typical omnibus bill, loosely aggregating a variety of programs and purposes, it purported to seek to eliminate blight and conditions detrimental to health and safety, to conserve and renew the older urban areas, to expand federal assistance to local authorities, to streamline programs and agencies, to conserve the nation's housing stock, to expand and improve the quality of community services, to promote more rational use of land, to restore and preserve properties with historic interest, and so on. Of more immediate importance to public housing, the act aimed to reduce the isolation of income groups (positively, to promote mixed-income occupancy in residential areas), to improve the quality of housing management, to further homeownership, to expand congregate housing for the elderly, and, rather ironically (since the net effect was precisely to the contrary), to "vest in local public housing agencies the maximum amount of responsibility in the administration of their housing programs." Having so said, the Congress proceeded to provide statutory authority for the most sweeping reduction ever made in the responsibilities and capacities of the local housing authorities. The act transferred virtually full control over daily operations to the owner; encouraged more direct participation by the states; and opened the way for HUD to serve as its own local agent, contracting directly with developers, owners, and tenants. All these changes were made at the expense of the local housing authority.

The 1974 act contained some surprisingly detailed provisions relating to housing operations. Families earning less than 80 percent of the median income for the area were defined as "low income families," while those earning less than 50 percent of the median were classed as "very low income families." Exclusions from income allowed in calculating rent were sharply cut and closely enumerated: income of family members under eighteen years of age, $300 for each minor child, the first $300 of a spouse's income, nonrecurring income, and 5 percent of family gross income made up the basic allowance. Extraordinary medical expenses, defined along lines followed by the Internal Revenue Service, and money received for care of foster children could also be deducted in computing net income. Such statutory limits created serious problems for areas such as St. Louis that had adopted much more liberal income-exclusion policies in an effort to restore occupancy in their conventional developments.

Moreover, the effort to detail operational limits in the basic legislation produced the almost inevitable anomalies. For example, the minimum rent for any public housing tenant was set at 5 percent of gross income. For tenants in leased housing, the limit was 15 percent of gross income or 25 percent of adjusted income. Further, the act required local housing authorities to allot at least 20 percent of their dwelling units to families with very low incomes; at least 30 percent of the tenants in leased housing should be very-low-income families. But section 9 of the act also required each local housing authority to collect at least "one-fifth of the sum of all the incomes" of all families for which HUD provided an operating subsidy. Bearing in mind that the Brooke amendment limited rent to one-fourth of income for all tenants (and much less for some, selected tenants), very little arithmetic is needed to demonstrate the dilemma in which local housing authorities were placed by the two provisions of the act.

A similar excursion into the details of operating standards in the HUD regulations produced the following example of bureaucratic incompetence and confusion, arising out of an effort to determine performance requirements and acceptability criteria for decent and adequate leased housing:

> (j) Access—(1) Performance Requirement. The dwelling unit shall be usable and capable of being maintained without unauthorized use of other private properties and the building shall provide an alternate means of egress in case of fire.
> (2) Acceptability criteria. The dwelling unit shall be usable and capable of being maintained without unauthorized use of other private properties. The building shall provide an alternate means of egress in case of fire (such as fire stairs or egress through windows).

Such intellectual malfeasance ought surely to be grounds for transfer (of the author) to the Internal Revenue Service.

The transfer of authority from local housing authority to the owner of leased housing was now provided with statutory justification. Subject to audit, the owner was given control over all management and renting functions, maintenance, rent collections, payment of utilities, and preparation of information required by HUD. The owner's functions could be delegated by contract to public or private agencies but not to the local housing authority that supervised the program.

While the Housing Act of 1974 enumerated the local housing authority's areas of responsibility at much greater length than before, its de facto control over leased housing was very much reduced. The one potentially effective instrument remaining was the right of periodic inspection. Once the initial lease authorization was made, the local authority had little more to do than inform, to publish and disseminate information to owners, prospective tenants, eligible persons, and so on. It had the right to authorize evictions, but that was limited to examining the grounds for eviction to make certain they fell within the terms of the lease. Beyond that, the local authority was an accounting agency for HUD, reviewing applications, issuing certificates of eligibility, calculating family rents and assistance payments, and so on. The functions tended to be routine, involving little discretion in program direction.

Expectations and Likelihoods

Judging by the content of the housing legislation passed in the 1970s, the leased-housing program was the official legislative–executive response to the question, "What should be done about public housing?" The benefits to be expected from leasing, the reasons it was preferable to conventional or turnkey development, were never made very clear. Much was made of the virtues of "direct cash assistance," but little was said about how it produced its benefits in relation to public housing.[2] The virtues of leasing alleged in statute and regulation referred to vague, general social features rather than specific effects for specific populations. It was claimed that leasing would disperse subsidized housing through the community, encourage mixed-income residences, increase economic efficiency by using up more of the capital locked into housing, and reduce costs. The accuracy of such expectations is uncertain. Cost reduction, for example, was unlikely; it would be more reasonable to expect costs to increase. Perhaps the best

2. Secretary George Romney in 1973, for example. See *HUD Newsletter* 4, no. 40 (1 October 1973) or the even earlier *HUD Newsletter* 3, no. 44 (30 October 1972). Similarly, the demand for income mixing appeared in 1973 (*HUD Newsletter* 4, no. 53 [31 December 1973]).

argument for leasing is the potential reduction of capital loss, but that ignores side costs associated with neighborhood conditions. In some circumstances, building abandonment might be wiser given the expected effect of neighborhood on resident families. While leasing would certainly produce dispersal of assisted housing, that was not always desirable per se. And the value and feasibility of mixed-income residential areas, HUD "experiments" notwithstanding, are very uncertain.

Perhaps the best statement of the virtues of leased housing is found in the very positive "qualitative" review of housing subsidy programs made by Arthur P. Solomon of the Harvard–MIT Joint Center for Urban Studies.[3] Using five basic measures, not meant to be exhaustive, Solomon concluded that leasing existing housing was far and away the best available approach to subsidized low-income housing. There are some serious problems in the evaluation. For example, it is not always certain whether Solomon is asserting his own beliefs or reflecting the views of those who favor such programs. The following example is typical:

> Concentrating the poorest families in the worst housing creates negative spillover effects—above all, neighborhood environments characterized by vandalism, broken families, vagrancy, and other social pathologies. Also, there is an assumption, but little empirical evidence, that mingling households of different income levels not only provides the disadvantaged with better access to educational and employment opportunities and a better home environment but also helps moderate antisocial behavior attributable to enforced ghettoization.[4]

The first sentence is apparently a statement of Solomon's own views (highly tendentious at that); the second seems an assumption Solomon does not accept—though a citation to the Coleman report complicates the question of meaning.

The first continuum on which Solomon scores subsidy programs is the extent to which they enhance consumer sovereignty. The criterion is justified by the following: "Our culture places a high value on consumer sovereignty, and most of our national housing legislation implicitly assumes that free residential mobility contributes to individual well-being." Ignoring the logical error involved in elevating social custom and

3. Arthur P. Solomon, *Housing the Urban Poor: A Critical Evaluation of Federal Housing Policy.*
4. Ibid., p. 175.

legislative history into acceptable normative practice, the three indicators of performance used to measure the different types of subsidy really load the dice against any form of publicly owned housing: (1) is the initial package of housing chosen by the tenant? (2) can the tenant remain if his income increases above the program limit? (3) can a normal landlord–tenant relation be achieved "free of public supervision"? By definition, leased housing will outscore any form of publicly owned housing, whether conventional or turnkey developed, using these criteria. But have the criteria anything to do with the purposes of public housing? If nothing else, Solomon has conveniently forgotten that the reason for having public housing in the first place is that under a system in which the tenant did the choosing and a normal landlord–tenant relation existed free of "public supervision," the results were simply appalling.

The second question addressed to the subsidies—"Do they encourage racial and economic integration?"—is clearly relevant but not easy to answer. Solomon supports his preference for leasing by an astonishing argument: "The leased units are dispersed throughout the rest of the city. This is especially true for units that are from the existing stock." But the fact of dispersal does not imply integration. On the contrary, if local sentiment is strong and the urban area is not integrated, dispersal simply supports the existing pattern of segregation—as occurred in St. Louis.

Third, Solomon asks, "Does the program stabilize the low-rent housing market?" Whatever importance that question may have for housing economists, its relevance to the problems public housing must solve is uncertain. The reasoning used to make it apply involves a howling non sequitur: "New construction programs offer a long-term commitment to a single structure, but not necessarily a stabilizing effect on the low-rent housing market." In contrast, "rehabilitation and direct consumer subsidies (for example, the leasing of private dwellings) provide a guaranteed rent-roll over a short time period, enough of an inducement for a modest upgrading of the existing stock. Rather than construct a small number of large-scale developments, the modest rehabilitation of many dwelling units is a more appropriate activity for stabilizing declining neighborhoods." If the latter statement is true, it is nonetheless not implied by the preceding "evidence." In effect, the problem of supplying housing to low-income families has been confused with the problem of optimizing use of the existing housing supply.

The fourth base for evaluation is adaptability of the subsidy to local market conditions. Solomon rightly notes that new construction or rehabilitation, once completed, is inflexible and that serious underutilization of either public or private housing can have deleterious consequences for a whole area. From that set of assumptions, it follows that construction should not produce a total supply that much exceeds the level of normal use fluctuation. Leasing is an ideal instrument for adapting need to supply quickly. But it does not follow, as Solomon seems to imply, that leasing is always or generally superior to construction: that depends on supply, need, the level of fluctuation in use, and a range of other factors. Accepting his initial argument need not produce support for leasing.

Finally, the question, "Will the subsidy produce an acceptable home environment?" is considered. The results are taken to support leasing for reasons that again are fallacious. "In recent years, the environmental qualities of most subsidized construction . . . represents a distinct improvement over the past; however, because of cost constraints and in some instances, continued design restrictions, commonplace, if not sterile, architecture is still the frequent result. By contrast, the use of rehabilitated units or the existing stock at least ensures that the subsidized housing is situated in a more or less normal neighborhood environment." Professor Solomon cannot have taken very many trips into the "normal" neighborhoods in Boston that provide sites for leased housing, for unless they differ radically from St. Louis neighborhoods in which housing is leased, they are just as commonplace and sterile as any other slum neighborhood, and in many cases much worse.

Using these five criteria, Solomon shows leasing to be far superior to any competitors among the available subsidy patterns. Leasing earned nineteen points, as against fourteen points for leasing of rehabilitated housing and only six points for conventional new construction. If Solomon's criteria were related to the purposes of the public housing program, and the argument could link changes in the criteria to public actions in support of leasing, the evaluation would be a good reason for supporting that program. In fact, nothing of the sort follows from the evaluation. To put the argument per contra in lawyer's form: it is uncertain and in some cases unlikely that the proposed results would follow; even in those cases where the stated outcomes seem likely to occur, it is not clear they are desirable; even if their desirability could be established beyond question, there may be side effects attached to such policies that would more than outweigh the putative benefits of a commitment to leasing.

For example, lease of existing housing will certainly scatter the sites. But who benefits in what way? *If* concentration of low-income families produces vandalism, vagrancy, and social pathologies, then scattering the sites will inhibit those effects. But where is the evidence on the question? Again, scatter-siting may lower the profile of the public housing tenant, allowing him to lead a more normal life, but that is the case only if the tenant matches in some degree the population in the territory where he is planted. Leasing will hide racial minorities or very-low-income families only if racial or economic integration has already occurred (almost nowhere the case) or is not important. If leasing is used as an instrument of integration it will have the opposite effect, forcing the tenant into the limelight. And site dispersal can involve very significant costs, particularly for special groups such as the elderly. It inhibits provision of a range of collective services—health services, recreation, socializing; it reduces the local authority's capacity to protect the tenants; it forces the tenant to make use of nearby existing facilities, usually very inadequate. Such actions as site scattering can produce quite different effects in different situations.

Some of the developments currently operating can serve as natural state experiments in the effects of scattering and concentrating tenants of public housing. Tenants who have moved from individual houses into public housing in effect voted with their feet and their futures for concentration. They have subsequently reinforced their vote by remaining in the development, by not complaining, and by strong verbal support for the new environment, informally and formally. The evidence in St. Louis strongly suggests that aggregation, particularly of the elderly, is a vast improvement over scattering, at least so long as the scale of aggregation remains moderate. If scattering is combined with a serious reduction in the local housing authority's capacity to intervene in the landlord–tenant relation on the tenant's behalf, the result seems an open invitation to return to the same market conditions and landlord–tenant relations that generated the need for public housing in the first place.

The leased-housing program might be used to create mixed-income communities at some additional cost—for example, it might be possible to subsidize the higher-income members of such communities in order to get them to stay. Would the result justify the cost? What would the characteristic of the resulting socioeconomic structure be? Studies such as the Coleman report seem to suggest that the value of socioeconomic admixtures has been grossly exaggerated, even with reference to such critical areas as education. What benefits can be expected from the action? Or is this merely one more sociological "fad"? In a special survey in the *Journal of Housing*, published as the 1974 Housing Act was being signed (August–September 1974), Jack Bryan of NAHRO addressed the question, Can mixed-income housing be made to work? He concluded that it could, but he did not address the question whether it would justify the cost. The conclusion to the article says a great deal about the focus of concern:

> The over-all conclusion of the Massachusetts study, which is generally corroborated by the experience and findings of other mixed-income programs cited in this article, is that ". . . .income mix 'works' or does not 'work'" according to whether the mix occurs in well-designed, well-constructed, well-managed developments. These latter factors are the crucial determinant of satisfaction. Income mix and racial mix are, in themselves, of no particular relevance.

Precisely the same thing can be said about conventional or turnkey housing, private apartments, individual homes, and so on. The conclusion begs the question whether income integration is a worthwhile goal.

Finally, arguments for leasing usually assume, implicitly rather than explicitly, that leasing is somehow more economical than any alternative way of supplying housing for low-income families. Comparing housing costs is always treacherous, of course. In some cases, leasing can certainly be cheaper than building or purchasing, but much depends on amount, time span, conditions of lease or purchase, price, and so on. The overnight visitor to a city would be ill-advised to purchase a house for the occasion, but it is not always and obviously cheaper to lease than to own—one set of costs may include the other. When housing is owned by a public agency that can borrow at preferred rates and avoid most local taxes, the advantages of ownership multiply. The economist's insistence on charging "forgone" taxes against the "cost" of publicly owned housing is mere ideological warfare; if costs of that nature are to be levied, why are not the social benefits totaled and added to the score?

With reference to such capital goods as housing, which can be used over substantial periods of time, fixed-point measurements of costs are meaningless. A good illustration is found in Solomon's "useful criterion for contrasting the impact of alternative housing programs . . . . the number of inadequately housed families moved into decent shelter for any given expenditure of public funds." A "move into housing," like a wedding ceremony, is a relatively small part of the total cost of the action represented. Solomon's measure makes any type of new construction or major rehabilitation look very expensive and such short-run arrangements as leasing, which involve no capital expenditures, look relatively cheap. That may be true in private business, where the additional cost is simply passed along to society through tax remissions, and such features attract a Congress that is inordinately fond of any fiscal arrangement that minimizes short-run costs and thus gives the appearance of economy. Most basic errors in public housing were due to that preference. The only fair measure of cost involving capital investment is long-run performance, the total product of the investment, the costs, and the benefits, over the life of the product. Otherwise, measures of housing efficiency and cost will have the same quality to deceive found in conceptions such as the cost reductions associated with mass production. In one sense of the term, a cost reduction does follow from mass production—the price of one unit of the product is decreased. But the *cost* of mass production must also include the long-run drain on resources, the long-run benefits to human populations, and so on. Unit reductions in cost can be very expensive indeed, socially speaking.

Leasing or renting is cheaper than purchasing only in rather special circumstances, given constant need. If the economy is deflating slowly but steadily; if cost efficiency is improving in the industry; if technological change, product improvement, or cost reduction is so frequent that the cost of obsolescence is high, then leasing is advantageous. But surely in such cases the owner of the products leased will recognize the special conditions as an opportunity for profit and scale his charges accordingly? A leased product must compete against the current cost of new production and not against its own past costs.

In any case, none of the conditions that make leasing advantageous has been satisfied in the housing industry since World War II. Inflationary pressure has been the rule, cost efficiency has declined, technological change has not increased productivity, and product improvement has been slow (considered in terms of fixed costs). In these conditions, there is great advantage to investing as soon as possible in any long-life capital for which demand is constant or increasing. Conventional public housing in St. Louis provides a perfect illustration of the value of early fixed investment: the fixed debt retirement payments for each unit of housing built in the early 1940s are less than $30 per month; for units built in the 1950s, the cost is around $70 per month; units that entered the market in the 1960s now cost about $85 per month; those completed in the 1970s have fixed annual contributions of $100 or more. Even if the quality of the units is ignored, and there are good reasons to believe quality has declined, the relative advantage of the buildings completed earliest is fairly clear.

Of course, construction of new facilities or major rehabilitation does involve fixed costs and forgone opportunities. It follows that policymakers should construct only as much housing as is needed steadily, filling the gap between long-term supply and short-term need by such procedures as leasing. Unfortunately, the data needed for estimating need are usually not available, hence estimates are likely to be little better than guesses. Second, if that policy succeeded, the risk to the owners of marginal housing available for lease would also increase, and the cost of leasing would rise. That might justify still further construction, even if it meant that some of the housing would be idle for periods of time during the use cycle. In practice, the demand for public housing has exceeded the supply, except in two special cases: First, when external factors (nonhousing considerations) such as resistance to racial integration have interfered with population movements; second, when the quality of the housing, taking the term in its broadest sense, has been very deficient, whether as a result of poor construction, maintenance failure, vandalism, or operational breakdown of some form. While the gross evidence supports the view that not enough housing of good quality is available to fulfill current needs, it says remarkably little about how much more, if any, is needed or for how long.

If governments could enter the housing market at will and always find enough apartments to meet their requirements without disrupting the market, leasing would be economical even in the long run. But the facts are different: Governments operate under constant pressure from tenants on the one hand and supply constraints on the other. Large-scale leasing requires a relatively large housing supply with some surplus capacity, otherwise demand pressure will drive up prices, eroding the quality of the housing available at any given price. The effects of these pressures are severe yet impossible to calculate. In some cases, decent and usable housing must be ignored because environmental conditions are unsuitable and too costly to alter. It would be foolish to clean a large river at enormous cost merely to obtain a relatively small supply of cheap fish. From the buyer's point of view, the most efficient lease point comes when capital investment has been paid and the residual capital "overbuilt" into the housing units can be purchased without the additional interest burden. In the life of a typical housing unit, that margin seems to be decreasing. If the rule in construction really is "build for twenty and lease for forty," there may actually be "underbuild" in present construction—which has some very interesting implications for the long-term future of leasing and some even more interesting implications for the mortgage and financing industries.

In the light of such considerations, leasing is unlikely to be a long-run solution to the problem of low-income housing. Local housing authorities or some other public agency will have to finance new construction or rehabilitation, whether as owners or lessees, or ignore significant human needs. Rehabilitation faces the same long-run problems as leasing, particularly as the supply of solidly built housing worth rehabilitating at current prices dwindles. New construction for lease is certainly more expensive, in the long run, than either turnkey or conventional housing, if only because rent must include taxes, higher interest rates, and profits. Such higher costs would have violated the provision in section 23 of the 1937 Housing Act (which would not allow payments for lease higher than the cost of development), but that provision was not carried over into the 1974 Housing Act. There is therefore no legal constraint on HUD expenditures for leasing far in excess of what it would cost to develop and operate the housing by public agency. Which route the government will take can have very significant implications, both for program quality and for long-run costs.

Leased Housing in St. Louis

The test of any policy comes at the point of application to the concrete case. How readily the test can be made depends on the kind of policy involved. Leased housing provides a good example of an extremely broad and complex type of generalized policy expected to apply to all sorts of different conditions. Leased-housing policy differs from conventional housing policy as instructions for swimming applicable anywhere on earth differ from instructions applicable only to the Dead Sea or the Great Salt Lake. In conventional housing, many of the critical variables determining outcome can be controlled—location, type structure, quality of equipment, and so on. Leased housing, however, depends on a host of external factors—the existing supply and the operation of the local housing market, among others—wholly outside the local authority's control and very difficult to anticipate even under ideal conditions. The influence of these external factors can be devastating: there can be no leasing where there are no apartments to lease. That underscores one of the real conceptual difficulties introduced into public housing by the decision to allow lease of new construction. The economic rationale behind the section 23 lease program was solid; leasing or rehabilitation provided a way of extracting maximum use from existing capital. Since the base cost was fixed, calculation of the effects of different kinds of investments and costs was feasible over a range of possible situations. New construction for lease, on the other hand, involves creation of capital and not use of existing stock; such actions are guided by a wholly different set of considerations. In effect, leasing and construction are not comparable; their costs and benefits must be calculated on separate schedules and some common ground must then be found for making comparisons.

The St. Louis Housing Authority did not experiment with either lease of new construction or rehabilitation of existing facilities; all leasing was carried out with existing stock under section 23 of the Housing Act of 1937. Most of the St. Louis operations for which data are available began during the first phase of the leasing program. In mid-1976, when this study was completed, the Authority was just converting its lease program to fit section 8 of the 1974 Housing Act. Some indications of changes likely to follow could be found, but no adequate comparisons were possible with the data available at the time.

Background

St. Louis provides a classic example of the pattern of inner-city development common in virtually every large metropolitan area after World War II. The city government was influenced primarily by the set of interests controlling the old central business district. The city was struggling to survive out-migration, loss of jobs and resources, and a dwindling tax base, but was tied to the old politician's slogan—building means prosperity! The housing stock was old; neglect and overuse had produced serious dilapidation and extensive abandonment. Overall, neighborhoods were declining, economic distress and industrial stagnation were common, there were few signs of unsubsidized rehabilitation—commercial or residential.

The scope of concurrent changes in the inner city was really staggering.[5] Between 1950 and 1975, the city lost some 300,000 inhabitants, mostly from out-migration to the rest of the metropolitan area. The selective character of the out-migration accentuated its impact: employed whites and blacks hastened to the suburbs in search of better schools, neighborhoods, and environments, leaving behind the old, the weak, the dependent, the minorities. The result was a poverty corridor running along the east–west axis of the city with powerful radials thrusting to the south, northwest, and southwest. The resulting impact on housing conditions were predictable: Semiofficial estimates, likely to be somewhat high, claimed that in 1975 more than 60,000 families occupied substandard housing and another 20,000 substandard units stood vacant. Such estimates are reasonably consonant with the size of the population exodus charted by the demographers, though hard evi-

5. From a draft report by Gary A. Tobin, *Regional Housing Needs Study: 1976.*

dence is scarce. Construction and demolition rates are known more accurately, however; and they paint a dreary picture of the flow of events. Between 1971 and 1974, for example, more than 11,000 units of housing were demolished in the city and fewer than 3,000 units were built—mostly for low-income families. Between 1961 and 1974, fewer than 15,000 units of housing were built in the city all told; in the county, more than 35,000 units were constructed in a single year. The debilitation in city housing was democratic: With the exception of some few areas to the south and some minor pockets of prosperity in the north, the whole city was poor. And the poverty of the occupants ensured that it would remain poor. Those who owned could not afford improvements, and those who rented could not afford rents that would allow the owners to improve.

The severity of the poverty and the poor condition of the St. Louis economy increased the need for subsidized housing, particularly among blacks. Only Atlanta and Houston among the nation's major cities had a poorer track record with respect to the black population. The combination of an economy that failed to provide employment for minorities, particularly the youth, and a state welfare system whose payments ranked well to the bottom of the national scale, created an appalling situation in the inner city. By 1970, some 22 percent of the entire population (or 15 percent of all families), a total of about 150,000 people, were living below the official poverty level. About 30 percent of all blacks, 20 percent of all elderly residents, and 40 percent of all those under eighteen years of age lived in poverty—at the official level. The rate of suffering is beyond calculation.

A city with a massive poor population, an old and dilapidated housing stock, a weakening school system, a declining working population, a declining economy, an eroding tax base, and an inadequate welfare system is not a good place to launch a leased-housing program. In 1976, as in 1967, finding decent housing that could be leased by the Authority was difficult. In the places where decent schools and neighborhoods survived, there was virtually no possibility of leasing space. Moreover, the surviving neighborhoods tended to be racially segregated; any effort to introduce racial integration through leasing would have run headlong into community opposition.

The Leased-Housing Program

The St. Louis Housing Authority received an initial allocation of 600 units of section 23 leased housing in the early summer of 1967. The program developed very slowly, doubtless hampered by the poor conditions in conventional housing—and by a notoriously weak management. At the end of six months, fewer than 100 units had been located and leased; only 88 units were occupied. By June 1968, 221 units were under lease; at the end of 1968, there were 373 units available, just over 60 percent of the allocation. Even at its peak, the program could not use more than 90 percent of its allocation. Had it not been for the acquisition of 100 units of housing for the elderly in a single building in the downtown area in 1974, the performance record would have been poor through 1976.

The root problem was an inadequate supply of decent housing available for lease. The supply of potential tenants was embarrassing. By the end of 1968, there were 446 applications in hand and only 12 vacant units; one year later, there were 950 applications and only 6 vacant apartments. Early in 1970, all of the applications were reviewed and updated, reducing the total to about 300, but by the end of the year the Authority again had more than 1,000 applications in the files and only a small handful of apartments available, despite the unused allocation.

The weakness of the leasing program came through clearly in the 1969 HUD audit. Deficiencies were numerous and serious, indicating both weakness in management and problems in the available housing supply. More than 100 tenants were seriously delinquent in their rent. Too many apartments remained vacant while under lease. The turnaround time for rerenting was too long; more than three months in some cases. Rents were capricious and bore little relation to current market prices. Finally, too many of the units were significantly below standards: Of the forty-eight units inspected during the audit, twenty-seven contained major faults—fifteen lacked adequate plumbing, eight required major electrical work, four had leaking roofs, and so on. Further inspections by city authorities (100 units in May 1970 and 280 units in the following autumn) showed an average of 35 percent of all leased units in violation of the operative codes (*St. Louis Post-Dispatch*, 17 December 1970).

In fairness to those responsible for the program, not all of the problems arose from incompetence or unconcern. The Housing Authority tried to use the leasing program as a way of providing the extralarge apartments that many poor families needed but could not obtain. When the family's need was great, it was difficult to refuse to accept marginal or even poor housing; the number of available units in the city was small, and if the landlord promised to make changes, the gamble often seemed reasonable. And if the tenant failed to complain, it was difficult for the Authority to learn of the landlord's failures. The units were scattered, staff was limited, HUD required only an initial inspection of the premises, and there was a constant pressure to find new units. Moreover, the housing was invariably old and liable to deteriorate quickly under severe tenant pressure; again, there was no way for the Authority to learn of the problem unless the tenant complained—unlikely when the tenant was a cause of the damage. Leased housing suffered the same kind of vandalism that plagued conventional housing; units prepared for occupancy were in some cases vandalized before they could be occupied, particularly in the latter 1960s when public housing was in an uproar.

Those who extoll the virtues of scattered housing, lease of existing stock, and the private market would do well to examine the problems facing the Authority during this period. A brief extract from a report made in the spring of 1969 may convey something of the atmosphere in which the program was trying to function and the difficulties it involved:

> Since the housing stock in St. Louis is quite old, even with the units meeting the Minimum Housing Standards of the City these units require constant attention and maintenance. With units scattered all over the city, with our efforts to develop more units, with our efforts to replace undesirable tenants, with our involvement with social, domestic, and economic problems of the tenants (and we cannot delude ourselves of not getting involved) it becomes physically impossible to follow up completely. Social services are completely lacking and vitally needed. Burglaries are commonplace . . . . The great flood of families desiring subsidized housing is far in excess of our abilities to house. With the scattered site concept, we lose control over tenants. We do not know if the family still lives in the unit unless we get wind of a change.

Some of the conditions that created the poor situation in leasing were corrected in the section 8 program, but practice will have to demonstrate the long-run effect of the shift in authority from the housing authority to the private landlord.

Even in those cases where the Authority was able to obtain decent units of housing in good condition, the environment around the site was likely to be poor. Leasing was concentrated in the east–west poverty corridor. Indeed, it may have contributed to the impoverishment of that area by extending black occupancy into areas hitherto occupied predominantly by whites. Low-income populations, dilapidated housing, public housing, and the lease program all tended to concentrate in the same areas. Unfortunately, these same areas are also marked by high crime rates, poorer schools, limited access to shopping, poor transportation facilities, lack of recreational areas, and physical dilapidation. The areas had, from the Housing Authority's point of view, two virtues: They were accessible, often the "only game in town" for public housing; and they were cheap, within the capacity of the tenants and the Housing Authority—neither munificently endowed with income.

Economy was enforced. The tenants were very poor and could pay no more than 25 percent of income for rent; congressional allocations to HUD were also limited. The tenant contribution to rent, which averaged $45 per month in 1968, was only $59 per month in 1976. Given large families, and the serious shortage of large apartments, the gap between tenant payments and rental costs could be quite large. Leasing older buildings was an economic necessity. As late as 1975, the average monthly payment to the owner for leased housing was only $138 per month. The scale of payments for leasing was $107 for a three-bedroom unit and $141 for a five-bedroom unit; for comparison, the HUD "fair market rental" for a three-bedroom unit in 1976 was $157 and for a five-bedroom, $206 per month. Section 8 leasing, which makes use of the fair market rent levels, should attract more and better apartments than did the section 23 program, other things equal—providing the units are actually available in the city. In the past, HUD would not allow even minor cost overruns in leasing: In 1969, to take an example, the Authority was offered *new* four-bedroom townhouses in the west end at $185 per unit; HUD refused to allow more than $160 per month, and the developer rented his facilities on the private market.

The lack of racial integration in the city served as another barrier to an effective leasing program. Until 1974, leasing was used mainly to house large, very-low-income black families. Only a third of the leased facilities contained fewer than three bedrooms. A block of 100 units for the elderly, acquired in 1974, was already occupied by elderly white tenants. That addition changed the overall statistical character of the program, but in quite misleading ways. The number of elderly tenants in the leased program increased from about 17 percent to nearly 45 percent in one jump; but the elderly white tenants were very heavily concentrated. Similarly, since the 100 units were all one-bedroom apartments, the distribution of apartment sizes changed, and the "average" size of a leased apartment dropped markedly. Actually, if the 100 elderly units are left aside, the program changed very little. After 1974, the lease program was still used mainly to locate housing for very large, black families who needed large apartments. About 95 percent of the white families were elderly; some 60 percent of them lived in one apartment building in the city.

In most respects, the operation of leased housing paralleled the operation of conventional or turnkey developments. Levels of occupancy were excellent through the 1969 rent strike then declined steadily through 1972. A change in management within the authority then produced a strong upturn in occupancy that lasted through the end of 1975—the average occupancy was around 98 percent for most of the time. The transition to section 8 in 1976 made the records hard to interpret, but there is little doubt that occupancy remains very high. Turnover rates have been moderate: Some 80 to 90 new tenants have entered the program each year.

Demographically, the tenants in leased housing most resembled the tenants in family housing. Disregarding the elderly for the moment, about 45 percent of the heads of household were between forty-five and sixty-four years of age; another 35 percent were between thirty-five and forty-four; the remaining 22 percent were under thirty-four. Families tended to be large: again disregarding the elderly, the median was four minors per family and the average family size was slightly more than five—indicating a large number of children since only one family in ten had both parents present. About half of the nonelderly families in leased housing contained one or more workers, somewhat more than in conventional developments but a little lower than in turnkey family housing. Practically all of the elderly were totally dependent on public assistance for their incomes; among the families, some three-fourths of the total were partially or totally dependent on public sources. Incomes remained remarkbly stable among leased-housing tenants: About 40 percent received $4,000 or less per year, another 35 percent had incomes between $4,000 and $6,000; about 10 percent had incomes in excess of $9,000 per year. Those receiving public assistance usually averaged between $3,000 and $3,600 per year.

A close examination of 463 of the 548 families in the leased-housing program at the end of 1975 bears out the general impression conveyed by aggregate statistics. The sample contained 342 black and 121 white heads of household. Of the 342 blacks, 89 were elderly, 48 were male, and 294 were female (26, 14, and 86 percent respectively). Among whites, 115 (96 percent) were elderly, 22 were males, and 96 were females. Most of the elderly, whether black or white, lived alone. There were only 61 two-parent families in the entire sample. Among the nonelderly, families tended to be large, averaging more than five persons per unit and requiring an average of 3.6 bedrooms per apartment. Nearly 90 percent of the total population of the family units was less than eighteen years of age, an indication of the number of single-parent families. That is roughly the same proportion found in family housing in the turnkey program.

The detailed records underscore the extent of the poverty and dependence of elderly and family occupants alike. More than 93 percent of all white families (112) were wholly dependent on public assistance, and 57 percent of the black tenants had no earned income. Only 1 of 121 white families lived solely on earned income, and some 48 black families (about 14 percent) received no public assistance. The apparent unwillingness of *employed* white families to live in assisted housing is striking. Some 29 percent of the black families (100) and 7 percent of the white families received income from both earnings and public assistance or benefits; in most cases, the primary source of income was earnings. Nonelderly families tended to be large (average 4.6 persons) with relatively high family incomes (average, $7,056 per year). Families wholly dependent on earned income averaged best of all, about $7,778 per year. The low level of assistance payments is displayed very strikingly in the income statistics. Families that depended on assistance alone averaged just under $700 per person per year; those who received no public assistance or a mixture of public assistance and income averaged $1,740 per person per year. Low incomes clearly pressed hardest on those with very large families. A total of 73 families in the sample contained 5 or more persons—some 518 persons all told, or an average of 7.1 persons per family. Average income for those families was only $3,844 per year—just under $550 per person. At that time, the official poverty level for a family of four in St. Louis was about $5,500 per year.

The combination of large families, low incomes, weakened administrative control due to dispersion, and an acute shortage of funds in the Authority made for a difficult managerial situation. The effect is readily seen in the standard measures of administrative efficiency—accounts receivable and collection losses. In lease of housing, as elsewhere, the problems appeared mainly in the family dwellings. Elderly tenants in leased housing, like their counterparts in conventional or turnkey developments, were ideal tenants. They paid bills regularly, moved infrequently, did little damage to apartments. Large families fell behind in rent, moved leaving unpaid balances and no forwarding address, and were sued by their landlords more often than other tenants. In this, they most resembled tenants in conventional housing. Collection losses in leased housing were relatively high, averaging about $4.00 PUM in the 1970s as compared to perhaps $1.00 PUM in family conventional developments and less than $0.25 PUM in Blumeyer. In fact, collection losses were a significant part of total administrative cost of the leased program. Scattered sites clearly played an important part in the losses, for there were few major differences in tenant characteristics or other factors that might account for them.

Quality and costs

The quality of the leased housing supplied to the tenant varied greatly. Some of the facilities, particularly those rented in the late 1960s, were inferior to the housing available in the conventional developments; in other cases, they were in better physical condition and better equipped than their conventional counterparts. Since leased housing came entirely from the older housing stock, comparisons with the newer turnkey apartments would be unfair, though in some cases the leased housing had locational advantages. In most cases, however, leased housing was not particularly well sited, on a par, all things equal, with conventional developments, which is to say that both were inadequate.

How much did the leased facilities cost? How did their cost compare to the cost of conventional or turnkey housing? The major element in leased-housing cost was, of course, the payment to the owner, but there were additional charges for administration, maintenance, collection losses, and miscellaneous general expenses—insurance, employee benefit contributions, terminal leave payments, and so on. Before 1971, total expenses were about $110 PUM, the average rent about $43 PUM, the HUD contribution $65 to $70 PUM. The owner's share of total expenses amounted to about $100 PUM, roughly 92 percent of overall cost. Other expenses, chiefly administrative costs, amounted to between $9 and $11 PUM. Maintenance costs and general expenses were less than $1 PUM; there were no collection losses.

From 1971 through 1975, total expenses varied from $120 PUM to $140 PUM, peaking in 1973. Rent paid by the tenant increased steadily, from $43 PUM in 1971 to over $54 PUM in 1975. Payment to the owner was remarkably constant, ranging only from $107 PUM in 1971 to $112 PUM in 1974. The principal sources of increased lease costs were administration (which rose to around $12 PUM), ordinary maintenance cost (which jumped to around $10 PUM in 1972, then dropped back to about $6 PUM in 1975), general expenses (which increased to about $6 PUM), and collection losses (which averaged about $5 PUM after 1972). Administrative expenses continued to rise in FY 1976, increasing by about 35 percent over FY 1975. Administrative procedures grew more complex, and more inspections were required by federal regulations. Of course, such increases were in some measure counterbalanced for the Authority by the absence of tenant services and security and by lower utility bills—the allowance for individual utility payments was much less than actual expenditures in some of the conventional developments.

Major increases in the payment to the owner can be expected after FY 1975. Even with section 23 leasing, the effort to improve the physical quality and environment of the facilities led to some cost increases in the early 1970s. A comparison of the average rent to the owner for facilities vacated since the program began with average rent for units leased in the autumn of 1975 suggests the size of the changes involved. One-bedroom units rented for $92 per month were replaced at $109 per month, three-bedroom units formerly costing $101 per month were replaced at $125 per month, six-bedroom units formerly costing $121 per month jumped to $147 per month in 1975. Rent to the owner was 15 and 20 percent higher for all new leases negotiated in 1975 than it was for leases allowed to lapse.

The leasing program was affected in a very curious way by inflation during the 1970s. The cost-of-living index in St. Louis increased by about 50 percent between 1968, when the program began, and 1975. Neither rent paid by the tenant, rent paid to the owner, total expenses, or the HUD contribution kept pace with inflation. Relative price stability was due to the fairly stable payment made to the owner; the deflated value of that payment was reduced drastically after 1973. Tenant payments, in deflated prices, began at $39 PUM in 1968, dropped to about $37 in 1972, and then to $35 in 1975. Total cost was about $100 PUM in 1968, jumped to $108 in 1972, but fell to around $77 PUM, deflated, in 1975. The deflated income of the owners was reduced by 15 to 20 percent, tenant rents dropped by about 12 percent, total costs were reduced by over 20 percent. Who benefitted most? HUD! Support payments from HUD decreased from $62 PUM to $46 PUM between 1968 and 1975, a reduction of more than 26 percent.

In effect, the owners of leased apartments absorbed the bulk of the inflationary effect, the tenant and HUD were major beneficiaries. The reason landlords could do this, obviously, was that their older buildings had long since passed the mortgage-burning stage. Actual operating costs were far lower than the imputed costs used to calculate or justify market price. Inflation simply burned up some of the "windfall" effect associated with the extra usage built into their capital equipment. If the cost of leasing is compared to the cost of operating the two older developments in St. Louis, ignoring their capital costs or mortgage, some notion can be gained of the margins involved. While Carr Square and Clinton Peabody were somewhat newer than most of the units under lease, three decades of heavy use and prolonged neglect should have produced roughly comparable cost figures. Figures are given for leased housing, Carr Square, and Clinton Peabody:

	Leased Housing	Carr Square	Clinton Peabody
1968	$101	$66	$70
1970	$118	$49	$47
1972	$125	$59	$58
1974	$136	$84	$87
1975	$135	$95	$88

Clearly, the two conventional developments cost about 30 to 40 percent less to operate than did leased housing. Even if the total cost of all modernization carried out in the 1970s is added to the operating expenses in the two conventional development ments, the average total cost per month, excluding capital payments, is only $103. And to extend the comparison to the newer turnkey units, the cost of turnkey family housing such as 1–15 was only slightly more than half the cost of leasing— though that comparison is improper, given the difference in age.

Few better examples can be found of the validity of the old adage "you get what you pay for and pay for what you get" than the leased-housing program. There are no bargains in housing. The facilities leased under section 23 were roughly comparable to the older conventional developments; the similarity was reflected in costs. Assuming leasing costs to be equivalent to the sum of operating expenses and annual contributions, leased housing cost more than the two oldest conventional developments in St. Louis, underscoring the importance of financing according to the long-run cost of housing and the enormous value of the lower financing charges that governmental ownership permits. Truly there are no bargains in housing, and all of them can be leased.

VII.

Conclusions and Implications

If public agencies are judged by the policies they generate and policies in turn are evaluated by reference to their human consequences, then the people of the United States have a monstrosity on their hands—blundering, incompetent, insensitive, expensive, and unable or unwilling to learn and improve. The thirty-five-year history of public housing in St. Louis suggests institutional arrangements for creating and administering public policy that are grossly inadequate to contemporary needs and a value system distorted to the point of being perverse. Obviously, arguments from the particular case must be treated with caution, though policy must also take care of the particular case. But the major difficulties encountered in St. Louis public housing appeared concurrently in the other larger metropolitan areas and on all the evidence available to me can be attributed to a common source. Moreover, the track record in other areas where communal problems are handled by the central administration is apparently little better. An informal check of performance in education, transportation, and health care suggests precisely the same shortcomings. Finally, local peculiarities may have accelerated or expanded the effects of policy weakness but did not cause it.

In the circumstances, the disaster in public housing is much more than a simple indicator of the quality of policies developed for public housing. Suitably hedged against overextended generalization, the St. Louis public housing program can provide, inter alia, a test of society's capacity to deal with such matters as providing essential services for the less fortunate and, by extension, providing any services for the community, including its defense. Given the degree to which the various elements in modern industrial society are intermeshed, the extent to which public action in quite diverse areas is shaped and channeled by a set of common institutional arrangements and values, it is reasonable to assume that major action programs are more likely to reflect those commonalities than to confront them with institutional or normative alternatives.

The public housing program developed in the 1930s and formalized in the Housing Act of 1937 was a New Deal response to the effects of private-sector failure—massive unemployment, disrupted trade, financial chaos, vast slums in the cities, and so on—and that may have contributed to its downfall. Operation of the established production and distribution system had over time created a supply of housing too expensive for the many while it created the many for whom decent housing was too expensive. The response, which was expected to have multiple payoffs for society, was public development, ownership, and operation of low-income housing. The government was forced to abandon the prevailing economic ideology in favor of public ownership because the latter, other things equal, was far cheaper than either direct cash payments to low income families or lease of privately owned facilities—publicly owned housing could be developed with capital raised at lower interest rates, it paid no taxes, and it required no return to the entrepreneur.

The basic program design was flawed seriously in ways that should have been apparent to the designers. First, it was a multipurpose measure, intended as a stimulus to the construction industry, a way of assisting the cities to clear slums, and a source of needed low-income housing. In operation, the program focused most heavily on production of physical facilities, often at the expense of both the quality and amount of housing-in-use provided for the target population. Second, the fiscal arrangements incorporated into the act were foreseeably lethal. The federal government agreed to meet the mortgage payments on public housing as they came due; all other expenses, including capital replacement as needed, were to be met from rental income. Moreover, local housing authorities were much more tightly restricted than private landlords with respect to both the amount of rent collected and the type of expenses paid. Rent was tied to the tenant's income; tenant income was limited by the congressional requirement that no family be admitted to public housing unless its income was at least 20 percent below the amount needed to purchase housing on the private market (calculated as five times the cost of rent). When family income rose to the prescribed level, the facilities had to be vacated. Beyond regular operating expenses, the local housing authority was required to pay all utility costs in the developments, to pay 10 percent of its rental income after utility payments to local government in lieu of taxes, and to limit reserves to no more than 50 percent of one year's rent—surplus earnings were used to meet mortgage payments. Since LHA expenses were a function of construction quality, management, and local economic conditions that the LHA could not control, a period of prolonged rising costs created an impossible situation for tenant and LHA alike. To meet rising costs, the LHA was forced to increase rents. Tenant income usually increased much more slowly than other wages and prices, hence rent increases tended to take an increasingly larger share of total tenant income. The LHA was forced by its own policies to gouge the tenant, often quite horrendously. If the cost pressure continued, LHA income was almost certain to fall behind as higher rents drove out the tenants able to seek cheaper (if inferior) housing on the private market. The problem was still further complicated by the third major weakness in the basic program, the absence of control over the quality of the design and construction of the physical facilities.

The design errors in the public housing program were predictably lethal if allowed to continued unchanged, particularly if the overall economy suffered from severe inflation, or even moderately rising prices. Given decent design and quality construction, such as the row housing produced in most cities during the early 1940s, relatively minor changes would have made a world of difference in the outcome. Had the LHAs been allowed to cumulate larger reserves, for example, the need for large-scale assistance with major repairs and capital replacement would have been greatly reduced. Relatively small operating subsidies would have limited rent increases and reduced pressure on the tenants (many of whom were paying as much as three-fourths of their income for rent by the late 1960s) thus eliminating one major source of tenant frustration and anger and destructiveness. Modest subsidies, coupled with better training and greater emphasis on the need for good management, would have improved local performance immeasurably. The most intractable of the problems facing the policymakers was maintaining quality control over design and construction in the face of the known tendency of major industries to provide their customers, public and private, with a product designed to maximize profits rather than durability or performance. It would not be difficult to improve on the use of cost-per-room limits as a quality control system, but even the most careful specifications of performance criteria involve some risk of product failure and cost overruns, as the defense and aerospace industries learned to their sorrow.

The fundamental weaknesses in the 1937 Housing Act were hidden by a variety of circumstances. The standard product of the construction industry in the early 1940s was sound and sturdy and lasted well. Fiscal weaknesses were obscured by the artificial prosperity brought about by the influx of overincome war workers who paid premium rents. Management problems were minimal in an era when the legal machinery heavily favored the landlord and the value system strongly pressured the public assistance recipient to take what was offered and be grateful. Whether from ignorance or inertia, the basic policies of 1937 were reproduced with virtually no change in the Housing Act of 1949. But by then the overincome tenants were gone, the housing industry had changed, and the public attitude toward collective assistance to the individual was altering steadily if slowly. Within a decade, the effects of inadequate quality control, suicidal fiscal policies, and weak management could be readily observed in every major city in the country.

Whether or not responding to crisis builds character, as sports buffs and others like to believe, careful study of a society's response to crisis provides invaluable information about the adequacy of its fundamental institutions. Between the late 1950s and the mid-1970s, the federal government and the LHAs struggled vainly with the public housing program. Ultimately, they failed and it was abandoned for private ownership. In that time period, the physical structures deteriorated beyond all recognition, partly out of poor design and construction and partly out of tenant vandalism and lack of concern for the developments. The public reputation of public housing was ruined almost beyond redemption. The LHAs became the largest slum landlords in the country, squeezing, from necessity, an ever-increasing portion of total income from their poverty-stricken tenants until protests and strikes finally led the federal government to limit the portion of income that could be charged for rent and thus opened the way for operating subsidies. By the 1970s, the working poor for whom the program was originally designed had long since departed; the conventional developments were serving as a residual depository for the permanent poor and for those dependent on public assistance; the newer turnkey housing was occupied primarily by the elderly. After 1970, federal spending for public housing operations soared under the impact of severe inflation and policy changes that forced operating subsidies for rising utility costs, added social services, and capital replacement in long-neglected and ravaged buildings. The federal government then abandoned public ownership, inaugurated a holding operation in existing developments, and turned back to the same private sector whose failure had been responsible for the program in the first instance. Guaranteed lease of privately owned facilities, either built specifically for the program or taken from existing stock, was substituted for public ownership. The response was ineffective, inadequate, and inexcusable. The best available analogy is to a physician starting out to perform a simple appendectomy, making a mistake at the beginning that was corrigible but lethal if not corrected; ignoring the mistake and inflicting yet more damage on the body in a series of futile and misdirected efforts to remove the appendix; then, after trying belatedly and at great cost to repair the original mistake, abandoning the operation in despair, leaving the patient to die under sedation—and going on to the next patient.

The conclusions and judgments that an examination of the institutional response to crisis in public housing tends to support very strongly are conveniently and usefully discussed under three major headings: first, the normative considerations that influenced the substance of policy as well as its applications; second, the cognitive aspects of the various activities that affected program operations; third, the relevant characteristics of the social and political institutions that most influenced program success or failure.

The Normative Dimension

It cannot be too strongly emphasized that the chief obstacle to a successful public housing program was normative, a matter of values and priorities. It is not a question of judging the extent to which the intent of the program designers was good or evil or the degree to which the tenants were virtuous and deserving. What needs restatement and underscoring is the very ancient precept that laws or policies must be supported by the customs, beliefs, and values embedded in the social fabric. *Quid leges sans mores?* still holds; laws unsupported by norms will fail. Regardless of technology, good will, rhetorical skill, or depth of conviction, policies that lack support in the fundamental priority structure of the society cannot succeed, particularly if they involve significant costs. Efforts to circumvent the need for basic agreement on norms make for tokenism and sham, for resistance and disobedience and, ultimately, for violent resistance. When the social institutions responsible for making policy must create programs out of an interplay of conflicting and competing interests, the results will necessarily reflect the inadequacies and inconsistencies that characterize society as a whole. Such factors limit the life expectancy and potential for accomplishment of any policy proposal. It is both futile and irresponsible to ask a public agency, whether a school, a police force, or a local housing authority, to solve a problem that society at large has not yet resolved in its fundamental norms.

In that context, the public housing program was a victim of society's inability or unwillingness to come to grips with the problem of dealing with the poor and the powerless. What is the nature and extent of the public obligation to the poor and unfortunate? Even at the rhetorical level, there is no common response to the question, and where the rhetoric favors assistance it is rarely consistent with practice. The very problem is elusive, for the poor can be differentiated by income and by race, by geography and by sex, by age and by source of income, and the basis for the differentiation tends to influence the accepted conception of the nature of the social obligation. To the late 1970s, actions taken to assist the poor have been token and palliative and not serious. There was little or no indication that the society, acting through its political apparatus, is any more prepared to shoulder the massive cost of producing an equitably ordered distribution system than it was forty years ago. Yet, without a serious commitment to meliorative and remedial expenditures of an unprecedented order, social welfare programs such as public housing will remain marginal at best and unlikely to produce a significant reduction in the amount of need within society.

The kind of tokenism that characterized public housing legislation has appeared in numerous other low-priority social programs. The absence of real and significant planning for our cities and regions is largely a recognition of the pointlessness of serious planning. That has opened the door to, and even positively reinforced, reliance on fads and slogans, the substitution of public relations campaigns for serious research, and the widespread practice of civic emulation—the effects parallel the "chain-letter" phenomenon in that the last entrants into the round robin lose most heavily, whether the fad in question is constructing convention centers in decaying cities, building tennis clubs in the suburbs, or acquiring more and more public housing. Tokenism produces the kind of apathy and cynicism that permit local entrepreneurs to switch their focus from servicing the poor (which provides opportunity for gain) to servicing the elderly poor (which provides opportunity for greater gain at less risk) without being subjected to criticism or nagged by conscience. In public housing, tokenism led directly to the conversion of conventional housing developments into Indian reservations for the terminally poor and maximally helpless families in society, administered by Indian agents and their tribal accomplices or by local entrepreneurs who saw opportunity in misery. Tokenism's influence can also be seen in the society's tendency to rely on self-taxation for provision of important social services, in the failure to make any serious assessment of need (the 1970 census, for example, contained only one question even vaguely relating to the health of the population—how many days of work had been missed for health reasons in the previous year?), and in the degree to which latent functions dominate social programs ostensibly aimed at the very poor.

The fundamental prerequisite to any serious effort to improve the lot of the poor is ethical agreement, acceptance of a common set of priorities and willingness to further them by collective action at cost. The absence of such agreement is the primary impediment to providing all of the population decent housing, adequate medical care, equitable education, and so on. Beyond the need for agreement on specific priorities is an even greater need for a reasonable and undogmatic approach to matters requiring collective action, for that is the base from which specific agreements must come. The importance of that point for the future is past exaggeration. A people who have been taught to channel their individualism into housing, transportation, clothing, and pointless ritual destruction of resources must somehow restructure and redirect their aspirations through less costly channels. While the price of achieving equitable distribution of social benefits seems likely to increase dramatically in the future, the cost of failure is likely to escalate even more quickly. And the hope that technological innovation might somehow provide cost-free and sacrifice-free solutions to the maldistribution problem has foundered on the hard rock of increased energy costs. We are slowly being forced to recognize that society is the most important of all social products and to realize that a society worth having cannot be had without major collective costs. An equal distribution of such costs is both unlikely and undesirable. While a reasoned approach to value questions will not alter the cost of equity and fairness, it can lead men to accept them in preference to the much higher costs associated with life in a society that is not prepared to pay its dues to the human race.

Cognitive Inadequacy

The second major contributor to the breakdown of the public

housing program was the failure of the cognitive apparatus employed in policymaking. Far more is involved than the known weakness of social science theory. Despite the long time span, enormous expenditures, immense piles of cumulated data, countless reports, and so on, there was very little improvement in design, construction, maintenance, management, tenant relations, and other fundamentals of public housing operations between the 1930s and the 1970s. Yet in many cases both the data needed for such improvements and the required theoretical structures were readily available to the federal government—or were even required by the formal reporting system.

Organization for learning is contingent on both a clear conception of what learning involves and awareness of the conditions necessary for learning to occur. The institutional arrangements that controlled policymaking, the traditional procedures used to handle certain classes of social problems, the focus of the reporting system, coupled with the vagueness and even outright misconception of the nature of the learning enterprise, all contributed to the failure to learn. Analytically, knowledge is simply organized human experience. It is produced and improved, serendipity aside, when an organized set of assumptions is taken to the environment and used as a base for purposeful action. The sets of assumptions we hold make up the patterns or theories that are the substance of knowledge and the objects of learning. They are generated by creative human actions whose logic defies formal specification; they are tested in action against specific purposes that are themselves sets of assumptions relating to the desirability of various alternative modes of human existence. Without a theory, action tests nothing; without a human purpose, no theory can be tested. Improvement of the human capacity to deal with the environment, whether the object involved is public housing, particle physics, or poultry raising, requires action based on theory in a known situation; the relation between outcome achieved and outcome expected (on the basis of the theory) provides the grounds for improvement.

The public housing program was handicapped from the outset, so far as learning is concerned, because it was a multipurpose program in which housing was not the primary goal. Without a clear purpose to be achieved, program performance could not be assessed, particularly since a single action might further one purpose while retarding another. Considered as a means of providing decent housing for low-income populations, for example, the Pruitt–Igoe complex in St. Louis was a disaster. But as a make-work program for the construction industry it was an outstanding success since it produced minimum facilities for least time at maximum cost.

Beyond the absence of clearly defined purpose, the public housing program was saddled with operating procedures that were in many cases inimical with learning or ruled it out altogether. The relative absence of dependable theory in social science and administration, for example, made it difficult for those in charge of public housing to place much confidence in specific proposals for improving operations, particularly in the 1960s when all manner of different remedies were tried unsuccessfully. What theoretical inadequacy justified the society did not get—careful experimenting, the only means available for avoiding repetitive errors due to ignorance or false assumptions. Yet the policy decisions coming from the central administration and the legislature seldom reflected an "experimental" outlook. Actions touted as "experiments" tended to be public relations efforts to gain support and approval for decisions already made; there is seldom any evidence of a serious effort to modify procedures according to the consequences of applying them. The few field experiments undertaken by the administration tended to be pure laboratory tests, separated quite deliberately from regular housing operations. But the results of brief tests of complex assumptions carried out in highly artificial situations are at best preliminary indicators that justify further testing. They do not substitute for the results of sustained action under regular operating conditions. And, in any case, most of the major policy changes introduced into public housing had the appearance of finished products plucked full blown from the brow of some bureaucratic Zeus. Unfortunately, the "paper world" of the federal bureaucrat is a poor source for either inspiration or evidence, and slogans or fads are poor raw material for a serious experimental station. And, since most innovations were introduced into the formal legislation immediately, they could hardly have been regarded as authorizations to experiment—commands are not usually interpreted as orders to try and learn. The normal practice, in short, was Darwinian, not experimental: innovations were tried and allowed to die, whereupon another set of innovations was introduced. Nature operates in this way, of course, but nature kills the individual without learning and thus changes the species—there is no learning by either individual or species. That may be satisfactory for oak trees, but men can do better.

Some of the specific operating practices that contributed to the failure to learn are common in most social agencies. No effort was made to inventory population needs and thus provide a baseline for measuring accomplishment and testing performance. There was no market research. Little effort was made to determine the causes of either failure or success, particularly the latter, which amounts to studying the person discriminated against to get at the causes of discrimination. Near total reliance on aggregate statistics literally ruled out reasoned action on local problems. At best, the data were broken down to the level of the individual housing authority, and that was much too gross for adequate policymaking. Little effort was made, either publicly or privately, to determine the variations within and among cities and to adjust policies accordingly. The overall procedure resembled medical diagnosis and treatment characterized by aggregation of the symptoms of large numbers of patients and prescription for the averages. Finally, excessive dependence on the budget for controlling operations and evaluating performance guaranteed failure in both areas. No budget, however based, is an adequate foundation for policymaking, notwithstanding the extent to which it is so used in government and the sanctification provided by the Brookings Institution studies. Taken in conjunction with a clear set of purposes and a good reporting system linked to those purposes, the budget is a valuable administrative tool; standing alone, it is almost worthless. The reason is simple: every large budget incorporates at some point a conceptual transformation from the lines used in consolidation to the specific purposes for which resources are spent at the operating level. That transformation creates a conceptual gap in the chain of reasoning connecting budget authorizations (based on the concepts used in the budget) and the results of expenditure. Since the results of change using one set of concepts cannot be transformed into changes or effects measured in the other set, the structure is almost worthless for policymaking or policy control.

Cognitive failure heightened dependence on myth, folklore, and declamation, thus reducing the influence of reasoned judgment and experiential evidence. The practical effect was an appalling absence of foresight with respect to the impact of specific policies. Thus, the Brooke amendment that limited tenant rent to 25 percent of income was certain to reduce LIIA income, but no provision was made for a replacement subsidy. The same amendment was also certain to lead to a reduction in many welfare payments, given the content of much state legislation, yet that effect too was overlooked or ignored and a second amendment had to be passed in the following year in order to prevent or cancel such reductions. The decision to abandon the use of high-rise buildings was justified by the use of a gross post hoc fallacy; because some developments that failed were of high-rise construction, excess height caused the failure. That reasoning ignored the high-rise apartments that remained in good condition and the row housing (such as Harbor View in San Francisco) that had gone the way of Pruitt and Igoe. Scatter-siting was recommended in the legislation of the 1970s without reservation, yet its impact on elderly tenants was foreseeably and testably undesirable—it resulted in more expensive and less readily available services, loss of companionship, more limited access to the outside community, and so on. And in this case, there were a great many natural-state experiments available to provide advance information, since many previously scattered tenants had been brought together into single developments and the effects of the concentration were easily examined. The sale of apartments to tenants was authorized and encouraged by statute without prior trial and continued despite substantial evidence of misdirected effort (to higher income families) and outright failure of purpose. National policy encouraged development of congregate dining facilities for the elderly with little concern for the impact on tenant expenses. Tenant management was authorized for St. Louis, expanded within a year, and then extended further to a $20 million national trial while its value in St. Louis remained unclear. The lease program began in 1965, expanded enormously to include construction for lease in disregard of congressional intent, and then became the central thrust of the whole public housing program without any serious evidence of workability, with clear evidence of increased cost, and with no provision for change if the "experiment" failed. A massive expansion of elderly housing was carried out without any preparation for the enevitable transition of tenants from public housing to the nursing home. In states such as Missouri that provided very low monthly payments to the elderly, it proved impossible to find nursing homes willing to accept elderly patients in need of care and equally impossible for the housing authorities to provide such care within the developments. The list of such cognitive aberrations could be extended almost indefinitely.

Perhaps the most important consequence of the cognitive inadequacy demonstrated by the policymaking institutions was the reassertion of a powerful ideological influence on the future development of the public housing program. Publicly owned low-income housing had been a reaction to private sector failure, one of the few attempts at public ownership in society. Like the Tennessee Valley Authority, it drew the wrath of the economic ideologues; their influence focused attention on public ownership, ignoring the real fiscal and other weaknesses. Under the prodding of the "free market" interests, Congress responded to the breakdown of conventional and turnkey housing by moving to reliance on the private sector— for development, management, and ultimately, ownership of facilities that were then leased by public agencies for use as low-income housing. Privatization of the program was an unwarranted and costly error. Leasing added significantly to cost because rent payments had to cover local taxes, higher interest on borrowed capital, and a profit to the entrepreneur in the rental price. Disregarding the higher costs, the assumption that privatization was justified because public ownership had been tried and found wanting was grossly mistaken. In very few cases indeed could it be said that public housing was given a fair and serious trial; in most places where it was given even half a chance to succeed, it performed extremely well over long periods of time. Condemnation without benefit of trial is a more apt description of the treatment given the original program. The procedure was roughly analogous to starving some poor animal to near death, restoring it to minimal health at great cost, then abandoning the animal to its fate, pointing to the expense incurred as justification.

The cost advantage of public ownership is beyond argument; assertions of superior efficiency in private operations are rarely documented, and in any case the gain in efficiency would be unlikely to offset the added cost. Governments can borrow much more cheaply than private developers and they can avoid federal, state, and local taxes as well as profit to developers and owners. The economist's practice of adding forgone taxes to the "real" cost of public housing is mere cant. The improved service to members of the community that public housing brings with it, which is the result expected from any payment to government, much outweighs the value of either hypothetical local property tax yields or decreased federal income tax returns. Of course, as the supply of public housing approaches the total need of the community, it is probably more efficient to under-build slightly and fill short-run needs by leasing, and that was the strength of the original argument favoring lease of existing facilities.

Some opponents of publicly owned housing accepted the evidence relating to costs but argued on other grounds that private operations necessarily lead to superior performance, hence private development and management should be instituted. But that mistakes the nature of the program, as the St. Louis experience shows very clearly. First, local housing authorities did not design or construct apartments; those activities were carried out by architects and construction firms in the private sector, hence the mistakes and inadequacies that characterized that dimension of the program should be charged to the private sector account. The St. Louis data suggest that the cost of facilities, the quality of the design and construction, and the subsequent performance of the facilities are largely independent of the method of development or the mode of ownership. Local housing authorities tend to get the current industry product just as the car buyer gets the current product of Detroit's factories. The poor quality and performance of some of the conventional developments were no more a simple function of public ownership than the poor performance and quality of some recent turnkey developments were a simple function of private development.

One good reason for developing low-income housing by public agencies rather than by private operators is the opportunity provided for experimentation with design and construction procedures. Although that opportunity has not been exploited fully in the past, the principle remains sound. When a public authority controls development and has the opportunity to learn and improve by repetition, mistakes can be opportunities for learning. When control over development changes with each new project, there can be no cumulation of experience and even common errors are likely to be "repeated." Why public housing seemed unable to take advantage of improvements in design and construction here and abroad remains a mystery. The Ontario Housing Corporation in Canada, for example, has a very good record with respect to design, construction, and maintenance of public facilities, and its knowledge is clearly relevant to parts of the United States. Other countries such as France, England, or the Scandinavian countries have also experimented widely with public housing. Yet the U.S. government seems to have made little effort to use that body of experience. Indeed, it failed even to take advantage of the manner in which motel design and construction were improved and standardized by large U.S. corporations, though such improvements could easily and profitably have been borrowed, perhaps especially for the development of housing for the elderly.

In principle, the use of private developers who then sell the finished product to public authority (turnkey housing) should improve the possibilities of obtaining better and cheaper sites. However, the results obtained in St. Louis were mixed and inconclusive. The older conventional developments were clustered together in cleared slum areas on the periphery of the downtown business district. Given that one major purpose of the program was to clear slums, that was not unreasonable. But the cost of clearing the land was high, even if the turnover tax imposed by the landowners is ignored, and the environment was poor at best and sometimes unspeakably bad. By comparison, the turnkey developments were scattered and site costs were usually lower. But the overall effect remains uncertain: some of the turnkey sites were very expensive, most of the neighborhoods in which they were located were every bit as unsavory as those around the conventional developments. While there may seem no good reason a local housing authority could not develop its apartments as effectively as any private entrepreneur, there are some quite good "political" reasons not to expect that outcome. A standard technique for rewarding political supporters is to provide them with inside information or preferential treatment that maximizes profits. Opposition to public housing is often so strong that a neighborhood will resist any effort to purchase a site for public housing, however attractive and innocuous the development to be constructed there. And, since it is not very likely that Congress will provide HUD or the local authorities with the authority to make site purchasing a meaningful way of leavening the racial or economic mix (though they have already demanded that outcome without supplying the needed authority or wherewithal), improvements in siting would probably have to evolve by the same process used to eliminate racial segregation—the Congress did nothing, the local authorities followed the congressional lead, the courts finally intervened to force a change in policy. Unfortunately, there is little reason to expect private developers to purchase sites in ways that will reduce either racial or economic segregation, and there are several reasons to expect the contrary. In sum, even if use of private developers *could* make for better and cheaper sites, that effect would not follow automatically and the constraints needed to force such outcomes from private developers would operate equally well with public ownership. If siting of public housing is to be used for either racial integration or economic integration, policies will have to be stated much more precisely than at present—given the congressional track record with respect to such questions, that is extremely unlikely.

Private management of public housing, like private ownership of leased facilities, necessarily involves greater costs than does public management, other things equal. A management fee that covers both the cost of personnel and the profit to the contractor must be higher than a fee for management alone, whatever the level of training and experience required of managers. The relative simplicity of the private management contract is attractive to local housing authorities because it avoids many of the problems associated with recruiting and training staff, developing operating procedures, and so on. Moreover, the housing managers then provide additional support for the authority's pleas for increased allowances for management. But the added cost may be far too high to be practicable. In St. Louis, experience with private management was quite mixed. Very good performance was obtained from the various religious organizations willing to accept managerial responsibility for the developments, particularly the buildings for the elderly. Good private management, however, was difficult to obtain and retain, largely because the fees allowed by HUD were very low ($7.21 per unit per month at the end of 1976, for example), particularly in the smaller developments (twenty or thirty units) where hiring a resident manager was not economical and even using a tenant as part-time supervisor would have been too expensive.

Moreover, even if the additional cost of commercial management was offset by an increase in LHA time available for other activities, the opportunity to use public housing as a training center for upgrading the skills of the low-income population would be lost. The use of public agencies such as the post office, the local housing authority, or even the military services as employers of the first instance for unskilled workers is perhaps the most practical channel available for bringing substantial numbers of currently dependent persons into productive employment and off the public rolls. Housing authorities require a range of work skills that are relatively easy to acquire and have high potential marketability in the private sector (painting, maintenance and repairs, electrical and plumbing work, and so on); they have exceptional potential in this area if trade-union restrictions can be lifted and adequate training can be made available. That potential is much more likely to be realized efficiently if the LHAs remain in control of their own daily operations. While centralized operations mean larger staffs, more administrative and housekeeping problems, and more attention to matters not traditionally regarded as part of housing management, that is presumably a challenge rather than an obstacle to be avoided. In any case, the long-run alternative is likely to be still more fragmentation of an already overfragmented social service sector.

Social and Political Institutions

The last of the major factors to have a negative effect on the development of public housing was the set of beliefs, attitudes, and assumptions about the nature and function of the political apparatus and its relations with other social institutions widely held within the society. The area has not been very adequately explored, and nothing more is attempted here than a brief summation of the more important influences on public housing; nevertheless, the range of inconsistencies, paradoxes, and perverse incentives involved is staggering. At a time when the only possible remedy for the condition of the underprivileged is governmental assistance, the accepted conception of the proper role of government effectively precludes its use for that purpose. That democratic government is sufficiently important to risk annihilation is asserted as a matter of faith, but it is also agreed explicitly that national government is necessarily incompetent and local government is powerless. That government must deal humanely with the unfortunate is taken as axiomatic, but the humane impulse has been used mainly as an excuse for raiding the public treasury. Compromise has been extolled as the greatest of public virtues without recognition that it is only a device for avoiding immediate resolution of fundamental disagreements about values. Compromise has virtue when applied to issues that could wreck the society, but it is a recipe for moral stagnation when applied to every issue in society. The government is forbidden participation in productive enterprise yet condemned when its enterprises are unproductive. The government is denounced for excessive expenditure, yet the population persists in treating federal resources as cost-free manna and regarding it proper for the federal treasury to serve as milch cow to the private sector.

What has been identified as the "horse" theory of government behavior is very powerfully supported by the experience with public housing. On the theory, the government, which is operated by horses, is concerned primarily with supplying its friends, who are also horses. Since direct payment from the treasury is considered improper and even illegal, some excuse must be sought for feeding the horses from the public granary. That excuse is provided by building. The principal justifications for building are the needs of "progress," wars, and the unfortunate in society—the "sparrows." "Progress" justifies feeding the horses who build roads and airports and ships and such, wars provide the heroes and occasions to which monuments may be constructed as well as the dangers against which society can be insured. The "sparrows," who must be fed, provide the justification for feeding the service-oriented horses. The grain is fed to the horses; the horses, in due course, feed the sparrows. Though there are many sparrows, the capacity of the horses is monumental, and they have developed an astonishing ability to pervert good intentions toward the sparrows into still more horse fodder. In general, social service programs aimed at feeding sparrows contain a built-in, latent function of feeding horses, and the ratio of horse feed and sparrow feed seems roughly proportionate to their respective weights. The "horse" theory accounts perfectly for public housing that was very poor in quality yet extraordinarily expensive to build, for policies that concentrated on producing housing rather than supplying housing-in-use of good quality, for financing through bonds rather than taxation, for the use of expensive union labor in maintenance and repairs, for the construction-for-lease program, and even for the policy of leasing apartments in inner-city areas where tenants could no longer be obtained privately on advantageous terms.

The second striking feature of social performance was the extent to which the various supporting institutions in society failed to provide the functional assistance the housing authority could presumably have expected. The police were unable to maintain order, or even patrol the area reasonably, and the authority was forced to hire private mercenaries for the task. The architects did as poorly as the police and were duly awarded certificates of merit from the architectural journals. The construction industry managed to achieve decreased efficiency and poorer quality products while increasing costs. The universities advised and studied and published reports, none of which had any significant positive impact on the conduct of housing operations. The business community at various times convened committees of notables to discuss the housing program's problems, but their principal accomplishment was to design new ways to spend federal dollars. Hordes of consultants, public and private, social and economic, tendered their services to the housing authorities, for a price; few had any beneficial effect on the program. The Legal Aid Society managed to complicate the problem of dealing with contumacious tenants to a point where the local housing authority stood virtually helpless if the tenant chose to attack. Other federal and local agencies concerned with public welfare, community development, manpower training, education, child abuse, health, and so on provided services to the authorities or their tenants with no visible positive effect. Even the organization of organizations, the National Association of Housing and Redevelopment Officials, did little of any significant value for either the tenants or the program as a whole. Considering the resources consumed and the identifiable benefits, the performance of the supporting institutions was at best marginal and at worst positively pernicious, little better than social vulturism.

Where To Go From Here?

As late as the mid-1950s, a relatively simple and inexpensive set of policy changes would have sufficed to place the public housing program on a sound footing. Quality control, a modest operating subsidy, better management, and perhaps an improved reporting system would have gone far toward creating a viable operation. By the mid-1970s, the problem had become much less tractable. The prime requirements, of course, are a firm commitment to supplying decent housing to some specifiable population and an appropriate inventory of that population to determine the extent of need. That would make possible a reasoned program for developing the needed amount of housing in the right sizes and locations. For the basic housing supply, conventional development, involving public ownership and operation, seems far preferable to leasing, though it would be desirable to build less than total need and lease enough space to handle short-run variations. However, simply building more conventional developments without adding qualitative improvements in design, construction, and operation, as the Housing Act of 1976 authorized on a small scale, is to invite further disaster. Some very basic policy changes are needed before such developments can be expected to succeed.

First, the overall performance of the housing industry will have to be improved, presumably by the use of both carrots and sticks. The change from conventional development to turnkey development had little effect on the quality of the product, particularly in housing intended for family use. By 1976, some of the new turnkey family housing was already well along the road trod earlier by Pruitt and Igoe and moving at about the same rate of speed. Caveat emptor, let the buyer beware, is not an appropriate base for the relations between housing authorities and developers; some form of consumer protection is very badly needed in governmental purchasing as well as in private consumption.

Analytically, careful research is needed into the relations between mode of construction, design, cost, and long-run performance of multifamily housing. Hopefully, some of the lessons learned from the design and construction of schools and other public facilities regularly exposed to heavy use can be applied to public housing. Again, other nations may have valuable information about the "do's and don'ts" of public housing that should be incorporated into housing policy. From the wealth of experience available, it should be possible to develop guidelines for designing and constructing housing that would do much to increase its efficiency in use. Such things as the use of plaster walls rather than wallboard in housing intended for family occupancy, fencing to preserve grassy areas, adequate holders for garbage cans, and so on may seem minor but can play a major role in preserving the physical environment and reducing maintenance costs. If such initial specifications could be supplied and both architect and builder were tied to their product by contract with penalty for a period of years after construction is completed, purchasing efficiency would be much improved. Failing a satisfactory solution to the problem of purchasing housing design and construction on the private market, it would probably be wise to consider forming public corporations for developing public facilities, perhaps combining them with needed job training or preliminary employment for those with modest skills in some aspect of construction.

Increased efficiency in construction is in some measure contingent on the control of labor union influence on design, construction, and operation of public housing. Union actions have increased costs, directly and indirectly, in all phases of development and operation and have reduced the government's capacity to assist with training of the unskilled. The agreement reached in St. Louis at the end of the 1969 rent strike is a good illustration of the benefits to be obtained by limiting the scope of union influence. Given the fundamental dependence of all labor unions on legal support (the strike has never been an effective union weapon against large-scale industry; without federal support most unions would be hard pressed just to maintain their bargaining position), the extent to which the construction unions have been able to usurp the distributive function with respect to certain classes of governmental resources is surprising, anomalous, and unnecessary.

Finally, the role that financial institutions have played in the development of public housing needs reexamination. Financing costs have been a major part of the total bill for public housing; the soaring cost of debt servicing is a major indication of the price of delayed investment in capital goods. A comparison of the cost of repayment per unit for buildings built in 1942 and those completed in the 1970s indicates the magnitudes—the newer units cost about three times as much as the older units, expressed in constant dollars. The Congress, for obvious reasons, prefers to borrow against future taxation rather than make capital payments from current income—borrowing feeds the horses and makes congressmen look thrifty in the short run. Assuming that inflationary pressures continue at a high level over a long period of time, deferred payment is the course of wisdom. But, under those conditions, capital investments should be as large as possible and should be made as soon as need is foreseen, since that would maximize the benefits of inflation. Congress tends to accept the initial premise, implicitly at least, but ignore the corollaries. While this attitude is not surprising given the congressional performance record and the various forces that operate in the political arena, it remains an exasperating reminder of the hidden costs of ignorance and inconsistency.

If design, construction, and fiscal policies can be corrected, a major decentralization of the public housing program will be needed to take advantage of those improvements. Until the late 1960s, the principal burden of housing program operations fell on the LHAs; the federal administration shouldered most of the remainder. Neither the state governments nor the HUD regional offices were very deeply involved with program operations. After 1965, the emphasis shifted steadily away from the LHA to the central administration, mainly as a result of legislative changes introduced by the Nixon administration. A whole layer of HUD local offices was created; an augmented role was provided for state housing agencies; a steady and significant decline in the authority and functions of the LHAs followed. The trend to centralization and development of a state administrative apparatus was apparently another by-product of the "horse" theory. A Republican national adminis-tration was unprepared to feed Democratic horses in the vari-ous cities and chose instead to supply grain to the cities through the states where some Republican horses survived. The trend has some ominous implications for public housing and indeed for social services in general.

While there is no simple answer to the centralization–decentralization question, a great deal of confusion can be eliminated by prior consideration of two points. First, the effect of centralization–decentralization on the tax-gathering func-tion should be separated from its effect on program administra-tion and policymaking. By and large, centralized taxation has been both more effective and more equitable than local taxa-tion, but that does not imply that the same benefits can be obtained in policymaking or administration through centrali-zation. Second, the federal budget is necessarily assumed to be an adequate instrument for congressional and executive policymaking, and that assumption is faulty. If policymaking requires a comparison of outcomes for corrigibility, then use of the budget for that purpose is a gross non sequitur. In the process of aggregating the budget, the link between changes in the line budget and effects in the field is broken, unavoidably and irreparably. Programs can be changed, certainly, by budget alterations, but they cannot be improved systemati-cally through that instrument.

A significant attempt to supply the poor with decent housing at least cost will almost certainly require public ownership of the facilities. For that to occur, some local agency will be required to generate an inventory of needs, plan ways of meet-ing those needs efficiently, develop the facilities required, and operate them over time. Of the various candidates for the job, only the local housing authorities have the legal status and performance potential required. While the past performance of the LHAs has not always been impressive, that has been due mainly to the inadequacy of national policy rather than to local incompetence or venality. Given adequate resources, some managerial assistance, and proper supervision, they are quite an adequate institutional arrangement for the task they have been assigned.

There is an even more important reason for allowing local housing authorities genuine freedom of action and choice, including enough resources to enable them to both define their own task and develop the means for accomplishing it. The tokenism that has characterized public housing over the years has obscured the function that local agencies perform in national programs. At no time in history has the federal government examined the public housing program in reasoned terms, that is, tried to determine the amount and type of housing required and then chart a course of action that would supply it at optimal cost in least time. Instead, HUD and its predecessors served as a distributing agency for resources known to be inadequate. A distribution formula for inadequate resources is a very long way from serious planning and the kinds of projections it demands; the kinds of policies HUD has produced are a travesty of those needed to do the job seriously and efficiently.

The point is that where very large scale operations such as public housing are concerned, central administrative agencies *cannot* perform the planning function. Planning must be done at the point of contact between agency and client. The relation is more easily seen in a medical context where diagnostic activity is clearly tied to the single patient and development of plans for an adequate medical facility is obviously a local matter. There is no "central" medical facility; they are all local, just as all public housing is local. Even if it were possible to determine in advance the information that centralized planning requires (which it is not) and even if a suitable processing system were devised, the cost would be prohibitive and the margin of avoidable error would be too large. Centralized planning is the domestic analog to overseas assistance programs in which American nationals try to think themselves inside the skulls of foreign nationals (which is impossible) in order to solve the foreign nationals' problems instead of providing the foreign nationals with the skills they need to solve their own problems using the information already inside their respective skulls. That does not imply that a national plan for public housing is simply a bundle of local laundry lists aggregated by HUD and forwarded to Congress. There is plenty of specialized work for both levels of administration; each needs its own plans and each must make its own plans. But in the absence of an informed, independent, and reasonably competent local administrative unit to serve as planner, instigator, data gatherer, and evaluator and improver of policy, the task is impossible. In that context, dilution of the authority and function of the LHA is a cause for serious concern, whether the reason for the dilution is encroachment by state or federal agencies or simply excessive decentralization within a local housing authority brought about by excessive reliance on contract management and other specialized services.

Obviously, there are risks associated with local autonomy in a national program. Autonomy is the obverse of control; its best measure is the extent to which an agent can transform resources into goods and services of his own specification. The more narrowly circumscribed the range of choices open to the agent, the less autonomy he enjoys and the less he can contribute to the overall operation. The extreme autonomy of the blank check or even a check in which only the bottom-line figure has been written in is neither needed nor desirable. But freedom of action consonant with the scope and nature of the tasks to be performed is essential. Granting autonomy cannot guarantee that it will be used, let alone used productively or creatively; the danger from abuse increases with the level of autonomy and the size of the resource allocation. Given the past actions attributed to the LHAs and the low level of local competence that the failure of conventional housing is usually taken to imply, it is not surprising that the national administration tends to restrict local option to the minimum. But the costs of mistrust are in this case too high, so high that a test of the costs of increased trust is essential. Assuming a genuine desire for accomplishment, and the need for planning that implies, there is really no option to local autonomy, and it seems far better to grant freedom of action willingly and knowingly and then arrange to audit the results closely enough to prevent utter catastrophe. Since it is unlikely that any future housing catastrophe could equal what occurred with the generation of housing developed during the 1950s, it should not be too difficult to develop a set of early warning signals from prior experience.

Finally, local autonomy should be supplemented with appropriate local arrangements for integrating the various federal, state, and local activities that impinge upon common populations. To consider the "housing" problem in isolation from employment and income, education, transportation, and so on is to destine the program for failure. The challenge is to find means of avoiding the loss of yet one more generation of the poor and helpless, whether they are black or white, members of a minority or ethnic group, natives or migrants. Since the mid-1960s, the functions of public housing have expanded greatly. The early emphasis on providing housing services, very narrowly construed, gave way to a "social service" approach to public housing that brought together a number of agencies servicing the same clients. In the absence of integrating machinery for linking their activities to the wider community and to the work of other agencies, and faced with definite statutory requirements for the performance of certain services, the LHAs have tried to develop and expand their own program to include these services. But most LHAs do not command the kinds of trained and experienced staff needed for job training, personal advice, medical assistance, work orientation, and so on. And in many cases the tenant population is not large enough to justify creation of a single staff able to carry out these diverse functions. Even if the staffing problem could be solved, it would be improper to treat the residents of public housing as a special subclass of the poor entitled to preferential treatment and special facilities by virtue of place of residence alone—the effect is simply an unauthorized additional subsidy. In terms of efficiency and fairness, services should be distributed equitably with respect to the total population.

The need to develop local integrating machinery is clear enough; the type of institutional arrangements required to deal with the present mixture of agencies concerned with the low-income population is uncertain. It is not an easy question at best, for it involves agencies from every level of government as well as a range of private organizations, some deriving their livelihood from servicing the poor. The history of past accomplishments by coordinating bodies is unimpressive; there is little likelihood that a single, overarching agency could be created to subsume all others presently operating. But it is reasonably certain that a governmental agency is needed rather than an ad hoc or private organization, that its jurisdiction should be defined in terms of an eligible population rather than existing political divisions, and that it should have genuine capacity to force action by specific agencies regardless of their sponsors—otherwise, it would speedily become a mere facilitator subject to control by competing interests. Such generalities aside, the data suggest the need but provide few clues to a solution. If social services continue to expand, as seems likely, and the public housing program remains in operation, then the effort to bring dependent populations into the productive mainstream of society will require coordinating machinery quite unlike anything presently available. Otherwise, society can expect to pay an even heavier price for overlapping, replication, exploitation by special interests, and even counterproductive actions by agencies ostensibly pursuing parallel goals with respect to a common population.

It is relatively easy to suggest the kinds of improvements in policy that are required for public housing; how to make those requirements either administratively possible or politically palatable is a much more difficult matter. The question, What's wrong with present policy? is quite different from the question, What's wrong with the way we make policies? or How do we account for what's wrong with present policy? The answer to those questions lies in the administrative–legislative nexus, a region that is virtually opaque so far as the external inquirer is concerned. What data flow through which hands in the national administration and what effect do they have? How is the Congress affected by various types of reporting? How might certain kinds of changes in policy be brought about? A study of the consequences of applying specific policies to a real situation can demonstrate that something is very wrong, given the stated purpose of the policymakers, and can suggest means of achieving the purpose more efficiently. It cannot, however, suggest ways of obtaining the changes required. That takes further study, focused on the national policymaking apparatus and concerned with the reasons policies take their present form and how they might be altered. I do not believe such questions can usefully be answered in general terms; they require knowledge of the particular consequences of applying a policy to a specified situation. In that sense, the present study is a baseline for further inquiry.

*   *   *   *   *

Anyone unfamiliar with the operation of such programs as public housing may have found the tone of the study extreme and perhaps overly pessimistic. The validity of a pessimistic outlook is a matter of evidence. The danger, however, is that the reader may infer that those involved with operations should be characterized in the same way, that monstrous results indicate a population of monsters. Nothing could be further from fact. Most of the people in public housing are decent and well-intentioned, committed to the program, and doing their best to make it work. The fault lies in the program design and not with them. The lesson, however, remains melancholy: Decency and good intentions are not enough!

Table 1 Development Costs

Project	Date	Number of units	Total cost per unit	Total cost per unit deflated²	Site cost per unit	Site cost per unit deflated	Construction cost per unit	Construction cost per unit deflated	Type tenant	Rooms per unit	Cost per room	Cost per room deflated	Construction cost per room	Construction cost per room deflated	Equipment cost per unit	Equipment cost per unit deflated	Site cost per room deflated
1-1	1942	658	5,368	14,911	1,320	3,667	4,115	11,431	Fam	4.5	1,253	3,481	960	2,667	191	531	833
1-2	1942	657	5,277	14,658	1,367	3,798	4,065	11,292	Fam	4.5	1,167	3,242	899	2,497	190	531	844
1-3	1953	704	13,081	20,187	1,608	2,007	11,202	17,287	Fam	4.9	2,665	3,327	2,282	2,849	240	300	410
1-4	1955	1,736	14,057	20,255	1,991	2,486	12,293	17,713	Fam	4.8	2,392	3,460	2,564	3,201	227	283	518
1-5	1956	1,134	15,049	21,647	2,292	2,837	12,911	17,495	Fam	4.8	3,122	3,864	2,678	3,314	258	319	591
1-6	1957	656	14,306	19,019	2,707	3,238	10,835	15,133	Fam	4.7	3,067	3,649	2,323	2,779	219	262	689
1-6A	1963	112	19,716	22,688	4,458	4,904	15,014	17,277	Eld	3.8	5,258	5,734	4,004	4,405	253	278	1,291
1-7	1956	656	13,636	19,045	2,936	3,634	10,592	14,793	Fam	4.7	2,923	3,618	2,271	2,811	176	194	773
1-7A	1961	580	15,894	19,219	2,197	2,469	12,325	14,093	Mix	4.4	3,587	4,030	2,782	3,126	218	270	561
1-9	1968	1,162	19,877	19,112	4,642	4,463	15,737	15,132	Mix	4.4	4,508	4,335	3,569	3,432	221	248	1,014
1-10	1970	155	17,969	14,941	1,736	1,452	16,604	13,883	Eld	3.2	5,638	4,714	5,210	4,356	277	266	454
1-11	1966	15	15,764	13,181	1,589	1,329	10,155	8,491	Fam	5.5	2,866	2,396	1,846	1,543	75	63	242
1-13	1969	222	19,039	15,919	3,029	2,356	16,285	13,616	Mix	4.3	4,398	3,677	3,762	3,145	264	221	589
1-15	1971	36	18,904	15,806	2,818	2,533	17,311	14,474	Fam	6.1	3,108	2,599	2,846	2,380	304	254	386
1-16	1972	34	19,086	16,195	2,962	2,422	17,817	14,568	Eld	6.1	3,253	2,650	2,926	2,392	288	241	397
1-17	1971	128	17,502	14,311	2,052	1,678	15,644	12,791	Eld	3.2	5,411	4,424	4,837	3,955	232	190	524
1-18	1971	147	18,252	15,261	2,158	1,864	17,194	14,376	Eld	3.2	5,697	4,763	5,366	4,487	232	190	564
1-19	1973	397	17,896	13,841	1,606	1,242	16,316	12,619	Eld	3.1	5,720	4,424	5,215	4,033	296	247	401
1-20	1973	201	18,307	14,159	135	104	17,109	13,232	Eld	3.1	5,892	4,557	5,507	4,259	197	152	34
1-21	1972	18	22,541	18,431	3,380	2,764	20,838	17,038	Fam	6.1	3,722	3,043	3,441	2,814	341	264	453
1-22	1971	32	16,808	13,743	2,547	1,919	14,917	12,197	Eld	3.2	5,273	4,512	4,680	3,827	258	211	600
1-23	1971	28	16,614	13,891	2,334	1,952	15,177	12,690	Eld	3.2	5,109	4,572	4,722	3,948	213	174	610
1-24	1973	124	19,262	13,546	65	42	19,015	13,372	Mix	3.8	5,087	3,577	5,022	3,532	295	247	12
1-28	1974	100	17,804	12,520	80	56	17,506	12,311	Eld	3.2	5,495	3,864	5,403	3,800	245	172	18
1-29	1971	45	25,508	20,857	2,548	2,083	24,219	19,083	Fam	6.3	4,063	3,322	3,858	3,155	309	253	331
U.S. Average for 1967			17,038			2,858		11,917		4.3		3,362		2,771		664	

1. Total costs are given for the most recent year. Since they change from year to year for accounting changes, the total may be either slightly more or slightly less than the sum of site and construction costs.

2. In 1967 dollars.

Table 2 Operating Expenses: 1968–1975 (PUM)

Date	Rent PUM[1]	Rent Defl[2]	Adm PUM	Adm Defl	Util PUM	Util Defl	Ord Main PUM	Ord Main Defl	Tot Exp PUM	Tot Exp Defl	Subsidy PUM	Subsidy Defl
1-1												
1968	55.36	53.23	7.76	7.46	19.23	18.49	16.90	16.25	66.31	63.76	4.43	4.26
1969	60.10	55.04	7.38	6.76	19.66	18.00	16.30	14.92	52.50	48.08	8.08	7.40
1970	43.25	37.55	6.27	5.44	22.16	19.24	14.46	12.56	49.30	42.80	19.46	16.89
1971	40.56	33.91	7.20	6.02	23.49	19.64	17.74	14.83	59.43	49.69	23.50	19.65
1972	40.21	32.88	7.98	6.52	25.18	20.59	15.94	13.04	68.84	56.29	19.67	16.08
1973	40.34	31.20	8.71	6.73	27.10	20.96	19.49	15.07	77.06	59.70	11.26	8.71
1974	44.74	31.47	9.69	6.81	31.59	22.22	23.86	16.78	84.22	59.20	24.83	17.46
1975	51.12	32.56	9.91	6.31	44.95	28.63	21.95	13.98	95.08	60.56	39.85	25.38
1976[3]	52.95	31.14	11.70	6.88	55.23	32.49	22.04	12.96	121.27	71.34	66.08	38.87
1-2												
1968	56.55	54.37	7.52	7.23	16.06	15.44	23.05	22.16	69.88	67.19	3.33	3.21
1969	62.18	56.94	7.89	7.23	16.93	15.50	19.88	18.21	51.72	47.36	6.35	5.82
1970	44.96	39.02	6.20	5.38	19.19	16.66	14.19	12.32	46.76	40.59	19.58	17.00
1971	41.34	34.57	6.26	5.24	20.73	17.33	19.65	16.43	58.09	48.57	19.51	16.31
1972	39.72	32.48	7.95	6.50	22.66	18.53	18.08	14.78	64.67	52.88	17.93	14.66
1973	40.73	31.50	8.26	6.39	24.45	18.91	22.24	17.20	70.87	54.81	11.03	8.53
1974	42.12	29.62	13.23	9.30	26.25	18.46	25.44	17.89	87.15	61.29	27.86	19.59
1975	46.90	29.88	10.49	6.68	33.57	21.38	23.91	15.23	88.33	56.26	36.91	23.51
1976	49.26	29.98	11.62	6.83	50.94	29.97	23.24	13.67	129.90	76.41	59.98	35.28
1-3												
1968	55.31	53.18	7.84	7.54	16.57	15.94	26.69	25.67	60.02	57.71	1.68	1.61
1969	55.12	50.48	8.22	7.53	19.50	17.86	27.85	25.50	63.07	57.76	6.90	6.32
1970	31.69	27.51	6.74	5.85	21.05	18.28	22.37	19.42	64.43	55.93	18.56	16.11
1971	32.72	27.36	9.15	7.65	24.00	20.07	38.83	32.47	97.34	81.39	69.92	58.46
1972	33.77	27.61	10.63	8.70	25.84	21.13	37.17	30.39	105.78	86.49	54.67	44.70
1973	34.69	26.83	10.75	8.32	30.11	23.29	44.67	34.55	118.53	91.67	26.67	20.62
1974	33.68	23.68	15.59	10.96	44.31	31.36	54.52	38.34	138.13	97.14	67.96	47.79
1975	36.57	23.29	14.83	9.45	56.83	36.20	41.43	26.39	139.75	89.01	96.32	61.35
1976	38.65	22.73	16.73	9.84	62.43	36.73	41.57	24.45	155.66	91.56	123.51	72.66

Date	Rent PUM[1]	Rent Defl[2]	Adm PUM	Adm Defl	Util PUM	Util Defl	Ord Main PUM	Ord Main Defl	Tot Exp PUM	Tot Exp Defl	Subsidy PUM	Subsidy Defl
1-6												
1968	51.50	49.52	8.00	7.69	17.12	16.46	23.35	22.46	57.45	55.24	3.52	3.39
1969	53.54	49.03	7.54	6.90	17.95	16.44	23.42	21.45	56.13	51.40	7.74	7.08
1970	30.75	26.70	6.28	5.45	17.16	14.90	17.21	14.94	52.15	45.27	19.52	16.94
1971	25.93	21.68	7.16	5.99	21.56	18.02	26.45	22.12	64.90	54.26	46.34	38.75
1972	24.78	20.26	8.39	6.87	23.82	19.48	22.20	18.15	74.84	61.20	35.93	29.38
1973	25.82	19.97	8.99	6.96	26.22	20.28	26.72	20.66	87.57	67.72	19.45	15.05
1974	32.46	22.83	12.70	8.93	31.17	21.92	39.48	27.76	102.51	72.09	46.35	32.60
1975	37.27	23.74	13.47	8.58	37.71	24.02	39.14	24.93	112.59	71.08	65.27	41.57
1976	38.68	22.76	14.88	8.75	52.20	30.71	44.71	26.30	159.59	93.88	103.42	60.84
1-7												
1968	48.23	46.38	7.69	7.39	14.40	13.85	22.34	21.48	53.28	51.23	3.68	3.54
1969	47.25	43.27	7.99	7.32	14.53	13.31	21.31	19.51	50.73	46.46	6.37	5.83
1970	28.78	24.98	6.31	5.47	15.67	13.60	15.29	13.28	45.04	39.10	18.04	15.66
1971	25.77	21.54	6.41	5.36	19.25	16.09	22.57	18.87	63.27	52.90	40.28	33.68
1972	24.31	19.88	8.50	6.95	21.01	17.18	23.04	18.84	69.64	56.94	32.33	26.44
1973	24.26	18.76	9.71	7.51	24.35	18.83	29.19	22.58	87.25	67.48	20.08	15.53
1974	30.80	18.66	12.88	9.06	33.05	23.24	37.84	26.61	110.67	77.83	52.01	36.58
1975	34.25	21.81	16.12	10.27	42.95	27.35	38.56	24.56	127.08	87.31	97.25	61.94
1976[3]	36.29	21.35	16.12	9.48	65.86	38.74	39.54	23.26	158.15	93.03	120.83	71.08
1-9												
1969	65.46	59.94	7.06	6.47	14.55	13.32	8.45	7.74	54.93	31.99	1.51	1.38
1970	51.64	44.82	5.62	4.88	16.15	14.02	8.83	7.67	55.19	30.55	19.60	17.02
1971	48.64	40.67	6.55	5.47	17.15	14.34	15.53	12.98	61.59	43.13	6.47	5.41
1972	47.88	39.15	8.41	6.88	18.83	15.40	16.24	13.28	61.16	50.01	11.84	9.68
1973	49.70	38.44	7.59	5.87	20.56	15.90	23.22	17.96	69.79	53.98	5.44	4.21
1974	53.45	37.59	12.26	8.62	22.09	15.53	22.26	15.65	74.03	52.06	5.38	3.78
1975	53.99	34.39	11.98	7.63	28.01	17.84	19.64	12.51	73.59	46.87	14.17	9.02
1976[3]	54.90	32.30	13.18	7.75	33.70	19.82	21.49	12.64	91.50	53.83		

1. PUM means per unit *available* and varies; averaged from end of month figures.
2. In 1967 dollars.
3. Estimated from 31 March 1976 data.

Table 3 Income and Expenses: Turnkey (PUM)

Project/ fiscal year	Rent	Administrative costs	Utility costs	Ordinary maintenance	Total expenses	Subsidy	Residents
1–10							
1972	38.57	6.99	18.09	15.01	43.09	9,082	3,111
1973	42.16	7.57	20.01	18.36	49.55	3,723	(4,668)
1974	48.27	13.61	20.16	13.91	52.00		30,209
1975	51.05	13.50	25.30	16.59	60.67	26,722	56,174
1–11							
1972	60.88	7.31	8.49	19.43	47.72		25,048
1973	62.56	8.94	9.57	17.49	48.74		31,156
1974	63.22	6.67	10.04	14.06	45.99		39,751
1975	63.06	12.19	16.13	25.43	67.57	1,373	42,619
1–13B							
1972	39.82	7.95	17.33	18.11	49.85		9,772
1973	41.43	6.54	20.71	15.53	46.20	19,780	6,121
1974	46.91	10.67	21.13	9.46	45.74	1,775	43,355
1975	49.64	12.59	26.18	18.76	66.50	22,096	40,324
1–15							
1972	79.29	9.81	33.71	10.99	59.72		9,508
1973	84.72	7.39	43.09	22.68	78.69		13,664
1974	102.36	13.45	40.84	13.21	74.47		36,666
1975	103.68	12.89	54.81	26.27	110.71	2,366	39,336
1–16							
1973	85.53	8.05	37.55	17.75	69.40		12,356
1974	95.45	13.75	38.92	15.76	75.10		31,990
1975	92.94	13.08	49.40	16.43	85.50	4,472	42,812
1–17							
1973	48.44	7.72	22.70	21.86	57.57	17,495	19,916
1974	53.14	14.76	24.26	15.61	59.96	14,177	60,378
1975	56.26	13.48	30.80	16.56	71.79	18,920	52,100
1–18							
1972	36.84	7.09	16.91	12.82	40.02	6,330	3,456
1973	39.06	7.29	18.88	20.20	49.79	5,048	(5,673)
1974	42.47	13.43	20.57	15.99	53.73		14,969
1975	47.36	12.91	25.77	17.17	61.08	31,900	26,519
1–19							
1974	59.30	14.08	16.56	10.08	45.37		180,381
1975	58.56	13.36	19.46	13.51	52.67		166,388
1–20							
1975	50.84	16.83	20.30	23.26	66.95	28,030	(1,925)
1–21							
1973	90.78	7.92	34.20	14.94	63.13		10,183
1974	106.28	7.16	36.57	14.81	65.00		25,318
1975	97.12	9.25	45.43	30.46	94.85		16,614
1–22							
1973	44.23	6.82	21.59	11.64	44.08	5,499	7,294
1974	49.84	13.14	20.96	10.07	48.04	3,233	20,137
1975	51.59	12.57	27.61	11.68	56.59		10,997
1–23							
1972	42.95	9.69	14.29	4.44	32.87		5,367
1973	44.97	9.99	15.26	11.57	40.74	2,110	10,101
1974	47.21	13.75	16.29	10.68	44.78		17,325
1975	50.33	12.98	20.10	11.91	50.64		20,081
1–24							
1975	70.52	13.09	33.67	16.42	68.69		7,033
1–28							
1975	72.33	14.89	28.31	10.79	58.88		17,095
1–29							
1973	82.66	7.38	41.74	11.90	66.54	1,163	20,748
1974	93.03	11.76	44.01	9.99	71.12		51,950
1975	91.14	12.20	50.20	27.23	101.09		17,434
U.S. average for 1974	45.27	11.52	19.52	22.87 Routine	70.23 60.23	25.42	

Selected Bibliography

Major Works

Aaron, Henry J. *Shelter and Subsidies: Who Benefits from Federal Housing Policies?* Washington, D.C.: Brookings Institution, 1972.

Bingham, Richard D. *Public Housing and Urban Renewal: An Analysis of Federal–local Relations.* New York: Praeger, 1975.

Burchell, Robert W.; Hughes, James W.; and Sternlieb, George. *Housing Costs and Housing Restraints.* New Brunswick, N.J.: Center for Urban Social Science Research, Rutgers University, 1970.

Committee for Economic Development. *Financing the Nation's Housing Needs.* New York: Committee for Economic Development, 1973.

de Leeuw, Frank, assisted by Eleanor Littman Jarutis. *Operating Costs in Public Housing: A Financial Crisis.* Washington, D.C.: Urban Institute, 1970.

de Leeuw, Frank, assisted by Sue A. Marshall. *Operating Expenses in Public Housing, 1968–71.* Washington, D.C.: Urban Institute, 1973.

de Leeuw, Frank, and Leaman, Sam H. *The Section 23 Leasing Program: Progress Report.* Washington, D.C.: Urban Institute, 1971.

Downs, Anthony. *Opening Up the Suburbs: An Urban Strategy for America.* New Haven, Conn.: Yale, 1973.

Dubman, Sue. *Poverty in St. Louis.* St. Louis: Center for Metropolitan Studies, University of Missouri–St. Louis, 1973.

Edson, Charles L. *1975 Supplement to the Leased Housing Primer.* 2d ed. Washington, D.C.: National Leased Housing Association, 1975.

———. *A Section 23 Primer.* Washington, D.C.: Section 23 Leased Housing Association, 1973.

Fisher, Ernest M. *Housing Markets and Congressional Goals.* New York: Praeger, 1975.

Fisher, Robert M. *Twenty Years of Public Housing: Economic Aspects of the Federal Program.* New York: Harper, 1959.

Flaum, Thea K., and Salzman, Elizabeth C. *The Tenant's Rights Movement.* Chicago: Urban Research Corporation, 1969.

Freedman, Leonard. *Public Housing: The Politics of Poverty.* New York: Holt, Rinehart, and Winston, 1969.

Fried, Joseph P. *Housing Crisis USA.* New York: Praeger, 1971.

Frieden, Bernard J.; Solomon, Arthur P.; et al. *The Nation's Housing: 1975 to 1978.* Cambridge, Mass.: Harvard–MIT Joint Center for Urban Studies, 1977.

Friedman, Lawrence M. *Government and Slum Housing: A Century of Frustration.* Chicago: Rand McNally, 1968.

Fuerst, J. S., ed. *Public Housing in Europe and America.* New York: Wiley, 1974.

Hartman, Chester W. *Housing and Social Policy.* Englewood Cliffs, N.J.: Prentice-Hall, 1975.

Isler, Morton L.; Sadacca, Robert; and Drury, Margaret. *Keys to Successful Housing Management.* Washington, D.C.: Urban Institute, 1974.

Keith, Nathaniel Schnieder. *Politics and the Housing Crisis Since 1930.* New York: Universe Books, 1973.

Leaman, Sam H. *The Leased Housing Program: A Statistical Review.* Washington, D.C.: Urban Institute, 1971.

Malozemoff, Irene K.; Anderson, John G.; and Rosenbaum, Lidia V. *Housing for the Elderly: Evaluation of the Effectiveness of Congregate Residences*. Boulder: Westview Press, 1978.

Mandelker, Daniel R. *Housing Subsidies in the United States and England*. Indianapolis: Bobbs-Merrill, 1973.

Meehan, Eugene J. *The Foundations of Political Analysis: Empirical and Normative*. Homewood, Ill.: Dorsey Press, 1971.

————. *Public Housing Policy: Myth Versus Reality*. New Brunswick, N.J.: Center for Urban Policy Research, Rutgers University, 1975.

Mendelson, Robert E., and Quinn, Michael A., eds. *The Politics of Housing in Older Urban Areas*. New York: Praeger, 1976.

Moore, William. *The Vertical Ghetto*. New York: Random House, 1969.

Muth, Richard F. *Public Housing: An Economic Evaluation*. American Enterprise Institute for Public Policy Research, 1973.

National Committee on Urban Problems. *Rebuilding the American City*. Washington, D.C., 1969.

Newman, Oscar. *Defensible Space: Crime Prevention Through Urban Design*. New York: Macmillan, 1972.

Prescott, James R. *Economic Aspects of Public Housing*. Beverly Hills: Sage, 1974.

Pynoos, Jon; Schafer, Robert; and Hartman, Chester W., eds. *Housing Urban America*. Chicago: Aldine, 1973.

Rabushka, Alvin, and Weissert, William G. *Caseworkers or Police: How Tenants See Public Housing*. Stanford: Hoover Institution, 1977.

Rainwater, Lee. *Behind Ghetto Walls: Black Family Life in a Federal Slum*. Chicago: Aldine, 1970.

Real Estate Research Corporation. *Federal Housing Subsidies: How Are They Working?* Written by Anthony Downs. Lexington, Mass.: Lexington Books, 1973.

Reeb, Donald J., and Kirk, James T., Jr., eds. *Housing the Poor*. New York: Praeger, 1973.

Rydell, C. Peter. *Factors Affecting Maintenance and Operating Costs in Federal Housing Projects*. Santa Monica, Calif.: The New York Rand Institute, 1970.

Sadacca, Robert; Isler, Morton; and DeWitt, Joan. *The Development of a Prototype Equation for Public Housing Operating Expenses*. Washington, D.C.: Urban Institute, 1975.

Sadacca, Robert; Louz, Suzanne B.; Isler, Morton L.; and Drury, Margaret J. *Management Performance in Public Housing*. Washington, D.C.: Urban Institute, 1974.

Scobie, Richard S. *Problem Tenants in Public Housing: Who, Where, and Why Are They?* New York: Praeger, 1975.

Solomon, Arthur P. *Housing the Urban Poor: A Critical Evaluation of Federal Housing Policy*. Cambridge, Mass.: MIT Press, 1974.

Steiner, Gilbert Y. *The State of Welfare*. Washington, D.C.: Brookings Institution, 1971.

Sternlieb, George, and Indik, Bernard P. *The Ecology of Welfare: Housing and the Welfare Crisis in New York City*. Brunswick, N.J.: Transaction Books, 1973.

Sternlieb, George, and Sagalyn, Lynne B., eds. *Housing: 1970–1971*. New York: AMS Press, 1972.

Sternlieb, George, with Paulus, Virginia, eds. *Housing: 1971–1972*. New York: AMS Press, 1974.

Sweet, Morris L. *Mandatory Housing Finance Programs: A Comparative International Analysis*. New York: Praeger, 1976.

Taggert, Robert, III. *Low Income Housing: A Critique of Federal Aid*. Baltimore: Johns Hopkins University Press, 1970.

Urban Institute. *The Development of a Prototype Equation for Public Housing Operating Expenses*. A working paper. Washington, D.C.: Urban Institute, 1973.

U.S., Congress, House, Committee on Banking and Currency, Subcommittee on Housing. *Compilation of the Housing and Community Development Act of 1974*. Public law 93–383. 93d Cong., 2d sess., October 1974. Washington, D.C.: U.S. Government Printing Office.

U.S., General Accounting Office. *Leased Housing Program Needs Improvements in Management and Operations*. Report to the Congress by the Comptroller General of the United States. RED–75–380, 11 July 1975. Washington, D.C.: U.S. General Accounting Office, 1975.

U.S., President's Committee on Urban Housing. *A Decent Home*. Washington, D.C.: U.S. Government Printing Office, 1969.

————. *Technical Studies*. 2 vols. Washington, D.C.: U.S. Government Printing Office, 1968–1969.

Ward, Colin, ed. *Vandalism*. New York: Van Nostrand Reinhold, 1973.

Welfeld, Irving H. *America's Housing Problem: An Approach to Its Solution*. Washington, D.C.: American Enterprise Institute for Public Policy Research, 1973.

Welfeld, Irving H., et al. *Perspectives on Housing and Urban Renewal*. New York: Praeger, 1974.

Whiffen, Marcus, ed. *The Architect and the City*. Cambridge, Mass.: MIT Press, 1966.

Wolman, Harold L. *Housing and Housing Policy in the U.S. and the U.K.* Lexington, Mass.: Lexington Books, 1975.

————. *The Politics of Federal Housing*. New York: Dodd, Mead, and Co., 1971.

Woodyatt, Lyle J. "The Origins and Evolution of the New Deal Public Housing Program." Ph.D. Dissertation, Washington University, 1968.

Articles

Aaron, Henry J., and von Furstenberg, George M. "The Inefficiency of Transfers in Kinds: The Case of Housing Assistance." *Western Economic Journal* 9:2 (June 1971):184–91.

Ahlbrandt, Roger S. "Delivery Systems for Federally Assisted Housing Services." *Land Economics*, August 1974, pp. 242–50.

Aiken, Michael, and Alford, Robert J. "Community Structure and Innovation: The Case of Public Housing." *American Political Science Review*, September 1970, pp. 843–46.

Angrist, Shirley S. "Dimensions of Well-Being in Public Housing Families." *Environment and Behavior* 6:4 (December 1974):495–516.

Bailey, James. "The Case History of a Failure." *Architectural Forum* 123:5 (December 1965):22–25.

Baron, Richard D. "St. Louis Tenant Management Corporations Bringing Major Transformation of Public Housing." *Journal of Housing* 31:6 (June 1974):263–69.

Bish, Robert L. "Public Housing: The Magnitude and Distribution of Direct Benefits and Effects on Housing Consumption." *Journal of Regional Science* 9:3 (December 1969):425–38.

De Salvo, Joseph S. "A Methodology for Evaluating Housing Programs." *Journal of Regional Science* 11:2 (August 1971):173–86.

Downs, Anthony. "Moving Toward Realistic Housing Goals." In his *Urban Problems and Prospects*, pp. 115–55. Chicago: Markham Publishing Co., 1970.

————. "The Successes and Failures of Federal Housing Policy." *Public Interest* 34 (Winter 1974):124–45.

Edson, Charles L. "Leased Housing: Evolution of a Federal Program." In *The Politics of Housing in Older Urban Areas*, edited by Robert E. Mendelson and Michael A. Quinn. New York: Praeger, 1976.

Ellickson, Robert. "Government Housing Assistance to the Poor." *Yale Law Journal* 76:3 (January 1967):508–44.

Genung, George R. "Public Housing—Success or Failure?" *George Washington Law Review*, May 1971, pp. 734–63.

Gilson, R. J. "Public Housing and Urban Policy: Gautreaux v. Chicago Housing Authority." *Yale Law Journal* 79:4 (March 1970):712–29.

Hartman, Chester W., and Levi, Margaret. "Public Housing Managers: An Appraisal." *American Institute of Planners Journal*, March 1973, pp. 125–37.

Hirshen, Al, and LeGates, Richard T. "Neglected Dimensions of Low-Income Housing and Development Programs." *Urban Law Annual* 9 (1975):3–32.

Knox, Michael D., et al. "Community Development in Housing: Increasing Tenant Participation." *Public Welfare* 32:3 (Summer 1974):48–53.

Lefcoe, G. "HUD's Authority to Mandate Tenant's Rights in Public Housing." *Yale Law Journal* 80:3 (January 1971):463–514.

Lampert, Richard, and Ikeda, Kiyoshi. "Eviction from Public Housing: The Effects of Independent Review." In *Housing, 1970–1971*, edited by George Sternlieb and Lynne B. Sagalyn, pp. 433–41. New York: AMS Press, 1972.

Long, Norton E. "The City as a System of Perverse Incentives." *Urbanism Past and Present*, Summer 1976, pp. 1–8.

———. "Making Urban Policy Useful and Corrigible." *Urban Affairs Quarterly* 210:4 (June 1975):379–97.

MacMillan, James A., and Nickel, Edith. "An Economic Appraisal of Urban Housing Assistance: Rent Supplements Versus Public Housing." *Canadian Public Administration* 17:3 (Fall 1974):407–42.

Marcuse, Peter. "Housing Policy and Social Indicators: Strangers or Siblings?" Center for Urban and Regional Development, University of California, Berkeley.

Palmer, Robert G. "Section 23 Housing: Low Rent Housing in Private Accommodations." *Journal of Urban Law* 48:1 (1970–1971):255–78.

Roisman, Florence W. "The Right to Public Housing." *George Washington Law Review*, May 1971, pp. 691–733.

Scobie, Richard S. "Problem Families and Public Housing." *Public Interest* 31 (Spring 1973):126–29.

Solomon, A. P. "Housing and Public Policy Analysis." *Public Policy*, Summer 1972.

Starr, Roger. "Which of the Poor Shall Live in Public Housing?" *Public Interest* 23 (Spring 1971):116–24.

———. "A Reply." *Public Interest* 31 (Spring 1973):130–34.

Tilly, Charles, and Fagen, Joe. "Boston's Experiment with Rent Subsidies." In *Housing, 1970–1971*, edited by George Sternlieb and Lynne B. Sagalyn, pp. 570–76. New York: AMS Press, 1972.

Welfeld, Irving H. "Toward a New Federal Housing Policy." *Public Interest* 19 (Spring 1970):31–43.

Yancey, William I. "Architecture, Interaction, and Social Control: The Case of a Large-Scale Public Housing Project." *Environment and Behavior* 3:1 (March 1971):3–22.

Basic Legislation:

Housing Act of 1937, P.L. 75–412, 75th Congress.
Housing Act of 1949, P.L. 81–171, 81st Congress.
Housing Act of 1961, P.L. 87–70, 87th Congress.
Housing Act of 1965, P.L. 89–117, 89th Congress.
Housing Act of 1968, P.L. 90–448, 90th Congress.
Housing Act of 1969, P.L. 91–152, 91st Congress.
Housing Act of 1970, P.L. 91–609, 91st Congress.
Housing Act of 1971, P.L. 92–213, 92d Congress.
Housing Act of 1974, P.L. 93–383, 93d Congress.
Senior Citizen's Housing Act of 1962, P.L. 87–723, 87th Congress.

Circulars

FHA 7430.3. *Low Rent Housing: Flexible Formula and Revision of Leased Housing Programs*. 24 September 1971.
HM 7475.12. *Subsidies for Operations: Low-Rent Public Housing*. 28 November 1972.
HM 75–20. Appendix 1, subpart A, "Performance Funding System." May 1975.
HM G 7475.1. *Low Rent Housing: Financial Management Guide*. March 1972.
HUD 7495.3. *Low-Rent Housing Homeownership Opportunities*. November 1974.
RED 75–380. *Report to Congress: Leased Housing Programs Need Improvements in Management and Operations*. 11 July 1975.
RHA. *Section 23 Leased Housing*. 6 October 1965.
RHA 7430.1. *Low Rent Housing: Leased Housing Handbook*. November 1969.
RHM 7465.8. *Leased Housing*. 21 February 1971.

Reports

Baron, Richard D. *Tenant Management: A Rationale for a National Demonstration of Management Innovation*. St. Louis: McCormack Associates, n.d.
Center for Urban Programs, St. Louis University. *Interim Tenant Management Corporation Evaluation Report*. December 1973.
————. *Tenant Management Corporations in St. Louis: Final Report*. July 1974.
————. *Tenent Management Corporations in St. Louis Public Housing: The Status After Two Years*. December 1975.
Division of Welfare, Missouri Department of Public Health and Welfare. *The ADC Families of Pruitt–Igoe: A Descriptive Study*. February 1964. Mimeographed.
National Association of Home Builders, National Association of Housing and Redevelopment Officials, Council of State Housing Agencies. *Section 8 Workbook: 1974 Housing Act*. February 1975.
Tobin, Gary A. *Regional Housing Needs Study: 1976*. St. Louis: East-West Gateway Coordinating Council, n.d. Mimeographed.
Tulsa Housing Authority. *Experimental Housing Allowance Program: Final Report*. October 1975.
U.S., Bureau of the Census. *General Social and Economic Characteristics, Missouri, 1970*.
U.S., Department of Housing and Urban Development. *Housing Allowances: The 1976 Report to Congress*. Washington, D.C.: Government Printing Office, February 1976.

Index